Sun Records

The Brief History of the Legendary Record Label

Colin Escott and Martin Hawkins

New York   London

Sun Records is a revised edition of *Catalyst,* first published in 1975. No part of this book may be reproduced or transmitted in any form or by any means, electronic or mechanical, including photocopying, without permission in writing from the publisher: Quick Fox, A Division of Music Sales Corporation, 33 West 60 Street, New York, NY 10023

International Standard Book Number: 0-8256-3161-0
Library of Congress Catalog Card Number: 79-65940

In Great Britain: Book Sales Ltd., 78 Newman Street, London W1P 3 LA

In Canada: Gage Trade Publishing, P.O. Box 5000, 164 Commander Blvd., Agincourt, Ontario M1S 3C7

Book design: Suzanne Newman

Cover painting: Roman Szolkowski

The authors are grateful to the following for supplying the photographs used in this volume, and copyright is acknowledged: *Billboard,* Johnny Bragg, Bill Cantrell, *Cashbox,* Jacques Demetre, Johnny Dickens, Colin Escott, Martin Hawkins, Mike Leadbitter, Robert Loers, Memphis *Press-Scimitar,* MGM, One Niters Inc.-Nashville, John Pearson, Mick Perry, Tom Phillips, Johnny Powers, John Singleton, Warner Bros., WDIA Radio – Memphis, Webb Photographic Agency – Memphis, Onie Wheeler, Jim Williams, WMPS Radio – Memphis, Malcom Yelvington.

Contents

Authors' Foreword

It was no fun growing up in England in the early 1960s. It rained a lot and there was far too much homework. It also seemed that virtually all of the good records we played after school came from the States and most of them were issued on the London-American label. After a while we began to notice that most of the records we liked best had a little inscription below the London-American logo which read, "Recorded by SUN, Memphis." That casual observation led to an investigation that occasionally became an obsession and eventually led to the appearance of this book.

It is now established that rock music did not originate with the Beatles or even with Elvis Presley a decade earlier and much rock literature has rightly emphasized the importance of the many forms of ethnic music that preceded the rock revolution.

"Rockabilly" was there at the beginning. It was basically hyperactive country music which borrowed in mood and emphasis from commercial rhythm and blues. Rockabilly has become identified with Sun Records and this book uses a study of Sun—its distinctive sound, its artists, and its market—as a starting point for a wider study of rockabilly music.

Throughout the swinging '60s a minority of record collectors retained their enthusiasm for blues, rockabilly, and vintage rock & roll which laid the foundations for the rock literature, television specials and university credit courses which have sprung up in the last few years. This book was originally written in 1971 and a lot has happened in the interim. A few of the leading characters have died, others have seen their careers reborn. When we sat in the listening rooms of the Shelby Singleton Corporation, owners of the Sun repertoire, in 1971, we did not foresee the vast rockabilly reissue industry that would grow up, particularly in Europe. We were convinced that we were hearing tapes which would never see the light of day. At the time of writing this revised edition there are probably more rockabilly records available than in 1957 and rockabilly revivalist Robert Gordon is in the charts.

All this seemed even more inconceivable fifteen years ago when we sat in our bedrooms and all the rockabilly music available to the discerning young fanatic was contained on a handful of scratched up singles and half a dozen albums. We're glad that it turned out this way and that rockabilly has not been overlooked in the quest for the next supergroup.

Among the people who helped in the production of this book we are especially indebted to Mike Leadbitter and Bill Millar. Mike helped us at every stage and edited the earlier version. Sadly, he died in 1974 and those who knew him still miss his boozy amiability.

We are also grateful to the following who helped with facts, ideas and photographs: Dave Sax, Steve LaVere, Ray Topping, Malcolm Temple, Hank Davis, Erik Larsson, Simon Napier, Tony Russell and Ralph M. Newman. The editors of *Time Barrier Express*, *Blues Unlimited*, *Hot Buttered Soul*, *New Kommotion* and *Billboard* gave us permission to reproduce parts of their publications. We would also like to thank Shelby and John Singleton and Paul Martin of the Shelby Singleton Corporation in Nashville, Knox Phillips in Memphis, Leon Campadelli of Phonogram (London) and Joop Visser of Charly Records (London). At the risk of becoming boring we would like to extend a final round of thanks to the people who are, or were, involved in the record business in Memphis and Nashville during the period covered by this book who took time out to speak to us.

COLIN ESCOTT, Montréal, Québec, Canada.
MARTIN HAWKINS, Lenham, Kent, England.
April 1979.

Elvis Presley

"My brother Lester had a recording studio in Memphis. Some guys came into his studio to record. Lester told them, "I think Sam Phillips can do a better job for you than I can. Why don't you go and see Sam?" As it turned out, the guy who was interested in recording was Elvis Presley."

—Jules Bihari

Downtown Memphis, Tennessee, July 1954. A small rectangular one-story building set back from the road at the junction of Union and Marshall Avenues, partially hidden by a car lot. Inside, three musicians, no onlookers and one engineer-accountant-record company president. They're working on a record in the white summer heat in a world concerned with Suez, Indochina and the first hydrogen bomb.

The guitarist, using a tiny 12″ x 12″ amplifier, has a shy gaunt face and says virtually nothing. The bassist, fatter, more ebullient, cries out, "Man we was hittin' it that time." The singer, with a nervous smile and a voice that leaps from a low register to a high whine has all the time he needs. So, they try the song another way, slow it down. He strums his acoustic guitar, a present from his parents to keep him off the streets, while his accompanists improvise a delicate melody line and find the tempo. The sound halts abruptly after one minute and the group looks toward the engineer at the console for encouragement.

They're all in a studio, the rented premises of the Sun Record Company and the Memphis Recording Service—"We Record Anything-Anywhere-Anytime." The company president, engineer, accountant, salesman and shipper is Sam C. Phillips, the bassist is Bill Black, the electric guitarist is Winfield "Scotty" Moore and the singer is Elvis Presley, hungrier, more nervous and, as always, disarmingly humble. "Fine, fine, man, hell that's different. That's a pop song now little guy, that's good" says Phillips. Somebody else in the background mutters something like "Sounds like a goddamn nigger."

Among the white kids who had no business hanging around clubs on Beale Street was Elvis Presley, just out of school, who picked a guitar some. "I knew Elvis before he was popular," said B. B. King. "He used to come around and be around us a lot. There was a place we used to go and hang out at on Beale Street. People had like pawn shops there and a lot of us used to hang around in

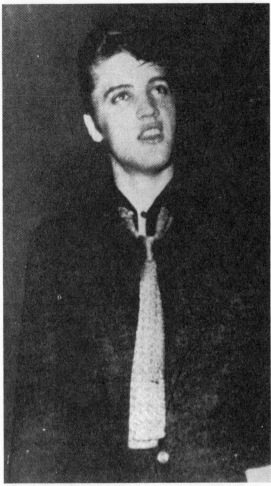

Hoodlum friends outside: Elvis in Memphis, 1954

Elvis — a period study

Elvis, Natalie Wood and Dewey Phillips

certain of these places and this was where I met him." Both entertainers returned to Memphis in December 1956 for the WDIA Goodwill Review, and the *Tri State Defender* for December 22, 1956, carried a photograph of Elvis Presley, no longer hungry, shaking hands with B. B. King, who was trying to come to terms with the stir that Presley had created in the Rhythm & Blues market.

One night in July 1954, Dewey Phillips (no relation to Sam Phillips) played a dub of Presley's first record, *That's All Right Mama/Blue Moon of Kentucky* on his Red Hot and Blue show which was broadcast from WHBQ in Memphis. The result was orders totalling 7,000 copies for a record, the product of many weeks work, which was finally released on July 19, 1954.

White singers had tried to sing the blues before Presley but there had always been a conscious effort to copy vocal styles and harmonic patterns. Presley achieved a natural fusion of the many influences that surrounded him and, as Sam Phillips said of Presley after he had left the label, "He sings Negro songs with a white voice which borrows in mood and emphasis from the country style, modified by popular music. It's a blend of all of them."

Elvis' first major influence had been gospel music. He deeply admired the music of the Blackwood Brothers and the Statesmen Quartet and had been on the point of joining the junior branch of the Blackwoods, the Songfellows, when he signed with Sun Records. Elvis also liked hillbilly, country boogie and the powerful early '50s R&B typified by Wynonie Harris, Roy Brown and Big Mama Thornton. When he approached Sun, however, he saw himself as a singer in the Dean Martin mold, and the discs he cut for his mother in late 1953 and January 1954 were in the slow popular crooning style. Phillips also thought that Presley was better suited to this style and tried him with *Casual Love Affair*—a song sold to Phillips by an inmate of Tennessee State Penitentiary in Nashville.

The first record was the product of experimentation by Elvis, Scotty and Bill. *Blue Moon of Kentucky*, for example, was attempted in a variety of styles which got further and further away from the slow bluegrass lament originally recorded by Bill Monroe. In fact, the first record created a lot of interest throughout the mid-South and *That's All Right* was covered by Marty Robbins for Columbia who added a fiddle to the sparse instrumentation employed by Presley. It became the first Sun release to achieve anything like national distribution since Junior Parker's *Feelin' Good*.

Later in the Summer of 1954 Elvis was interviewed by Dewey Phillips who had helped to make Presley a minor celebrity in Memphis. "I asked him where he went to school," recalled Phillips "and he said 'Humes'. I wanted to get that out because a lot of people listening thought he was colored." Sam Phillips, however, got a different reaction. "You can't believe how much criticism I got from my friends in the disc jockey business. I recall one jockey saying to me that Elvis Presley was so country that he shouldn't be played after 5:00 AM. Some people said they couldn't play him because he was too country and country stations would say that he was pop. The first break came when Alta Hayes of Big State Record Distributors in Dallas helped get the record moving in that area."

Elvis was getting mixed reactions but Sam Phillips decided that he should go on tour, which meant the country music circuit. Before long Elvis would be headlining with country stars like Marty Robbins, Hank Snow, Onie Wheeler and Cowboy Copas, but, like everyone else, he started off small time. His first gigs after he started recording for Sun were at the Bel Air club in Memphis with Scotty, Bill and their former band, Doug Poindexter's Starlite Wranglers. Poindexter recalls that, "We were strictly a country band. Elvis worked hard at fitting in but he sure didn't cause too many riots in them days."

These early gigs were organized by Scotty Moore, Presley's first unofficial manager. Other people showed an interest, including deejay Sleepy Eyed John. He organized shows at the Eagles Nest club on the south end of Memphis where Elvis later played with Malcolm Yelvington's band. Yelvington recalls that, "Elvis wasn't at all professional in those days. He was a kid, full of enthusiasm but with a lot to learn. Sleepy Eyed John let him go. Lucky for Sam and Bob Neal."

Bob Neal was Presley's first professional manager. He was also a Memphis deejay and saw the potential in Elvis. He later placed an advertisement in the trade papers in September 1954 calling Elvis "the freshest, newest voice in country music."

That month Elvis moved up to the big time for a show at the Overton Park Shell in Memphis. Billed as the "King of The Western Bop" he came on early in the show and sang a couple of slower numbers that got minimal reaction. After the interval, however, he returned and sang *That's All Right* and *Good Rockin' Tonight*. He was flailing his arms and shaking his legs, playing faster, bluesier country music than anyone had heard before. Among the artists standing in the wings was Marty Robbins who was so impressed that he recorded *That's All Right Mama* the following month. Elvis had made his first impact.

This increasing level of interest did not noticeably increase Presley's fortunes. He had given up his job with the Crown Electrical Company to devote himself to touring but he still traveled in Scotty's Chevy Bel Air, bought on credit by Scotty's wife. Bill Cantrell who worked for Sun and their hottest competitor, Meteor Records of Memphis, recalled, "I heard the dubs of *Blue Moon of Kentucky* before it was released and I came by the studio one day and saw Elvis for the first time. He was wearing patched blue jeans not because it was the style but because it was necessary."

For his second release Presley chose Roy Brown's *Good Rockin' Tonight*, which had been a bigger hit for gravel voiced Wynonie Harris in 1948. It was coupled with a pop tune, *I Don't Care If the Sun Don't Shine*, recorded in three takes after Presley had fluffed the words on the second take. It was released on September 23, 1954 shortly before Elvis made his disastrous debut on the Grand Ol' Opry. Elvis wasn't ready for Nashville and Nashville certainly wasn't ready for Elvis. He went over very badly although his confidence was restored by a regular slot on the Louisiana Hayride, broadcast each Saturday night on KWKH (Shreveport). It was this valuable exposure that gave Elvis a solid base of support in the mid South and generated more radio station requests and plays.

Elvis on stage with Marshall Grant and Luther Perkins on a Sun Package Tour

Elvis on stage, 1954

Elvis and Bob Neal, 1955

The third release continued the successful pattern of coupling an R&B standard with a rocked up country ballad. *Milkcow Blues Boogie* was a vintage blues which was attributed to Kokomo Arnold. Elvis and the boys capitalized on their reputation for getting *real gone* by changing the tempo before the end of the first chorus. The revamped *Milkcow Blues* was coupled with *You're A Heartbreaker* and was issued on Presley's twentieth birthday, January 8, 1955.

The fourth, and possibly most interesting single was issued on April 1, 1955. One side was a cover version of Arthur Gunter's R&B hit *Baby Let's Play House* which had dented the R&B charts earlier that year. Presley made a telling change in the lyrics when he sang *"You may drive a pink Cadillac but don't you be nobody's fool"* in place of *"You may get religion but..."* The reverse side was *I'm Left, You're Right, She's Gone,* written by Stan Kesler and Bill Taylor. Years later, Taylor recalled the song's origins. "I wrote that thing in the bath. It was based on the Campbell's soup advert and was written as a western swing type thing. I'd almost forgotten that in the studio Elvis, Scotty and Bill tried it as a slow blues." The slower version, subsequently released on a number of bootleg albums, has a guitar figure lifted indirectly from the Delmore Brothers' recording of *Blues Stay Away from Me.* Elvis, his acoustic guitar heavily to the fore, sings in his slow blues style.

Even the bluesiest of the Sun singles were reviewed in the trade papers in the country section and it is probable that Elvis and Bob Neal were not setting their sights much higher. From October 1954 through 1955 Elvis continued to rush back to Shreveport every Saturday night to play the Hayride. He also played with other country package tours and headlined a Sun show which included Carl Perkins, Johnny Cash and Warren Smith. They mostly played within one day's traveling distance of Memphis although they ventured as far west as Texas where Elvis was starting to have a great impact. A recording has recently surfaced of a gig Elvis, Scotty and Bill played in Houston sometime in early 1955. They were obviously quite well known because there is some screaming as soon as Elvis is introduced as the "Bopping Hillbilly." Elvis ran through four Sun songs and also included *I Got a Woman* which had just been recorded by Ray Charles. He loved to sling the guitar behind his back and grab hold of the microphone stand but in those days the group needed him to carry the rhythm on his acoustic guitar. Occasionally he lets go of the guitar, shouts "Let's get real gone," shakes his legs and the girls in the audience go crazy. When they could ask a little more money for a show they were quick to bring in D.J. Fontana who could keep the rhythm moving and drop little bombshells while Elvis did his bumps and grinds. It was also starting to become obvious that Elvis might have a future outside country music but a lot of the older country performers felt threatened by Presley, mostly because they knew that they could not compete. Among these was Webb Pierce who observed somewhat resentfully, "That boy could put us all out of business."

Presley's last Sun single was *Mystery Train*, originally recorded by Junior Parker for Sun in 1953. Presley's version borrows the guitar riff from the flip side of Parker's disc, *Love My Baby*, and highlights Presley's acoustic guitar. There is no apparent reason why the song should be titled "Mystery" Train unless, as

Elvis woos 'em and wows 'em with his stage antics

Elvis on-stage, Louisiana Hayride

an English reviewer said in 1956, "it refers to a mystery train of thought." Countless versions of the song have appeared throughout the years but none have matched the effortless swing of Presley's first version or the compelling train rhythm and beautifully pitched vocal of Junior Parker's original.

In October 1955, just as the disc was beginning to sell, Elvis played the annual Country & Western Disc Jockey convention in Nashville and the haggling over his future began in earnest. Earlier in 1955 he had been signed to a management contract by Jamboree Attractions, Col. Tom Parker, President. Parker could see no future for Presley on a label like Sun with its limited capital for promotion and shaky distribution through the minor independent factors. "When I found Elvis," said Parker, "the boy had a million dollars worth of talent. Now he has a million dollars." Sun had already received an offer from an unlikely source, Mitch Miller, the king of the singalongs, who performed an A&R function at Columbia Records. Atlantic Records in New York had also expressed an interest but both companies balked at Phillips' asking price of $18,000, although the owners of Atlantic had been prepared to mortgage their little company up to the hilt to buy Presley's contract.

Among those watching the Disc Jockey convention in Nashville were Steve Sholes and Ann Fulchino of RCA Victor. They both agreed that they "hadn't seen anything so weird in a long time" and the negotiations started. Parker almost certainly played a big part in the negotiations because of his connections with RCA which stemmed back to the time when he managed Hank Snow and Eddy Arnold. Finally, in November 1955 Phillips flew to New York and the deal was signed. Sun received $35,000 and Presley received $5,000 which may have represented unpaid royalties. In any event, he used it to buy his first limousine. It was an unprecedentedly good deal for a singer whose appeal in the huge northern and western markets had yet to be tested. Some indications may have been received when deejay Bill Randle reportedly used Presley in a short movie he was making titled *The Pied Piper of Cleveland*. The response to Presley had been overwhelming and Randle became one of Presley's first boosters in that area.

It was a calculated gamble by Steve Sholes who had put his job on the line by signing Presley. It was probably only Sholes' enviable record that encouraged RCA to back him. He had signed an outstanding roster of hillbilly artists and helped establish Victor's pre-eminence in the country market. Sholes helped produce Presley's first Nashville sessions and remained active in Nashville until his death in 1968. He had been instrumental in setting up the Country Music Association and had been one of the first living members voted to the Country Music Hall Of Fame. Presley's own feelings about signing with RCA are unknown but he was reportedly upset at leaving Sun, possibly because of its "family" atmosphere.

Although Phillips did not have enough capital to promote Presley properly and even knowing that Presley would almost certainly have left Sun when his contract expired, one cannot disguise Phillips' error in releasing him this early. A Victor official commented, "Maybe it was a question of Phillips not wanting to stand in the kid's way, knowing we had the facilities to do so much for the kid.

Elvis on stage – a classic study

Or maybe he just liked the color of our money. Victor's money is so much greener than any other." Phillips himself always publicly maintained the attitude that "We had two up and coming stars in Johnny Cash and Carl Perkins under contract at the time we sold Presley. I haven't regretted selling his contract because I figured then, and still think, that you can't figure an artist's life for more than six months in advance." In any event, the sale of Presley to Victor was more than a financial loss for Phillips, it was an artistic disaster because Presley was never recorded in more favorable circumstances than at 706 Union.

From the time that Elvis signed with RCA there has been much speculation about what he did, or did not, record for Sun. All this speculation could be ended by RCA but they are not letting on. They have issued two boxed sets which contained a fragment of Presley's jump suit as the only previously unavailable item and three volumes of the "Legendary Performer" series have been devoted to greatest hits and esoterica from Presley's long career. The accompanying booklets have offered tantalizing glimpses of Sun tape boxes, containing such items as *Satisfied* and hinting at unissued takes of other songs. No doubt all will be revealed by the time we are old and gray.

Sam Phillips was supposed to hand over all recordings by Elvis Presley in his possession in exchange for $35,000 and limited sell-off rights. He complied but a few fragments have escaped including a false start of *I Don't Care If the Sun Don't Shine* and a trial run through *Blue Moon of Kentucky*, which offer fascinating glimpses of Presley in the Sun studio, interacting with Scotty, Bill and Sam Phillips. An acetate of a bluesy version of *I'm Left, You're Right, She's Gone* also came to light in the late '60s. Still in the Sun vaults is a tape fragment of a guitarist, who sounds amazingly like Scotty Moore, rehearsing *How Do You Think I Feel?* which Elvis later cut for RCA.

When RCA was putting together their first Presley album, after the initial success of *Heartbreak Hotel* they dug into the Sun recordings. They had received hours of tape from Phillips and some fully mastered songs, including *I'll Never Let You Go, Trying to Get to You, I Love You Because, Blue Moon* and *Just Because*. These were probably the "five unissued waxings" that *Billboard* mentioned when they announced his signing with RCA on November 26, 1955. From that point, RCA touched nothing in those boxes until 1973 when they issued *Harbor Lights* on one of the "Legendary Performer" albums. It was far being the finest thing Presley had recorded for Sun but it was interesting to see him trying to become a crooner. RCA has admitted having *Tennessee Saturday Night* on tape and various guesses have been made concerning the other songs left unissued. It might be a long time before we know the complete story because it was twenty years from the time he signed with RCA before all his Sun recordings were brought together in one package.

Sam Phillips probably still has the pages from his notebook which logged the session details, cash advances and the like and he definitely still has his original contract with Presley. The Sun International Corp., a division of the Shelby Singleton Corp. in Nashville, also has the tapes of the legendary Million Dollar Quartet, a session recorded in the old Sun studio in December 1956 just after

Elvis had finished his first dates in Las Vegas. Elvis played piano in the two keys he knew, Johnny Cash and Carl Perkins played guitars and Jerry Lee Lewis, just arrived from Louisiana, sang and played piano occasionally. "John was already there," recalled Perkins. "He stopped by to pick up a little money and Elvis . . . came to see us. We started singing old hymns and we did things like *Blueberry Hill, Island of Golden Dreams, I Won't Have to Cross Jordan Alone, Tutti Frutti, Peace in the Valley* and *The Old Rugged Cross*. I guess Sam must must have two hours of tape there with lots of laughing and joking on it." The tapes have been the subject of a lawsuit and it seems unlikely that they will be issued legally in the near future.

Presley's voice is also rumored to be present on Ray Harris's Sun recording of *Greenback Dollar* and on a series of duets recorded with Jerry Lee Lewis. It is anybody's guess whether Elvis is singing with Ray Harris and it is highly unlikely that he is participating in the duets with Lewis. Jerry Lee's comment on the album was typically irreverent, "That dead of son-of-gun is still riding on my coattails."

So much has been written about Presley, especially since his death in August 1977, that it is almost superfluous to comment upon his contribution to popular and rock music. He was also a pivotal figure in the development of country & western music. He was not doing anything radically different but he took some developments further than their originators had intended. White country singers had freely plagiarized and overtly covered R&B material since the War and many country boogie artists used black rhythms and black instrumentation. Wayne Raney and the Delmore Brothers, for example, had mastered the boogie idiom as successfully as any jump blues combo. It was only the cornball vocals and the plodding hillbilly rhythms on the slower numbers that identified the artists as country personalities. Even Presley's clothes, sometimes as loud as his music, were not unusual. Nudie's Rodeo Tailors in Los Angeles, for example, had outfitted most country artists at the height of garish bad taste for years.

It was unusual for country artists to gyrate to the music, though. A few uninhibited souls danced a solitary jig during a spirited fiddle solo and some tapped an immaculately studded boot on the stage but no one flailed and wailed or threw himself to the floor. Tex Ritter viewed this development with more detachment than most because Presley was unlikely to encroach upon Ritter's market for cloying western ballads. "That boy," he drawled, "sure gits audiences worked up and he sure gits himself worked up gitting 'em worked up."

Presley also freed country music from its plodding rhythms and gave it a freer blues style. In short, he was the first artist to bring a totally black approach to country music. This was partly because his background in poor downtown Memphis, close to the black neighborhoods, had given him a genuine feel for black music and partly because his voice was deep, which enabled him to adapt easily to black singing styles. "When I first heard him," said one girl in 1956, "I thought he was an old man." Presley, in common with many of his contemporaries was looking for something more exciting than half a dozen

Elvis cuts up on stage

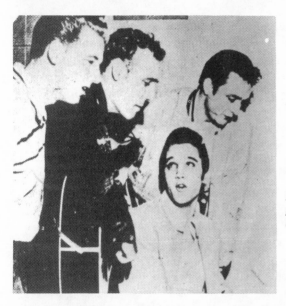

Most Sun records were stored at the pressing plant and drop-shipped to distributors. Elvis is the big seller.

The Million Dollar Quartet. Left to right: Jerry Lee Lewis, Carl Perkins, Elvis Presley and Johnny Cash

stately choruses of the *Tennessee Waltz*. He looked for a medium through which he could express his youthful vigor and sensuality. Sam Phillips was one of the few producers who would have encouraged this hybrid style. "Take your hats off to Sam," said the anonymous writer of "Your Record Stars." "He recognized talent where most people would have winced."

At Sun, Presley was recorded in exactly the same way as the R&B acts who passed through the door. Reverberation was used to create a stark, lonesome and incisive sound which was not lessened by the addition of vocal groups or choruses which became the bane of many of his later recordings. Moreover, Scotty Moore, an exciting and inventive guitarist, was able to adapt to both country and R&B styles. After a few months with Presley his playing took on the harsh tone and searing runs characterized by B. B. King. This fusion makes Scotty one of the founding fathers of modern rock guitar playing. His solos on *Baby Let's Play House*, for example, are among the finest in '50s rock & roll.

The limited instrumentation brought the acoustic guitar into greater prominence and highlighted the powerful support of Bill Black's upright bass. Drummer D. J. Fontana was recruited from the Louisiana Hayride in the Spring of 1955 but he is hardly noticeable on the Sun recordings because the pulse is sufficiently strong to make a drummer almost redundant. D. J.'s day of glory was to come with *Hound Dog* a year after Elvis left Sun.

Presley's group continued to work with him after he left Sun and are seen and heard to particularly good advantage in his second movie *Loving You*. Sadly, the sound they had forged with Phillips became partially submerged when the Jordanaires began their association with Presley which stretched over twenty years. Scotty Moore, Bill Black and D. J. Fontana quit Presley's line-up in September 1957, claiming that their $100 a week salary was insufficient, but they returned for the occasional live appearance and to make the "King Creole" soundtrack.

After Presley's induction into the army, Bill Black formed his own combo and was one of the first artists to record for Joe Cuoghi's Hi label. He led the group until his death in October 1965. Scotty Moore returned to session work and produced many later Sun sessions in addition to work for Fernwood and his own Music City Recorders in Nashville. He has played on countless other sessions and even recorded an album of Presley's greatest hits for Epic in 1962. In 1968 he joined Elvis and D. J. Fontana for a nostalgic romp through their old hits on Presley's NBC comeback special.

Elvis and country star Faron Young

Scotty Moore, Bill Black and D. J. Fontana

Elvis didn't make the front page so he checks inside

Presley's career in the twenty-two years after he left Sun has been formidably well documented. He never quite gave up on his country, blues and gospel roots but he rarely managed to recapture the effortless excitement of his earliest records. Twenty years after he chased around the mid-South playing *That's All Right Mama* twice a night for peanuts, he was sitting on his bed in the International Hotel in Las Vegas, bloated, bored and paranoid waiting for his love bath with the blue rinse set. No one will know the thoughts that passed through his mind on those nights any more than we will know the thoughts that passed through Hank Williams' head on the night before he died. We just know that Elvis Presley rarely tried to make records with the same magic formula that he used in his early days. The formula does not sound dated; in fact, it's still used as a point of reference by countless musicians around the world.

The last word belongs to Sam Phillips, who watched some early footage of Elvis on a television documentary and said, "Wasn't he something? . . . He stood on his own. I'll see it in my mind's eye until the day I die—and then I'm not so sure that I won't see it after that."

Ike Turner's Kings of Rhythm

Joe Hill Louis and B. B. King, WDIA

*A classic song and a classic car: The 1951 Olds
Rocket 88*

Earl Zebedee Hooker

B. B. King

Where it all began — The old Sun studio at 706 Union Ave, Memphis

Sam Phillips

The Memphis Recording Service

"The Negroes had no place to record in the South. They had to go up to Chicago or New York to get on record and even the most successful of the local entertainers had a hard time doing that. Rhythm & blues men like Jules and Saul Bihari would come south into Tennessee from the West Coast and set up studio in a garage to record the Negro blues singers of the South. So I set up a studio in 1950 just to make records of those great Negro artists."

—Sam C. Phillips

Sam Phillips saw himself as a "frustrated criminal defense lawyer," but his ambition was thwarted when he had to drop out of high school in Florence, Alabama, in 1941 to support his aunt and newly widowed mother. He had played in high school bands but admits "I never was a musician." Phillips was spotted, however, by Jim Conally of WLAY (Muscle Shoals, Ala.) while conducting a summer concert and he joined WLAY as a disc jockey in 1942. In the following year he switched to WHSL (Decatur, Ala.) and then to WLAC (Nashville, Tennessee). It's worth noting that WLAC later became the home of Gene Nobles whose Randy's Record Shop Show promoted R&B and early rock & roll into a white market. Phillips quit WLAC in 1945, however, and moved to Memphis, joining WREC in 1946.

Sam was also a promoter for the Hotel Peabody in Memphis and by 1950 he had built up enough capital to form a company, the Memphis Recording Service, and open a small studio at 706 Union Avenue, Memphis. The building was leased for $150 a month and recording and mastering equipment was installed on a piecemeal basis.

Phillips' first venture was to cut a custom taping session on jazz pianist Phineas Newborn for Modern Records of Los Angeles in June 1950. He followed this with a session on Joe Hill Louis in July 1950. Dubs were sent to Modern but recalled on August 7 because Phillips had another venture in mind. He had been approached by his namesake, but not his relative, Dewey Phillips with a plan for going into the record business. Dewey was a prominent disc jockey on WHBQ in competition with another early white R&B jockey, Bill Gordon was WMPS. Dewey was an early screamer and yeller and his theme song was *Write Me a Letter*. He had the idea that he would find blues singers without record deals and get Sam to record them. Dewey would run the label and it would be called 'The Phillips'. Sam agreed to a trial run and the two dubs he had recalled from Modern, *Boogie in the Park* and *Gotta Let You Go* were the first and only release on The Phillips later in August 1950. It was obviously unsuccessful because only a handful of copies have been found and Sam proceeded to negotiate a contract with Modern for Joe Hill Louis in November 1950, recording approximately fifteen songs for that label, twelve of which were issued over the next two years.

Phillips continued working for Modern, cutting sessions with B. B. King on January 9, 1951, Walter Horton on January 17 and Rosco Gordon in February 1951. Later that same year he began his association with the Chess brothers in Chicago. The relationship began in a highly successful way with Howling Wolf and Jackie Brenston. The Bihari brothers who owned RPM/Modern were understandably irked that Phillips had given the first option on Brenston and Wolf to Chess and they took virtually nothing from him after 1951.

Jackie Brenston was a saxophone player with Ike Turner's Kings of Rhythm. At that time, Ike was a disc jockey on WROX, located in his home town of Clarksdale, Mississippi. He had put together a jump blues combo on the lines of Amos Milburn and Roy Brown with some more local boys and Brenston had come up with a really sharp automobile song, *Rocket 88*. Ike and the boys trekked off to Memphis to see Sam Phillips who leased *Rocket 88* and an undistinguished blues, *Come Back Where You Belong*, to Chess in March 1951 after Sam had got Jackie's mother to sign the contracts because Jackie was under age. The record was issued under the name "Jackie Brenston and His Delta Cats" and became one of the biggest R&B discs of the year. Sam Phillips later characterized the disc as "the first rock & roll record. It really started pulling those things—blues, country and pop—together." It was not the first eulogy to the automobile but this slab of unsolicited advertizing for Olds' latest product predated Chuck Berry by almost five years and was a fine rollicking example of contemporary commercial R&B. Phillips overamplified Willie Kizart's guitar, which laid down a rolling boogie rhythm in unison with Ike Turner's piano. Raymond Hill played the muscular tenor sax solos which had been in vogue since Illinois Jacquet screeched his way into jazz history on Lionel Hampton's *Flying Home* ten years earlier. The song even attracted the attention of a small western swing outfit in Chester, Pennsylvania, named Bill Haley and the Saddlemen who chose it for one of their first releases on Holiday Records, adding auto noises and hooters to enhance the novelty appeal. When *Rocket 88* became a hit in May 1951 Brenston began to front the band and they went on the road. Phillips signed Brenston to a personal contract and cut several more songs, all of which failed to attract any significant attention. Phillips later secured the rights to *Rocket 88* from Brenston for $910.00. Brenston soon parted company from the rest of the Rhythm Kings and Ike Turner returned to the Tri-State area. In July he had been signed to a contract by RPM/Modern to scout out new artists because the relationship between Phillips and the Biharis had soured considerably. Turner made sure, for example, that B. B. King remained a Modern artist, despite the fact that Phillips had recorded him up to that point.

B. B. King had come to Memphis in 1947 and secured a job with WDIA in 1949. A radio show meant steady work both on and off the air, "If you wasn't with a radio station," recalled James Cotton, another outstanding blues singer working in Memphis at this time, "then the people didn't know you. . . . If you had been with one you could get work." B. B. King started off by singing jingles for Peptikon, a patented cure-all. "This Peptikon," recalled King, "was supposed to be good for whatever ails you, y'know, like toothache. Anyway, they put me on from 3:30 to 3:40 and my popularity began to grow. I sang and I played by myself and later I got two men with me . . . Earl Forrest playing drums and Johnny Ace playing piano." King had made his first recordings for the Nashville based Bullet label in 1949 using the WDIA studios and he went on to join RPM who usually coupled a fast jump blues with a slow one. Many of the earliest titles were recorded in Phillips' studio and on up-tempo songs the guitar was again over amplified to produce an early fuzz box effect. Although King's vocals were not as distinctive as they later became, his guitar playing with its ringing tone and dazzling runs was instantly recognizable. He recorded for Phillips between January and June 1951 with limited success but later that year Ike Turner recorded him at the Memphis YMCA and the song, *Three O'Clock Blues*, became a massive hit in December of that year. This success encouraged King to give up his radio shows and hit the road on the black one-nighter circuit, which he traveled for fifteen years before his manager, Sidney A. Seidenberg, took him off the chittlins circuit and directed him toward the more lucrative college and concert hall audiences.

Another major source of contention in the battle between RPM/Modern and Chess was Howling Wolf, one of the most original and distinctive blues talents of all time. Wolf was born in West Point, Mississippi in 1910 and learned his blues listening to Charlie Patton, Son House and Tommy Johnson. He moved to Arkansas in 1948 and put together a band that included James Cotton, Willie Johnson and Willie Steel. At Ike Turner's instigation Wolf came into Phillips' studio and recorded *How Many More Years*, which was leased to Chess, giving them an immediate hit in November 1951. Ike Turner was now under contract to RPM/Modern as a talent scout and to make amends he recorded Wolf on portable equipment in West Memphis, reworking the Chess songs and trying some new material. When Phillips re-recorded Wolf for Chess Records, he began appearing on both labels simultaneously but Wolf just continued farming and playing his regular spot on KWEM, sponsored by grain and tractor dealers. He laced his powerful blues with weather and farming information and is remembered by western swing artist Clyde Leoppard whose show preceded Wolf. "I don't know who called him the Howling Wolf but the name kinda fitted. He'd sit there—a huge guy—with his legs apart in front of the microphone and just howl those blues."

Wolf continued to record for both Phillips and Turner until December 1952 when his employment with KWEM ended and he was finally tempted north by Chess. His early sides are among his finest. Phillips' liberal use of reverberation complements Wolf's falsetto and the ferocity of Willie Johnson's guitar playing.

Moreover, his work had not yet taken on the air of self parody and exhibited a crudeness that made him an heir of the country blues tradition.

Howling Wolf went on to receive overseas recognition and tour campuses where he looked strangely out of place amid a sea of freshly scrubbed white faces. He was in ill health throughout the 1970s and died in January 1976. He received this tribute from Sam Phillips: "He had no voice in the sense of a pretty voice but he had a command of every word he spoke. When the beat got going in the studio he would sit there and sing, hypnotizing himself. Wolf was one of those raw people. Dedicated. Natural. His message was definitive. Few people can say that."

Phillips managed to form a more lasting relationship with another highly distinctive voice in the post-war blues scene, Rosco Gordon, a member of the Beale Streeters. Rosco was first recorded in February 1951 and the results were sold to RPM/Modern. The first single, *Rosco's Boogie/City Women*, was a primitive effort featuring Rosco's distinctive insinuating vocal, a rasping sax solo and a clattering drummer. In November 1951, after two more singles on RPM, Phillips recorded *Booted* which he sold to Chess, to the amazement of RPM/Modern who considered that they had Rosco under contract. Gordon had a hit on his hands and promptly cut three more sessions for Chess for which he received $210. RPM/Modern did not let this pass, however, and asserted their rights to Gordon and on February 15, 1952 the rights to *Booted* and four other masters reverted to RPM, who paid Phillips $150 for his studio time. *Booted* was a great record; it featured Rosco's distinctive loping beat and slurred vocal together with another appropriately booting sax solo from Raymond Hill. Although they had lost the rights, Chess slipped their version onto a 1964 blues compilation "Walking By Myself." A second single, *Decorate The Counter/I Wade Through Muddy Water,* was already in the works at Chess but it was abandoned, although Rosco makes an unbilled appearance on Bobby Bland's first and only Chess single, issued in January 1952.

Rosco's tortuous recording career did not end there. In July 1952 Phillips recorded him for the fledgling Duke label, which had been formed in Memphis by Bill Fitzgerald of Music Sales One Stop and James Mattis of WDIA earlier that year. Again, *RPM / Modern* leapt in with a cease and desist order to stop production. On August 2 the situation was resolved when Fitzgerald and Mattis sold Duke to Don Robey's Peacock label in Houston.

Rosco returned to record for Phillips in 1956/57 after the formation of the Sun label. Phillips obviously had a lot of faith in Gordon's abilities and he frequently noted in his files that a song was to be recorded "with Rosco's rhythm."

Another Beale Streeter who began his career in Memphis in the early '50s was Bobby Bland. During his early years in rural Tennessee Bland absorbed many influences. "We used to listen to the radio every morning to people like Roy Acuff, Lefty Frizzell, Hank Williams and Hank Snow. I think hillbilly has more of a story than people give it credit for. We were taught that hillbilly wasn't the thing but I guarantee they were wrong."

Bland began his career on the amateur hour at the Palace Theater in

A page from Phillips' log

"Lest Get Booted"
Rosco Gordon, 1951

Chester Burnett, The Howlin' Wolf

Rosco and Elvis

Memphis. "I had started out with B. B. King as a valet and from him I went to Rosco Gordon who encouraged me to go out alone." He made his first record soon after the session that produced *Booted*. The disc coupled *Crying* with the highly topical *Letter from a Trench in Korea* on Chess. The record was eclipsed by the success of *Booted* and in 1952 Bland switched to Modern under the guidance of Ike Turner. He was finally signed by Duke Records shortly before he entered the army. He has stayed with Duke through three changes of ownership, seeing success in the black market during the late '50s and early '60s with storming soul ballads and then mellowing out to produce his "California Album" and the subsequent follow-ups that have kept him more or less in the public eye.

Another blues giant who wandered in and out of Phillips' little studio during the early '50s was Walter Horton. He went under various pseudonyms including "Mumbles" and "Shaky," both of which suited his wavering vocal style. He was resident in Chicago throughout most of the 1950s but he had relatives in Memphis and visited the city frequently. In 1951 he cut *Little Boy Blue* and *Now Tell Me Baby* for Phillips who leased them to Modern. He went on to make other recordings, which were issued under various names on the Sun and Chess labels. Throughout, his trademarks are well in evidence; the full toned harmonica and wavering vocal, highlighted to good effect by Phillips' liberal use of reverberation.

Earl Hooker, another Chicago resident, also recorded a few extended demo tapes for Phillips in 1952/53. *Earl's Boogie Woogie* and *Guitar Rag* display his formidable command of the guitar. The flowing improvisations display the influence of both T-Bone Walker and Lowell Fulson, who influenced most post war guitarists, as well as Hooker's mentor, Robert Nighthawk who is identifiable by the clear, whining, single note slide sound. Hooker was born in Clarksdale, Mississippi, and died in Chicago on April 21, 1970 after a long struggle against tuberculosis. Shortly before his death he started to receive some long overdue acclaim for his work with Blue Thumb Records.

There were those artists who did not play in the popular jump blues style of Roy Milton or Roy Brown. Instead, their work harked back to an earlier era. Charlie Burse and Sleepy John Estes had both recorded before World War II and they also came into Phillips' studio. Phillips made special efforts to place Estes' recording of *Registration Day Blues* with various companies but he failed and it remained unissued together with Burse's recordings. It was a different story with Joe Hill Louis.

Joe Hill Louis was a manservant to a local family of politicians and construction company owners, the Italo-American Canale family. He was also a part-time kitchen hand at the Hotel Peabody and a womanizer whose reputation has endured almost as long as his music. Phillips first recorded him as a one-man band and leased the results to RPM/Modern after "The Phillips" label failed to get off the ground. *I Feel Like a Million* reportedly sold well but Louis never moved far from home, probably because he had a regular gig at WDIA, fifteen minutes before B. B. King, together with employment at local black ball games.

In 1952, however, he came up with a new style. The accompaniment was provided by other musicians and Louis just sang and played guitar. This allowed his dazzling guitar style to be brought into sharper focus and he improvised searing runs on the guitar which transcended bar lines with a ragged tone and uncommon emotional intensity. Perhaps the finest blues in this new style was *When I Am Gone*, leased to Checker, a Chess subsidiary, in July 1952. Louis was recorded again in November. Two titles were quickly issued in the second batch of releases on the Sun label. His talents were also used by Phillips in support of other artists such as Rufus Thomas and the novelty singing group, the Prisonaires. He died in August 1957, aged 35 from tetanus. He was too poor to afford a preventative injection.

By the end of 1952 several unforeseen problems were beginning to bear upon Phillips. The first was that the Chess brothers in Chicago were proving less and less willing to buy Memphis recordings, although they utilized some of Phillips' masters when they were setting up their Checker subsidiary in 1952. They still depended heavily upon the Southern market but by early 1953 several of the key figures in the Memphis blues scene had already made their way north to Chicago. The second factor was that Lester Bihari, youngest of the entrepreneurial Bihari family who owned RPM/Modern and Flair, had extended the activities of the Memphis branch office to include a new label, Meteor. Lester founded the company in December 1952 and installed primitive equipment at 1794 Chelsea Avenue, the center of the black neighborhood in north Memphis.

For Sam Phillips the foundation of his own label was the next logical step along the dollar highway. He had recorded hits for Chess and Modern and had also leased some recordings by Tiny Kennedy to Trumpet Records in Jackson, Mississippi, and further recordings by slick nightclub performer Tuff Green to Bullet in Nashville. He had even tried to interest a few of the major companies in his product, sending dubs to Mitch Miller at Columbia. At the same time he recorded weddings, bar mitzvahs, club meetings and similar events onto single-faced LP records for $9.00 a time. By working closely with the Chess and Bihari brothers he had learned much about the operation of independents in the highly competitive R&B market. He had learned from the mistakes he had made in setting up The Phillips label and, having been joined by his brother Judd, he must have hoped for greater things when he commissioned a design for a "Sun" logo from a small commercial artist on Beale Street in 1952.

Sunrise

"I thought I could maybe make a go of a company that just recorded R&B numbers, so I quit my announcing job and opened my record company. I had a wife and two children and it was a big move, but I was sure that I could do it. Everybody laughed at me for recording black people but those were great artists...I never fooled with anyone who had recorded before I found them."
—Sam C. Phillips

There were many factors which caused the proliferation of smaller independent record companies after the Second World War. The groundwork had been laid when Broadcast Music Inc. (BMI) had been founded in October 1939 as a rival to The American Society of Composers, Authors and Publishers (ASCAP). These rival bodies collected performance fees from radio stations and other organizations licensed to perform or play music. BMI was instantly more flexible in accepting new members and it paved the way for minority interest music to get exposed on the radio. In particular, it spurred the growth of hillbilly and R&B music. Between January and October 1941 the National Association of Broadcasters refused to accept ASCAP protected works for broadcast which was another stimulus to the growth of BMI and several important publishers signed with BMI during this period, including Fred Rose who signed Hank Williams in 1946. Acknowledging the fact that hillbilly and R&B music were becoming more important, *Billboard* inaugurated a "Western and Race" section in 1942.

In addition, the majors were holding to a fairly inflexible A&R policy, spearheaded by Mitch Miller who had joined Columbia from Mercury in 1950. Ballads were in the driver's seat and no one was really catering to the burgeoning black and hillbilly markets.

It was in this climate that the first independent jazz, blues and hillbilly labels were formed during and after the War when the shellac shortage was beginning to ease. The first black owned and oriented radio stations also commenced operations at about this time. There was WEDR (Birmingham, Alabama), WSOK (Nashville, Tennessee), WERD (Atlanta, Georgia) and, of course, WDIA in Memphis. Among the first labels to spring up were Apollo, Savoy, Black & White and Jubilee in New York, Juke Box (later Specialty), Dial,

RPM/Modern/Flair in Los Angeles and King in Cincinnati. These labels also got an initial boost from the Petrillo recording ban, which had been called by the American Federation of Musicians (AFM) from August 1940. The major record companies eventually signed new contracts with the AFM between 1943 and 1944 but by that time many of the new companies, who had signed immediately with the AFM, were well established.

It was another few years before the first independent record companies started appearing in the South. Jim Bulleit of Nashville founded Bullet in 1945 and inspired and aided Randy Wood to form Dot in Gallatin, Tennessee, in 1950. He also paved the way for other Nashville labels such as Tennessee, Nashboro and Excello. Down in Jackson, Mississippi, Lillian McMurry and Johnny Vincent formed the Trumpet and Champion labels during 1952. In regional centers throughout the States localized recording operations emerged with national hopes and aspirations. It was in this climate that the most famous independent of them all, Sun Records of Memphis, Tennessee, was born in February 1952.

Sam Phillips was label manager. The records were pressed by Buster Williams' Plastic Products Inc. at 1746 Chelsea Avenue and distributed by Bill Fitzgerald who ran Williams' Music Sales One Stop. Promotion was co-ordinated by Judd Phillips who had worked in country music promotion with Roy Acuff before moving out to the West Coast to work on radio station publicity with Jimmy Durante. By 1952 Judd had acquired a thorough knowledge of exposing product through radio and was being introduced to techniques of ground-level selling which, in the South, meant peddling records from the back of a car. Sam Phillips also logged thousands of miles attempting to break his new label. "I recall leaving on a Sunday afternoon," he said, "to visit distributors and radio stations. I'd sleep in my car. No one drove more in a three year period than I did." Nervertheless, early sales were slow and the label was left dormant for almost a year after the first three releases bombed out in the spring of '52.

During the hiatus Phillips advertised for partners in the local press and eventually Sun was gotten off the ground with the help of Jim Bulleit of Nashville. During this period a legal wrangle over the use of the name "Sun" was settled in Phillips' favor and against the Sun-Ray Company of Albuquerque, New Mexico, who had started their operations in February 1952. Unknown to both parties, there was also another Sun record label, founded in the late '40s in New York which only issued Jewish folk songs.

"We were with Sam at the beginning of Sun," recalled Jim Bulleit, "before he took it all over. I did all the initial distributing because we were the only company with the setup and the know-how. I later sold my share of Sun for $1200 and at the time it really wasn't worth any more than that. Judd traveled with me to set up distribution in New York and other cities. It was his introduction to the record business."

The first Sun issue had been scheduled as number 174, *Blues in My Condition* by Walter Horton and Jack Kelly. The latter had been prominent in the Memphis blues scene of the 1930s. The record was circulated to local radio stations and had a poor reaction. So, the first Sun record was not issued.

A screaming alto sax duet, the lead taken by Johnny London, became the first disc to appear in Memphis record stores on the Sun label. It was recorded on March 1, 1952 and acetates were given to Dewey Phillips on the same day. There was obviously a good response from Dewey's WHBQ audience because masters were cut the following day. On March 8 dubs were given to WHHM in Memphis, on March 10 to KWEM is West Memphis and finally on March 11 to Rufus Thomas at WDIA. In each case they were aired as the introduction to the new Sun label and the first pressings were made on March 27, 1952. A record by Walter Bradford was issued almost simultaneously but neither enjoyed the success for which Phillips had been hoping.

The second batch of releases did not appear until March 1953 but this time they featured men with established reputations in the city. A record by Joe Hill Louis was assured of solid local sales and Willie Nix was well known through his work on WDIA. He had recorded previously for Phillips and the results had been leased to Modern and the new Checker label. Nix, in an interview with Steve LaVere, claimed that his Sun record was so successful that Muddy Waters invited him to Chicago but little else was heard from him. As far as we know, he is still playing in the Tri State area.

The one acknowledged classic to emerge from the early releases was Walter Horton's *Easy*, possibly one of the finest blues harmonica solos on record. Again, the steadily mounting echo that Phillips employed was integral to the success of the disc. Horton recalled, "We cut that thing in three or four takes but my box started screechin' and we had to cut it. I played real loud on that one. I like to play loud." Phillips remarked in his notebook that Horton had brought in Jimmy DeBerry as accompanist and DeBerry was featured on the flip side of *Easy* and on his own excellent solo recordings, which were probably too acoustic and primitive to attract positive sales.

Success finally came in the form of a novelty jump blues by Rufus Thomas, who was certain to secure good local sales through his exposure on WDIA. Thomas had first recorded for Star Talent in 1949 and *I'll Be a Good Boy* is in the rocking jump blues style. Phillips had previously recorded Thomas in 1951, leasing the results to Chess, whose releases usually coupled a slow blues with a novelty song. *No More Doggin' Around*, issued by Chess in 1951, features the distinctive over-amplified guitar and honking tenor sax which had brought overnight success to Jackie Brenston earlier that year. Limited success on Chess, however, had not tempted Thomas to make the familiar pilgrimage north, possibly because of his four regular shows on WDIA: "Sepia Swing Club," "Cool Train," "Hoot 'n' Holler" and "Boogie for Breakfast."

His first Sun recording, *Bear Cat*, was a thinly disguised answer disc to Big Mama Thornton's immensely popular recording of *Hound Dog*, on Peacock. Thomas had been signed to a contract on March 13, 1953 and recorded *Bear Cat* the same day, just as *Hound Dog* was beginning to break into R&B charts. *Bear Cat*, replete with the appropriate animal noises, began to break into the national R&B charts in April. Don Robey, owner of Peacock, saw *Bear Cat* as an infringement of his copyright on *Hound Dog* and on August 1 *Billboard*

Billy Emerson

Little Junior Parker

Willie Nix

WDIA Goodwill Revue, December 5, 1952. Amongst those taking part were Rufus Thomas (top right) and Rosco Gordon.

WDIA Goodwill Revue, December 22, 1956. Left to right: Jr. Parker, Elvis Presley, Earl Malone (Spirit of Memphis Quartet) and Bobby Bland.

Walter Horton (right) with Muddy Waters

reported, "Don Robey's Lion Music is suing Sun over *Bear Cat* . . . although the practice of freely cutting answer discs has been common in the R&B field, the United States District Court ruled that Sun's *Bear Cat* was an infringement. Broadcast Music Inc. denied Sun clearance, Sun thereupon agreed to pay two cents royalty per record on all discs sold plus court costs. The Lion Publishing Company agreed to allow the Sun Record Company to continue the manufacture of the disc rather than force a withdrawal."

The follow up was *Tiger Man*, another novelty song highlighted by more animal noises, a jungle rhythm and a dazzling guitar solo from Joe Hill Louis. At this time Thomas made live appearances dressed in tiger skins and worked out a rain dance routine which he was still using in the movie *Wattstax* almost twenty years later. By that time he had been performing for forty years, starting his career with the Rabbit Foot Minstrels in his home town of Collierville, Tennessee, six miles east of Memphis. His dance craze albums of the 1960s contained some solid contemporary blues mixed in with more funky animal dance numbers and he never stopped broadcasting over WDIA. In the revolutionary atmosphere of the late '60s he held an ambivalent attitude toward black power, declaring "It takes black and white keys on the piano to play the *Star Spangled Banner*," although he never went as far as James Brown in publicly supporting Nixon for re-election.

In any event, the success of *Bear Cat* and *Tiger Man* enabled Phillips to start consolidating national distribution deals. Sun continued to be distributed locally by Music Sales on Chelsea Avenue and in other major outlets by Alpha in New York, Central Record Sales in Los Angeles and Gramophone Enterprises in New Orleans.

It became clear that the path toward solvency did not lay with the delta blues which Phillips had hitherto done much to foster but with commercial jump blues, an area largely neglected by the major record companies. Art Rupe, owner of the virile independent Specialty label, explained: "The majors kept on recording primarily what we call country blues. The black people I knew—the urban blacks—looked down on country music. To them country music was demeaning. They didn't want to be a field nigger; they wanted to be in the city." Phillips, however, was still in a position to tap the vast rural market and made a gesture in this direction by releasing *Greyhound Blues* by D. A. Hunt, who had achieved a limited mastery of Lightnin' Hopkins' clichés. The record failed to sell and Phillips went immediately to the other end of the spectrum and issued a smooth supper club performance from Dusty Brooks and His Four Tones, which had been recorded by Jim Bulleit in Nashville on April 25, 1953.

Brooks had been an established name for years and had recorded on the West Coast with Bobby "The Sweetest Voice This Side of Heaven" Pittman. He had achieved limited success with *That Jive's Got to Go/Please Don't Tell Me We're Through* on Supreme but his record for Sun sold poorly. Brooks' disc, and another in a similar vein by "Big Memphis Ma Rainey", were designed to appeal to the sophisticated black habitués of the night club scene in Memphis. "Big Memphis Ma Rainey" was in fact a pseudonym for Lilian Glover who still sings in Memphis clubs today. On Sun she was backed by Onzie Horne, a schooled musician who led one of the most popular combos in the city. Horne worked with Sam Phillips when Sun was releasing R&B product and in July 1954 he produced an acetate mastered by the Memphis Recording Service. In his file Phillips wrote "to be worked out for Sun" but nothing became of it. Horne later worked behind the scenes with Isaac Hayes as an arranger and died in 1973, aged 50.

In another attempt to find a commercial style Phillips tried his luck again with "Dr." Isiah Ross from Tunica, Mississippi. Ross, like Joe Hill Louis, was a one-man band and worked with Ike Turner over WROX (Clarksdale, Mississippi). Phillips had recorded him in 1951 and leased two titles to Chess, *Dr. Ross Boogie* and *Country Clown*, but the over-all sound was too primitive and countrified to stand any chance of success. By the time he recorded for Sun in 1953 Ross had developed a harder driving sound and the four titles issued, together with the unissued titles subsequently made available on Arhoolie, are artistic high spots. Ross was also dropped, however, probably because of poor sales and he went to Detroit to work in an auto plant, resuming his recording career on Fortune, Testament and a variety of European labels.

On October 3, 1953 *Feelin' Good* by Little Junior's Blue Flames entered the national R&B charts and from that point until the flow of blues releases dried up in late 1955 Phillips released only commercial urban blues. "Little Junior" was Herman Parker who had begun his career in rural Arkansas. "I was promoted from the fifth to the sixth grade in school and then had to go back to the fifth because I had to stop to chop cotton and pick cotton and plow. My greatest idol was Mr. Sonnyboy Williamson and I played my first job with his band . . . There were two harmonicas. He'd play, then I'd play. That's where I got the name 'Junior' from 'cause everybody thought I was his son." In 1949 or 1950 Parker left Sonnyboy Williamson and joined Howling Wolf.

In 1951 he made his first recordings in a straight blues vein and in 1952 was an accompanist to Bobby Bland on a memorable session that included *Driftin' from Town to Town*. Johnny Vincent, producer for Specialty Records and founder of Champion and Ace Records, claimed that he recorded Junior Parker in 1952 singing the original version of *Mystery Train* and issued it on Champion but the South has been combed and no record has come to light. *Feelin' Good*, however, was Parker's first recording for Sun and for a follow-up he recorded another version of *Mystery Train*. His version has tended to be overshadowed by Elvis Presley's cover version (Presley's version was also considerably easier to obtain until Charly Records in England reissued Junior's original) but it is an outstanding record, a beautifully poised blues supported by a nifty guitar riff from Pat Hare. It was an ideal vehicle for Junior's smooth refined delivery.

In late 1953 Junior joined the Johnny Ace Revue and began his long recording association with Don Robey's Duke label. Parker stayed with Robey until 1966 when the hits were becoming few and far between. In December 1953, however, Robey lost a court case over Parker. *Billboard* reported that "Sun, through its attorney Morris Pepper, charges that Robey had induced Parker to breach his contract with Sun. Judge Connolly of the Federal Court,

South District of Texas, upheld that when an artist's name appears on a label he cannot be signed by another without agreement with the first label, and ruled that Robey was liable for damages." Parker continued to work for Duke/Peacock, however, and he co-led the Blues Consolidated Show with Bobby Bland after Johnny Ace's bizarre death. Throughout the '50s he tended to work in Bland's shadow and in 1961 he left to work as a solo attraction. His last records for Groove Merchant, United Artists and Capitol brought him some measure of belated recognition but he died during brain surgery at the St. Francis Hospital in Chicago on November 18, 1971. Despite Parker's continued success in the black market Phillips did not release the last few recordings he had made before Junior left for Houston.

In the wake of Parker's success Phillips recorded Billy "The Kid" Emerson who was working as a pianist with Ike Turner's Kings of Rhythm. Emerson's first session included his debut Sun single, *No Teasin' Around/If Lovin' Is Believin'*, and the fast rocking *Cherry Pie* which contained the sexual allusions common in the work of Roy Brown, Wynonie Harris and The Midnighters. Perhaps Phillips decided against releasing the latter because of the decision by WDIA and other stations to ban obscene recordings "in the interests of good citizenship and for the protection of morals and the Christian way of life."

Emerson's later songs included original versions of *The Woodchuck*, *When It Rains It Really Pours* and *Red Hot*. On most occasions he was backed by the Ike Turner band; they are all outstanding city blues. On *The Woodchuck* Phillips' recording techniques bring out the pounding bass sound while allowing Emerson's jive talking to remain out front. His remakes of the Sun recordings for Chess and his own Tarpon label tend to be characterless by comparison. He made the familiar pilgrimage to Chicago where he worked with fading R&B star Willie Mabon. He still records occasionally and works in small bars. His last record to attract any attention was a mid '60s dance craze, *The Whip* on M-Pac.

Sam Phillips was also the first to record Little Milton Campbell from Greenville, Mississippi, as a solo attraction. "I guess you might say that I was lazy from the start," said Milton. "I knew that there had to be something better than picking cotton in Mississippi." He started work with Eddie Kusick's band in Leland, Mississippi, and was later a session guitarist for the Trumpet label. Signed to a contract with Sun in July 1953, his first record was released in December. It was an attempt to capitalize upon the burgeoning success of Fats Domino with a rolling New Orleans rhythm. The second release was a copy of B. B. King, featuring a harsh biting guitar and a powerful vocal. A little later Milton recorded for Memphis-based Meteor; he sounded a lot like Roy Brown. In fact, it has been a problem for Milton throughout his career to establish an identifiable sound and it has probably been a block to the progress of his career.

After leaving Memphis, Milton went to St. Louis where he worked with Oliver Sain for Bobbin and then to Chicago where he worked with Phil Wright at Checker and finally began to taste national success. In 1971 he moved back to Memphis to record for Stax in a soul-blues style with some success. After Stax collapsed Milton moved on to the Florida-based Glades label.

One of the finest blues to be issued on Sun was James Cotton's *Cotton Crop*

Blues. Cotton, like Junior Parker, had begun his career as a disciple of Sonnyboy Williamson. "I'd been playing a number or two on the streets since I was ten and then I met Sonnyboy, or Rice Miller to give him his real name. I heard him play this harp you see and I was crazy about the way he got it and that's what started me to really trying. I had tried for about a year and a half and I was pretty sad but when I got with him he learnt me. I played like him at first 'cause we was always playin' together but after a while I developed a style of my own." By 1953 Cotton had played with virtually every well known blues man in the Tri State area. He had recorded with Howling Wolf and remembers gigging with Ike Turner, Willie Nix, Walter Horton, Elmore James and many others. In December 1953 he entered the Sun studio to record his first single, *My Baby/Straighten Up Baby*. It was a jump blues with a solid backing provided by the highly talented Billy Love on piano and two riffing saxes in the background. It went nowhere.

In May 1954 Cotton was back with a new band that included Pat Hare on

Johnny Bragg, 1957

The Prisonaires, 1954. Left to right: Marcell Sanders, Johnny Bragg, William Stewart, Ed Thurman and John Drue

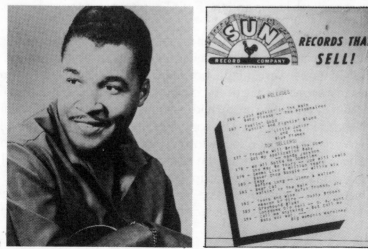

Little Milton

Sun publicity sheet, 1953

guitar. They recorded at least two songs, of which *Cotton Crop Blues* and *Hold Me in Your Arms* were chosen for release. *Cotton Crop Blues* attracted the attention and even today it's possible to see why. It was a blues on a decidedly rural theme with a sharp city sound distinguished by a furious guitar solo from Pat Hare who played in a crude, over-amplified, intensely angry style that contrasted sharply with the smooth jazzy style of T-Bone Walker that was in vogue at the time. Hare came from Parkin, Arkansas, of mixed Irish and black ancestry. He later went on to play with Muddy Waters and Mojo Buford before the implied violence of his guitar work spilled over into his personal life and he killed his girl friend in Minnesota. He is still serving the jail term. This act was presaged in the amazing *I'm Gonna Kill My Baby*, recorded by Hare in Phillips' studio in 1954.

The last artist to be recorded by Phillips in the urban blues style was Rosco Gordon who was re-signed in 1955 after an absence of three years from Memphis. His recordings for Sun included some driving R&B such as *Just Love Me Baby* but more often he settled with novelty numbers such as *Weeping Blues* and *The Chicken*. On his last recording, *Sally Jo*, he was accompanied by a white group in something approaching a rockabilly style but perhaps the strangest single of all was *Shoobie Oobie/Cheese and Crackers*, recorded under the direction of Sun's new producer, Jack Clement, in 1956. *Crackers* was written by rockabilly singer Hayden Thompson and freely adapted by Gordon.

In the black music world of the early '50s the most saleable product was jump blues or novelty blues and vocal groups. Sun made some concessions to the vocal group style and a study of the session files reveals that more groups were recorded than released. Gospel was a heavy seller in the South, of course, but the secular form of vocal group music, dubbed "doo-wop", was more popular in the bigger cities of the north and west. It was never really a part of the Memphis scene at this time.

The only black gospel group to have a record issued on Sun in the early '50s was the Jones Brothers, *Look to Jesus*, in 1954. The only secular black groups to have records issued were the Prisonaires and the Five Tinos who recorded in 1955 and employed a decidedly more blues-oriented sound. Other recordings by such groups as the Vel-Tones and the Four Dukes were in the more popular greasy style and remained unissued.

Phillips' most successful group recordings were made in a variety of styles by some inmates of the Nashville State Penitentiary who called themselves the Prisonaires. Negotiations were made between Red Werthan and Warden James Edwards to record them and recording equipment was taken to the Penitentiary in August 1953. The group had previously recorded *Just Walkin' in the Rain* under guard in Memphis. The song was later covered by Johnny Ray on Columbia Records who took it to the top of the popular charts in November 1956. Royalties were held in trust for the composer, Johnny Bragg, until his release on parole. The success of the group reached the ears of State Governor Frank G. Clement who remarked, "The Prisonaires represent the hopes of tomorrow rather than the mistakes of yesterday. They are a part of the program of rehabilitation and their musical message is for people everywhere and not merely for themselves." The group responded with a song, which Phillips did not issue, called *What About Frank Clement (A Mighty, Mighty Man)*.

For subsequent sessions the group was again allowed to make the two-hundred-mile trip to Memphis. The guards sat next door to the studio in Taylor's Café while Phillips taped the group, bringing in local musicians such as Joe Hill Louis and Ike Turner to supplement the sparse guitar chords of William Stewart, the original accompanist. The quality of the Prisonaires' records transcends their questionable novelty value, which was enhanced by pressing some copies of the discs on red plastic with black stripes. Most of the group was released on parole in 1954–55 and reformed as the Marigolds, recording for Excello in Nashville. Bragg joined them for one record and made a solo recording of *Beyond the Clouds* on Excello before being inducted back inside the Penitentiary for a parole violation. The group once supported Elvis Presley in a five hour charity marathon in Nashville and Presley later visited Bragg in jail. When we talked with Bragg in 1971 he was scuffling, still hoping to land another record contract. Most of all, he wanted to get back in touch with Elvis to borrow some money.

The importance of Sam Phillips in the post-war-blues scene has often been obscured by his success with rock 'n' roll artists and by a trend within blues scholarship which seeks to find "true blues" in arthritic rediscoveries. The decade after the War was the last time that the black market bought blues records in any appreciable quantity and the kind of blues they were listening to was slick urban jump blues. The commercial R&B of the '50s is now being seen as an important phase in the cultural shift of black taste after the War and Phillips was one of record label bosses who recorded the blues during this period.

Phillips was recording the Memphis blues scene in its most vital and interesting phase since the 1920s. Many black night spots preferred to showcase the smoother sounds of Onzie' Horne, Al Jackson, Sr. and Tuff Green but the blues could be heard loud and clear every day on WDIA, WROX and KWEM. These stations provided Phillips with his artists, his market and his most effective means of promotion. He did not have to look for talent; it came looking for him from all over the Tri State area.

Most of Sun's bluesmen not only contributed to the thriving blues scene on the airwaves but also to the clubs and bars of Memphis and West Memphis, Arkansas. The Chelsea area of Memphis and Beale Street were alive and jumping most nights. It was in Pee Wee's Saloon in 1909 (legend has it) that W.C. Handy wrote the first published blues, *Mr. Crump,* later retitled *The Memphis Blues*. Although Beale Street, the home of the blues, was cleaned up by police commissioner "Holy Joe" Boyle in 1940 there were enough bars, theaters, hustlers, prostitutes, pimps and punters throughout the '50s to provide a focal point for local musicians looking for a place to play and hang out.

Memphis in the '50s also bred some fine jazzmen who paid the rent by honking and screeching for Phillips and "walking the bars," a popular feature of a performance in the '40s and '50s when the sax player would walk along the bar, being careful not to step on paying customers' hands and drinks, making barnyard noises on his instrument. John Coltrane and Ornette Coleman, who went on revolutionize jazz in the late '50s, began their careers "walking the bars" throughout the South and in Memphis. The city itself bred the Newborn brothers, Calvin and Phineas, as well as George Coleman, Booker Little and Frank Strozier who went on to make dents in the jazz world.

In the early '50s Memphis became a cradle of the post war blues scene. There was a confluence of styles ranging from country blues to urban shouters; from gospel to the profoundly secular. Many facets of the Memphis scene were echoed in the Chicago blues of the '50s. There was a harshness and violence reflected in the distorted sound and heavy amplification of much post war blues. This violence is mirrored in the work of Willie Johnson and Howling Wolf but is epitomized in Pat Hare's work with Jimmy Cotton. This "feel" struck a responsive chord in Phillips who used his technical expertize to capture it.

By 1954, however, most of the leading characters had gone away. Dr. Ross was in Flint, Michigan, James Cotton, Walter Horton and Willie Nix were in Chicago, Junior Parker and Bobby Bland were working out of Houston. So Phillips had to find some other way to keep his little record company on a stable footing. He turned to country music and he discovered Elvis Presley and nascent rockabilly.

Beale Street, Memphis

Country Roots to Carl Perkins

Memphis had a reputation for being a center of jazz and blues but it also supported an interest in country music which grew rapidly during the early years of Sun Records. Big business had moved into the country market. *Newsweek* remarked in 1949 that "Ten years ago if a country sold 10,000 it was a hit; today a 50,000 sale is mediocre." New companies such as M-G-M and Capitol leapt immediately into the country market and the big companies were forced to sit up and take notice.

This was a time when the terms "country and western" or "folk and western" were coming into common use, uniting a growing number of musical styles. Western ballads and western swing music were being assimilated with the traditional folk ballad and hillbilly styles of the mountains and plains east of the Mississippi. Older styles were hived off into folk, bluegrass or gospel and although the influence of Jimmie Rodgers, the "singing brakeman" of the early '30s was still strong, a new breed of country star was emerging.

In the 1940s many singers tried to remove the "hillbilly" tag and the "hills and stills" image. Bob Wills, king of western swing, told *Time* magazine in 1946, "Please don't confuse us with none of them hillbilly outfits." He should also have included the many artists who adopted the singing ranger image in the wake of Gene Autry, an image that had very little to do with country music.

Of the new wave of country & western singers, Ernest Tubb and Eddy Arnold were the most popular with country audiences while Bob Wills and Hank Penny were the major western swing artists and Tex Ritter was starting to get a reputation for his cowboy ballads. Roy Acuff still dominated Nashville but overshadowing everyone was Hank Williams. During the years before Presley turned the country music scene upside down it was Williams' style which had the greatest impact in Memphis or elsewhere. His influence should not be underestimated. He died in the back seat of his '49 Cadillac on New Years Day 1953 and was only slightly less influential, although considerably less troublesome, in the years that followed.

Born a farm boy in Mt. Olive, Alabama in 1923, Williams won national acclaim in 1946. His widespread following grew although the hillbilly influences remained in his style. Success stemmed from the universality of his lyrics which, like those of Johnny Cash, reflected the feelings of many rural southerners who had moved to distant cities amid the growing urbanization of their homeland.

Smilin' Eddie Hill

Hank Williams

Sonny James, lead singer with the Loden Family, one of the few country acts to escape Phillips in Memphis.

W.M.P.S. in the 50s

Left to right: Red Foley, Minnie Pearl, Ernest Tubb, Cowboy Copas, Rod Brasfield and Hank Williams

Harmonica Frank Floyd

Such people often needed to find an outlet and expression for their traditional upbringing and an explanation for their conflicting ways of life. Many Sun artists were to share the emotions which Williams expressed in such songs as *Your Cheatin' Heart*, *Honky Tonkin'* and *Jambalaya*. The four main themes of lament, merriment, devotion and religosity were well covered in Williams' unique and much copied style. There was blatant sincerity too, particularly evident in his religious recordings and the painful honesty with which he chronicled his marital problems. Hank was a man for all moods and he had a profound effect on all of the major Sun artists.

During the '40s radio took hold of country music. Every Southern town had at least one country station and Memphis, the eleventh largest market in the Country, had WMPS, the first of a chain owned by Plough Broadcasting which would later stretch across the nation. WMPS went country in 1939, when it changed from its original call letters of WGBC and changed ownership from the *Memphis Press Scimitar*, who had founded it in 1925. By the time Plough took over in 1945 and Sam Phillips arrived to work as an announcer on the rival station, WREC, there had grown a steady country music business based on artists working short, sponsored radio spots. There was no local recording activity. The only label in Nashville was Bullet. The major recording centers were Cincinnati, Houston and Atlanta.

Memphis produced some country music personalities during the '40s although their recordings were made outside the city. Chief among these were Curley Williams and Eddie Hill. Williams ran a group called the Georgia Peach Pickers who performed in the western swing style but their repertoire emphasized the hillbilly connection concentrating on the steel guitar, fiddle and piano as lead instruments but the rhythms often derived from bop jazz. They recorded for various labels but primarily for Columbia in Nashville. Williams is probably best known for his interpretations of country standards such as *My Bucket's Got a Hole in It* and *Half As Much* which were both hits for Hank Williams. The Curley Williams band used Memphis as a base but spent much time touring the mid-South and Texas. Sometimes they were billed with the influential Wayne Raney and Delmore Brothers.

Eddie Hill made an even greater contribution to the Memphis scene. He was known locally as "Smilin'" Eddie Hill and broadcast regularly over WMC, performing at many venues around Memphis and Nashville. Hill's Apollo and Mercury recordings sold well around Memphis and his catch phrase, "gonna squall and ball and climb the wall" is found on several country and rockabilly records made later.

Charlie Louvin recalls that the Louvin Brothers moved to Memphis in 1947 and that Eddie Hill was already installed. "Eddie had the gift of the gab like no one I had met before or since. He was a mixture of emcee and comic. Eddie's fame in Memphis when we were there was unparalleled. We would get 6,000 letters a day requesting songs. My brother, Ira, Eddie and I had a trio called the Lonesome Ramblers doing three shows a day (country and gospel) for four years. We toured all through the mid-South."

A member of Hill's touring troupe during the '40s was Harmonica Frank

Floyd, a seasoned medicine show entertainer who became the first white singer to record for Sam Phillips. Frank recalls his early days in Memphis, "I began playing at Frank's liquor store and bar at the corner of Vance and Main where Joe Manuel, who is dead now, played guitar and yodeled. He worked with Eddie on WMC like I did. In fact, he got me in there. Eddie had Paul Buskirk and a piano man called Billy Simmons and Tony Sentola on accordion. Lightnin' Chance was on bass. I played with the Caradine Boys who advertized flour with Charlie Dial. Also, the Louvin brothers, Ira and Charlie, who were in Memphis then, the Swift Jewel Cowboys, Kitty Scott, and Zeke Martin all played on WMC too. I can remember the Memphis Jug Band and Ramblin' Red Lowery being around too but Eddie Hill was the biggest."

Eddie Hill also worked as an announcer from WMC, the second most important station in Memphis. Operating from the Godwin International Building on Third and Madison Avenues, near downtown, it had regular live shows featuring local country artists and big names like the Delmores. Curley Williams and Eddie Hill were the leading lights on WMC although there was competition in the shape of Curley Fox, a well known fiddle player, who, like the Delmores and Wayne Raney, was contracted to King Records in Cincinatti, the only Southern independent record label as successful as Sun during the '50s.

The longest running show on WMC belonged to Slim Rhodes and his band. It was aired regularly from 1944 through to the late '60s, even after Rhodes' death in 1966. The Rhodes family has been one of the most influential in Memphis country music although Rhodes himself only made a few recordings for Sun, Gilt Edge and Cotton Town Jubilee. The band of Clyde Leoppard was popular in the city for a shorter period during the early and mid '50s when they played over WMC and KWEM in West Memphis, Arkansas.

KWEM was a newer station, founded in May 1947 by J. C. Johnson and taken over in 1952 by Dee Rivers, an entrepreneur who owned a chain of stations. Rivers brought in Texas Bill Strength during the early '50s as a jockey spearheading the country programming. Strength was also an artist for Coral in Nashville and later Sun.

Memphis was by no means swamped with country radio, however. Sam Phillips' employers at WREC programmed little music in that style although Swift and Company's Jewel Cowboys led by Jim Sanders were a popular feature for some years. Until the rockabilly revolution in the mid '50s, the most important jocks in the city were "Sleepy Eyed" John (Lepley) on WHHM, Dewey Phillips on WHBQ and Bill Gordon on WMPS. Smaller stations in nearby towns were bigger on country music, for example KLCN which featured Jimmy Haggett who later recorded for Sun.

The most important station in the city, consistently top of the ratings, was WMPS, based in the Columbia Tower on Main Street. It had programmed country music since the late '30s, live and prerecorded, and after it moved up to 10,000 watts in 1947, it could be heard clearly within a radius of 125 miles. Its top liners were the Carlisles and the Loden Family, who featured Sonny James, probably the most famous pop and country artist in the area to have not recorded for Sun. The leading country deejay was Bob Neal, who also doubled on children's hour as Uncle Pudgy. In 1958 Neal quit to manage Johnny Cash full time, having previously managed Presley and other Sun artists. He also ran a record store on Main Street but he kept on deejaying until 1958 because the powerful 10,000 watt station helped him to book acts contracted to his own Stars Inc. "Those were pioneering days," said Neal. "Mine was one of the first country radio shows. 'Live' radio was the policy with the bands in the studio."

Clyde Leoppard, leader of the Snearly Ranch Boys, and one of the first country artists to record for Phillips, recalled, "All this time, from 1950 up until 1960, the whole music thing in the city of Memphis was just growing. More and more people were getting involved until today there's a band on every corner. My band was playing western swing or hillbilly dance music, whatever you want to call it. We played mainly the Cotton Club. My regulars included Smokey Joe, Stan Kesler, Bill Taylor, Barbara Pittman and Warren Smith. Later Ace Cannon and Gene Simmons—all top record artists. Others played with me occasionally. Eddie Bond was one, Charlie Feathers even Jerry Lee Lewis."

The Cotton Club in West Memphis was the main spot for country music. Opened in 1949 by a music fan named Grady Lofton, it presented most of the musicians in the Memphis area at one time or another, until its demise in 1960. Other country acts found bookings in Memphis itself; there was the Five Gables Club on Bellevue Avenue, The Beaufort Inn, the Eagles Nest and the Bel Air, where Elvis Presley played for a short time with Doug Poindexter's hillbilly

Bob Neal moves to WMC. Left to right: Slim Rhodes, Dusty Rhodes, Spec Rhodes and Bob Neal.

band. Then there were the out of town spots such as Jackson's El Rancho club, early haunt of the Carl Perkins band.

Most of the bands had no chance to get on records unless they got lucky and were taken to Nashville by a large company. From talking to the musicians working in the city in the early '50s it seems that a wide range of music was being played. A lot of popular bands were not recorded, including the Bob McNight band, a western swing outfit. The Garrett Snuff Boys were also an important influence on later bands such as Sun artists Malcolm Yelvington and Doug Poindexter. A lot of other smaller bands contained men who were to make an impact on the music scene in later years. There was Slim Wallace's Dixie Ramblers, Jim Stewart's Band and William Diehl's Band. Jim Stewart later founded Stax Records, Diehl did a lot of session work for Sun and Slim Wallace founded Fernwood Records, a fairly successful record label which harbored Ramon Maupin and Jack Clement and struck gold with Thomas Wayne's *Tragedy* in 1959.

The Loden Family played a type of music more sacred in lyric and smoother in rhythm than that of western swing bands. They were popular but never recorded, although, of course Sonny James has recorded consistently for over twenty years. The band also included Luther "Pee Wee" Suggs who went on to make some fairly undistinguished records for Sun.

Two other important country music styles were evident in Memphis at the time. Groups led by Malcolm Yelvington and Red Hadley, both from Covington, ten miles north of Memphis, and Lendon Smith from Florence, Alabama, excelled in a style of music that has become known as "honky tonk." It was dance music, often relying on a pianist and drummer to strengthen the rhythm but it was essentially closer to the hillbilly sound of Hank Williams than to western swing. Another couple of bands of note were those of Bob Price and Dexter Johnson from Tishomingo, Mississippi, who worked at various times with the band of guitarist Quinton Claunch who was also to play a large part in recording the country music of Memphis. Other young bands playing where they could on weekends included groups led by Bud Deckelman, Larry Price, Red Mathews, Jack Earls, Curtis Hobeck and Charlie Feathers.

Carl Perkins was also playing honky tonk music in Jackson's clubs and bars using the basic line-up of acoustic guitar, upright bass and lead guitar. During the decade before rock & roll almost every record company that catered to the country market had a band who derived their sound from Hank Williams. King Records had Jack Cardwell and Lattie Moore, Trumpet Records of Jackson, Mississippi, had Werly Fairburn, both labels had Luke McDaniels (later known as Jeff Daniels), Dot of Gallatin, Tennessee, had Jimmy Work, Jimmy Logsdon and Jimmy Newman heading an outstanding roster of hillbilly artists. It was no surprise, therefore, that when Sam Phillips started recording country music that most of the men who walked in through his doors sounded a lot like Hank Williams.

Sun Country

*"I really loved those Blue Suede Shoes. When you were as poor as
we were, you loved any kind of shoes."*
—Carl Perkins

When Sam Phillips sold Elvis Presley's contract to RCA Victor in November
1955 he did so in the knowledge that there were other young singers where
Presley came from: off the streets of Memphis, off the streets of a score of
nearby towns and from the farms for miles around. Sun Records had not yet
enjoyed a national hit but already the talent was knocking on the door and
hanging around waiting for a break. Hitherto they had mostly been blues artists
but already a few country singers had been tried. Presley was not typical; he was
not a country boy like most of the artists who were to follow him through
Phillips' front door. Carl Perkins, on the other hand, was the real thing. Several
times during 1954 he and his band had driven to Memphis in their beat up 1940
Plymouth convertible and tried for an audition but each time they had returned
to the farm or to dead end city jobs, playing the bars and honky tonks around
Jackson, Tennessee, on weekends for little more than beer money.

Eventually, late in 1954 Phillips listened to Perkins and, against the
newcomer's protest that he could do better than Presley in the pop field, Phillips
recorded him as Sun's answer to Hank Williams. Phillips was still preoccupied
at the time with the new white blues sound that he and Presley had forged but at
the same time he knew that there was a vast bread and butter country market in
the mid-South that he had not reached. Presley might be the answer to the new
young country pop market but Sam wanted to cover all the bases.

By the time Carl Perkins' first record was issued in early 1955 Phillips had
already released nine other records by white artists. Apart from Presley, there
was a religious disc, two one-man-band novelty items, two western swing, and
one Sinatra-styled nightclub performance by Buddy Blake Cunningham. Only
one had been a true hillbilly record in the Hank Williams style. Phillips was not
blindly recording the obvious but was searching for a hit style; something that
would put Sun Records and Memphis on the country sales map.

In searching for that elusive hit he had the help of Jim Bulleit in Nashville and,
later, his brothers Judd and Tom. In Memphis itself Sun had two main talent
scouts, Bill Cantrell and Scotty Moore. Scotty worked part time as a session

musician, pickup band member and scout between 1952 and 1954 before he joined forces with Presley. Bill Cantrell came to Memphis in 1954 by way of Florence, Alabama and Nashville from his home town of Hackleburg, Alabama. He was a country fiddle player who had worked on sessions and in bands for some years and had in fact met Phillips during the '40s when Phillips was an announcer on WLAY in Florence.

As it happened, most country artists who wanted to get on records found Phillips without his having to look too far. The first country release on Sun was *Silver Bells* by a vocal group from Ripley, Tennessee, called the Ripley Cotton Choppers. Their leader was Ernest Underwood and his group recorded only once on July 11, 1953. The resulting disc, released in October had "Hillbilly" stamped on the label of deejay copies. This practice was followed for some years because of Sun's reputation as a blues label.

Country sessions had been held before, however, the first with Harmonica Frank Floyd on July 15, 1951. Frank only had two sides issued on Sun but others were leased to Chess. Floyd was a rambler but has lived in Memphis for several periods during the '40s and '50s, especially when he had a regular gig with the Eddie Hill band. A multi-instrumentalist, he played acoustic guitar and harmonica and sang in a unique way. This was achieved by holding the harmonica in one side of his mouth and singing out of the other side, producing an old timey, slightly black sound.

Floyd's repertoire was taken from various sources in old-time music and blues and even vaudeville. His recorded performances reflect this to a great extent, varying from humorous narratives such as *Swamp Root*, released on Chess, or *The Great Medical Menagerist*, issued on Sun, to an up tempo, almost rockabilly sound on *Rocking Chair Daddy*, the flipside of his Sun release. *Swamp Root* was adapted from Buddy Jones' *Huntin' Blues* on Decca while the *Menagerist* closely follows Chris Bouchillon's *The Medicine Show*, both songs dating from the 1920s. Floyd was adaptable, however, recording *Rocking Chair Daddy* in response to Phillips' request for more contemporary up tempo country music and these days he includes even more contemporary material in his large repertoire. His philosophy remains liberal, "In the '30s I used to ride trains and hitch all over the South and play street corners, pool halls, country squares. It's different now. Once in a while one of the younger groups will sound like a dyin' calf in a hailstorm but music's music, what's the difference?"

The second country artist to be recorded was Bob Price from Tishomingo, Mississippi, who recorded in December 1951. His band had played around Memphis on many occasions with Dexter Johnson, Roy Cooper and Bob Smith. When in Memphis they joined forces with Harold Buskirk and Quinton Claunch. The Sun label had not been formed when Price recorded *How Can It Be* and *Sticks and Stones* which were sent to Chess on December 13, 1951 together with *Howlin' Tomcat* by Harmonica Frank. Price's record was issued on Chess in January 1952.

At the time, Phillips was merely dabbling in country music to test its potential but both he and Chess had high hopes for the success of such records and for the future of country music on Chess. A "Country & Western" series was instituted with a scarlet and white label replacing the usual blue and white one. These Memphis recordings did not turn hopes into sales, though, and the experiment was dropped until 1954 when Chess began leasing product from Stan Lewis in Shreveport, Louisiana. Again, a specially formed "4850" Country Series folded after a few releases by Jimmy Lee and "Country" Johnny Mathis and Carolyn Bradshaw, among others.

By 1954 Chess had virtually severed ties with Phillips, who had been offering his country product elsewhere. In May 1952 he recorded Red Hadley's Wranglers, committing four sides to tape and this time the dubs were sent to Lillian McMurry at the Trumpet label in Jackson, Mississippi. Although some of Phillips' blues recordings did appear on Trumpet at this time, it would appear that there were enough local country artists to keep Mrs. McMurry occupied.

Presley was recorded in July 1954 but during the previous March, April and May there was a rush of country recording activity that pointed the way toward the future. These sessions may have been made possible by the revenue generated from the sales of Rufus Thomas, Junior Parker and The Prisonaires.

The Harmonica Frank single was released in July 1954 but, of course, this had been recorded in July 1951. With it, however, came the fruits of the Spring sessions and Earl Peterson, a twenty-seven-year-old country singer from Lancing, Michigan, known as "Michigan's Singing Cowboy" who had previously recorded for his own Nugget label and had come to Memphis in March to record *Boogie Blues*. This up tempo song with an appealing semi-yodeled vocal was later recut for Columbia.

Issue # 198, in April 1954, was a religious item performed with acoustic guitar, harmonica and a marvellously expressive vocal by Howard Seratt. The artist was a thirty-two year old crippled singer from Manilla, Arkansas, who graduated from harmonica to guitar and by 1943 was playing over KLCN in Blytheville, Arkansas. After spells in Michigan and California, Seratt returned home and in 1953 local deejay Larry Parker took him to Sun to make a custom recording of *"Make Room In The Lifeboat For Me."* This came out of the St. Francic label. Sam Phillips thought that it was good enough to warrant Sun releasing a gospel recording and *"Troublesome Waters"* was the result. It got a good review in *Cashbox* and then sank without a trace. Seratt could not be persuaded to record other than religious material, although he did play several Sun country shows with Slim Rhodes and others. In particular, Seratt, now a watchmaker in California, recalls with pride the night in January 1955 when he played a big show in Clarksdale, Mississippi with Elvis Presley and Jim Ed and Maxine Brown.

Phillips' country sessions continued and eight discs were issued between March and September 1954. Phillips still seemed to be searching for a new sound to break into the country market and sessions with fairly established country artists such as the Kirby Sisters and Luke McDaniel remained unissued. Nevertheless, a semi-popular singer became the next country artist on Sun. Hardrock Gunter, famous for his recording of *Birmingham Bouce* on Bama Records in 1948, was one of the few country artists who tried to rock their music and in releasing *Fallen Angel* and *Gonna Dance All Night* Phillips was moving closer to his goal of finding a country artist who could sing the blues.

Gonna Dance All Night was the up tempo side and while the country influence was strong, the point of the record is stated loud and clear, "We're gonna rock 'n' roll while we dance all night." The addition of a saxophone to Gunter's western swing and hillbilly influences mark this record as Phillips' only concession to the Bill Haley sound that was just becoming very popular.

A second artist, recorded on the same day as Gunter, May 25, 1954, produced the nearest thing to rockabilly that Sam Phillips had heard so far. Part time talent scout Scotty Moore had been playing guitar with a band led by singer Doug Poindexter which also included Bill Black. Essentially, it was a hillbilly band but Moore and Poindexter had been working on a song called *My Kind of Carryin' On*. There were no drums or rock 'n' roll backbeat but there was a hurrying bass rhythm akin to the style Black would perfect with Presley and some hot guitar from Scotty Moore. One verse was surprisingly salty for a country record:

> I took my baby out to the park
> We fussed and fought 'till it got dark
> You wanna give me little sugar
> You cute li'l booger,
> Then it will be so plain to see
> That you're gonna like my kind of carryin' on

Poindexter was a Hank Williams fan and went to see Bill Fitzgerald, who was the main record distributor in the city at that time and told him that he wanted to get on M-G-M, like Hank. "He didn't exactly laugh out loud," recalled Poindexter, "but he sent us down to see Sam Phillips. That was just what we did, Scotty, Bill, myself, guitarist Clyde Rush, steel player Tommy Seals and fiddler Millard Yeow." By May 1955 Doug's disc had sold 330 copies, earning him $8.06 in royalties. His disc may now be seen as possibly the best example of the passing of one era in hillbilly music and the arrival of countrified rock 'n' roll—rockabilly.

Poindexter epitomizes the many hillbilly singers who could handle embryonic rockabilly but not the newer, driving, sexual Presley-style product. Many singers preferred to remain semi professional—unknown but secure— and Poindexter turned down Phillips' suggestion that he run a country radio station out of Memphis to publicize artists. He is philosophical that his bass player and guitarist were used for Presley rehearsals and in his estimation he was better off sticking to his regular job because "I knew some professional musicians out there who were better than I was but who were not making it. At that time, the record business was in a funny state and I wasn't sure that I wanted to go with it. Scotty and Bill had the chance to go to Shreveport with Elvis and they wanted to go ahead with it but I stayed in Memphis. Eventually Sam forgot about me and I guess it was for the best. There was no way of knowing that success was coming to Presley. Frankly, I thought the boy would starve to death."

Presley, of course, did no such thing. In July and September, with his fourth and fifth discs, he achieved the breakthrough into the national country charts. He had not done it with straight country music but the point was that he had done it and that Phillips had the faith and ambition to maintain his assault.

In November, Johnny Cash's first record, *Cry! Cry! Cry!*, followed Presley into the *Billboard* chart and Phillips' output of records by white artists started to increase. Now he had developed the musical synthesis he had been seeking which allowed him to record the best he came across, without a need to experiment continually with up tempo songs. From this point, his success in both country and pop markets did not depend on his ability to pinpoint a new sound but on his ability to spot talent. He tried to adapt the style of anyone whom he thought had an aptitude for rockabilly music but he also recorded other artists in the mainstream country idiom.

After the release of Presley's fourth and fifth records in 1955 Phillips slowed down the recording activity, possibly because he wanted to put his little company's limited promotional resources behind Presley. In fact, from the recording of *That's All Right* until the end of 1954 only three other records were released. These came in November and comprised a blues by Dr. Ross, a western swing item by Malcolm Yelvington and His Star Rhythm Boys (who were later to mold the echoey rockabilly feel achieved on *Drinkin' Wine Spo-Dee-O-Dee* into a developed sound) and a black gospel issue by the Jones Brothers, whose *Look to Jesus* sold as poorly as Howard Seratt's disc, leading Phillips to turn down requests by Johnny Cash and others to record gospel music.

By the beginning of 1955 the wheels were starting to get in motion once again. Promotion of Presley had largely passed into the hands of Bob Neal. The new issues included some blues by Sammy Lewis, Billy "The Kid" Emerson, Eddie Snow and Rosco Gordon, but mostly the new artists were country artists.

A second label was started, Flip, which was designed to test new artists locally. Any potential hits could be transferred to Sun. Four fine country discs appeared on the Flip label during 1954–55 and the first was by Carl Perkins who had finally been auditioned and accepted. In general, the country releases were by artists living in Memphis: Johnny Cash, Slim Rhodes, Clyde Leoppard with Bill Taylor and Smokey Joe, and Charlie Feathers. The three exceptions, Maggie Sue Wimberly was from Muscle Shoals, Alabama, the Miller Sisters from Tupelo, Mississippi and disc jockey Jimmy Haggett from Blytheville, Arkansas.

The Slim Rhodes band saw three releases on Sun in 1955. The group consisted of Slim on rhythm guitar, his relatives Dusty on fiddle, Spec on bass, Dot on vocals, Brad Suggs on guitar and John Hughey on steel guitar. There was another group, however, that was virtually the Sun houseband, led by Bill Cantrell. Quinton Claunch was on guitar, Stan Kesler on steel guitar and Marcus van Story, Bill Black or William Diehl on bass. The sound they forged was almost as distinctive as the Sun rockabilly sound. There was a strong walking bass sound derived from picking the bass strings of the electric guitar together with the double bass and around this simple backdrop there was the interplay of fiddle, steel guitar and high-pitched hillbilly vocal. It was modified Hank Williams and it was very effective.

This "electric hillbilly" sound was not a startling innovation; nowhere near as startling as rockabilly. It also had its precursors in the work of Jimmy Work on Dot, Jimmy Swan or Luke McDaniels on Trumpet and Bobby Roberts on King. The song that crystalized and epitomized the sound came from Memphis in the fall of 1954. It was *Daydreamin'*, issued on Meteor, by Bud Deckelman. It had been written by the team of Claunch and Cantrell in conjunction with Deckelman. Bill Cantrell recalls, "Sam cut the masters on that disc, using Les Bihari's rough demo tape. Deckelman was a mechanic and he had to patch up the old recorders that Meteor used before he could record but *Daydreamin'* was mastered at Sun."

The record sold well in the mid-South although it did not enter the *Billboard* charts. A cover version by Jimmy Newman on Dot did enter the charts and Claunch and Cantrell worked on three follow-ups. The first was *Daydreams Come True* on Meteor by the Hayriders, with backing provided by the Claunch–Cantrell band, the second was the same song on Sun by the young teenage Maggie Sue Wimberly (who would later become country star Sue Richards) again with the writers providing the instrumentation. A rockabilly version of *Daydreamin'* was also recorded in 1956 by Carl McVoy on Hi Records but the saga ended for Deckelman when a contract was offered by M-G-M and he disappeared from the local scene for a few years. In the '60s he returned to Memphis to run Shelman Publishing with Cantrell and in the '70s he became emcee at the mid-South Jamboree.

Also very much a part of the local scene was the band of Clyde Leoppard, a steel guitarist who switched to bass and then drums. During that time he led a band at the Cotton Club in West Memphis. The contribution of Leoppard and his Snearly Ranch Boys to Sam Phillips' country releases was important and varied. Basically they were a western swing band in 1949 when Leoppard and his boys moved to a boarding house on McNeilly St. run by Alma Snearly but their three records for Phillips were somewhat removed from that style. Their first was straight hillbilly, *Lonely Sweetheart*, with trumpeter and local songwriter Bill Taylor taking the vocals and the up tempo *Split Personality* which featured Smokey Joe Baugh as pianist and vocalist. This was the second release on Flip and a solo session was arranged for Smokey Joe in the fall of 1955.

"Smokey" Joe came from Helena, Arkansas, and moved to Memphis in 1947, joining Leoppard as a pianist two years later, aged 17. He attracted the

Doug Poindexter

Hardrock Gunter

Bud Deckleman, 1954

Bill Cantrell, 1948

The Slim Rhodes Band on stage in West Memphis, for WMC in the 50s. Left to right: Spec Rhodes, Dusty Rhodes, Slim Rhodes (possibly) and John Hughey.

Maggie Sue Wimberley (Sue Richards)

Clyde Leoppard

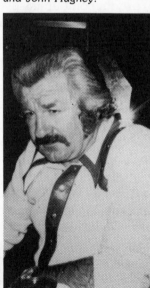

Bill Taylor

Charlie Feathers

attention of Sam Phillips and a two year contract was signed early in 1955 not only because he was an excellent pianist but also because of his voice. Bass player Marcus van Story, who joined Baugh on one-niters with Warren Smith from 1956, recalls that "Joe had a fantastic personality and a hell of a piano style. He really played the hell out of that thing and this was before Jerry Lee Lewis came on the scene, but what Sam liked, man, was his vocalizing. Now Joe had an accident a few years before and this affected his windpipe or something with the result that he sang real deep, almost like a negro. Sam really dug that."

It was not only Phillips who went for Smokey Joe's style, especially on his debut disc, *The Signifying Monkey*, a blues based song written by Stan Kesler and Bill Taylor. When the record reached New York, Phillips received a call from the booking agent of the Apollo Theater wanting to book the artist. Baugh's country roots were too deep, however, and he decided against making the trip. In 1974 he was working in a group called the Midnight Cowboys out of Waco, Texas, with Buddy Holobaugh, Leoppard's guitarist.

The Snearly Ranch Boys' final appearance on record was with Warren Smith, one of the more successful offshoots of a band that included, at one time or another, Sun vocalists Barbara Pittman and Jean Chapel and session men Ace Cannon and Bobby Woods. The band continued with rapid changes in the 1960s but was never under contract to Sun because of a disagreement with the local branch of the Musicians' Union. Leoppard explains, "We went down to the offices on Young and Parkway and the guy said it was nothing personal but they didn't want our kind, since at that time we were playing with a black band out at the Cotton Club, Drummer Red's Band, or something."

According to Bill Cantrell, Phillips had high hopes for three acts to break in 1955: the Miller Sisters, Charlie Feathers and Carl Perkins.

In April 1955 Flip 504 appeared. It was a pair of country duets by Elsie Jo Miller and Mildred Wages, the Miller Sisters, who had been newly signed. The record was a Claunch–Cantrell hillbilly production but its special feature was the unerring vocal harmony of the sisters. Phillips thought that this sound was a sure-fire winner and was always puzzled why it did not catch on in the wake of the success of the Fontane Sisters on Dot. "Maybe they were just too perfect," he concluded. In any event, Phillips did not give up easily and the Sisters had two other releases on Sun, one hillbilly and one with an added drum and saxophone and a pronounced rockabilly beat, *Ten Cats Down*. After this failed to make it the group returned to their home in Tupelo, Mississippi, with guitarist Roy Miller. They did not record again, as far as we know, but some excellent unissued recordings that they made for Sun have been unearthed and used in European reissue programs.

Commercial failure also befell the artistically successful discs of Charlie Feathers, who became a cult figure for rockabilly freaks. Feathers was used by Phillips as a session musician, songwriter and musical arranger. During this time, in 1954 and 1955, he evolved a distinctive hillbilly style and two records were issued. *I've Been Deceived* was a slow song with typical Claunch, Cantrell, Kesler and Diehl instrumentation, while *Peepin' Eyes* was fast; if a backbeat had been added it would have been rockabilly. Marcus van Story played the hustling upright double bass and the song was a perfect vehicle for Feathers' unique phrasing. *Billboard* reviewed both songs in May 1955, saying "The indie label Flip has found itself a major piece of talent in Feathers. This is one of the few distinctive voices to emerge in a country field that has long suffered from stereotypes. *Peepin' Eyes* is a bouncy little item that should do business in rural areas."

In November, Feathers recorded again and in December 1955 a second hillbilly record was on the market. This time Kesler was absent and Bill Black played the rhythm on his bass while Quinton Claunch provided the walking bass sound on the deadened strings of his electric guitar. Both sides, *Defrost Your Heart* and *Wedding Gown of White* were excellent examples of the hillbilly sound that had evolved in Memphis in the few years before rockabilly took over. It may have been issued on Flip as well as Sun, although this could have been a mistake at the pressing plant. The appearance of a cover version by Canadian Bob King on *Defrost Your Heart* suggests that the record must have attracted a little action but it was not reflected in sales with the result that it has become one of the most sought-after artifacts of the period. From that point was issued on Meteor under the pseudonym of Jess Hooper. It is not certain whether this name was used because Feathers was still under contract to Phillips or because "Jess Hooper" was a better name for an aspiring rocker than "Charlie Feathers."

Feathers also recorded demos of new songs. In return he was given half of the copyright. This usually did not amount to much except when the song was picked up by none other than Elvis Presley. This was the case on *I Forgot to Remember to Forget*.

Lately, a demo session has come to light which may have been recorded at the Sun studios on an unknown date; the titles include *I Forgot to Remember to Forget*. Feathers has said, "They were made before Elvis cut *Forgot*. I cut them on electric guitar and you can hear a boy playing bass behind me in some places and we had a Negro boy on drums there. I think Houston Stokes." Feathers' memory is not always so good when it comes to those far off days but it does not matter because what emerged was very fine music. Feathers was an uncompromising performer who retains his same basic style today, and still performs it in local clubs and bars where no one knows that he is virtually a legend in Europe.

The third of Phillips' most promising country artists of 1955 was more successful. Carl Perkins can certainly be seen as part of the Memphis country sound in that he joined the group of artists who recorded hillbilly in 1955. His music was also related to the honky tonk music played in the bars all over the South. It was dance music and cry in the beer music but it was loud enough to be heard above the rattle of glasses. Juke joints and bars had featured country music before the War but after 1945 they proliferated and moved into the cities bringing juke boxes and amplified groups with them. The repertoire of honky tonk singers still included traditional songs about railroads, great disasters and loves won and lost, but boogie rhythms were coming into demand. All of these elements and more were to come together in the music of Carl Perkins.

The Rockin' Guitar Man

Carl Lee Perkins was born the second of three brothers on a welfare aided tenant farm near Tiptonville, Tennessee, on April 9, 1932 and spent his early years in that north western corner of the state on a plantation in Lake County where his family were the only white sharecroppers. These are circumstances similar to Johnny Cash and Elvis Presley, except that the Cashes were slightly better off and Presley became a city boy. These factors tend to tell in the music of all three artists, especially that of Perkins, whose songs are frequently autobiographical. In 1945 the Perkins family moved southeast to Bemis and after leaving school Carl found work at a battery plant and later at a bakery in nearby Jackson.

His early life was hard but he always insists that his leisure hours were happy and to this day he delights in the simple country pursuits of hunting and fishing. Music, too, has always been with him. He grew up in the Bible Belt with gospel music on weekends and the blues of the black sharecroppers during work hours. One of his best friends was a black boy named Little Charlie.

Carl also listened to country music on WSM, Nashville, and other radio stations by night and he showed an early aptitude for the guitar, although out of economic necessity his first instrument was constructed from a cigar case and broom handle. In 1945 he won a talent contest in Bemis and performed *Home on the Range* on WTJS in Jackson. The talent show earned him twenty-five dollars and allowed him to air his own composition, *Movie Magg*, which became his first record a decade later.

Encouraged by these events, Carl taught his brothers, Jay B. and Clayton to play guitar and they sought their first local engagements as the Perkins Brothers Band. After two years they were given a local radio spot on WTJS and soon obtained enough club work to consider turning professional. By 1953 Carl had bought his first real guitar, a one hundred and fifty dollar Les Paul with a tiny amplifier and younger brother Clayton took up the double bass while Jay B. played the acoustic guitar. Later that year, a local drummer was with the group whenever a fuller sound was required; this was W. S. "Fluke" Holland, who later joined Johnny Cash.

Holland lived in Parkview Courts in Jackson, Tennessee, a government subsidized housing project. Carl moved there in January 1953 with his wife Valda, from Corinth, Mississippi, herself a proficient pianist who encouraged

Carl to realize his musical talents. Another Parkview resident was a blind singer and songwriter, Curley Griffin, who also encouraged Carl's songwriting and was rewarded when Carl later used one of the songs they had written together. In 1953 the Perkins Brothers Band was basically a straight, play-any-request country band, relying on the strength of Carl's voice, which, like that of his idol Hank Williams, was pure expressive hillbilly. There was another side to his talent, however, that was to transform his style and career. The sound of the black sharecroppers had followed Carl and particularly the advice of one old Tiptonville field worker, John Westbrook. It was Westbrook who taught Perkins some of the rudiments of the guitar and he is mentioned in a demonstration tape Carl made in 1963, for Cedarwood, his publishing company. An autobiographical song, *The Lord's Fishing Hole*, tells of an Uncle Ben with whom Carl would go fishing as a child. He has always partly attributed his rhythmic sense to the sharecroppers such as Uncle John, or Uncle Ben, and partly also to the bluesmen that he heard occasionally on the radio. Carl says that he "liked Bill Monroe's fast stuff and also the colored guys, John Lee Hooker, Muddy Waters, their electric stuff. Even back then I liked to do Hooker's things Monroe style, blues with a country beat and my own lyrics."

Carl also liked country guitarist Arthur Smith and the Memphis bluesman B.B. King. Carl later adopted a singing pose similar to King's while playing licks from Smith's nationwide hit *Guitar Boogie*. The patrons of the El Rancho Club in Jackson, the Perkins Brothers' resident Saturday night gig, were witnessing the birth of a new musical style. Bob Neals of WMPS recalls that he "visited the club in the fall of 1954 with Elvis Presley and we were both struck by the sound Perkins was getting. It was very similar to Elvis's own." Presley's first disc had just been released and Carl can remember hearing it on the radio and being very excited. "It was identical to what our band was doing and I just knew that we could make it in the record business after that."

Late in 1953 Perkins had sent demo tapes to various record companies in Nashville, New York and to Dot in Gallatin, Tennessee, but without success. He continued playing local clubs but now his bookings were farther afield. Malcolm Yelvington, who was the first to record for Sun after Presley, said, after hearing Carl play the clubs around Covington, that "he had a real unusual way of electric lead picking. He was always known as 'one string Perkins' because of his clear picking style. He was a terrific guitarist, even back then." It would seem that Perkins, like Scotty Moore in Memphis, was using the guitar solo to develop his ideas in the manner of the blues guitarist, although the overall sound of the band was still decidedly hillbilly. There was another factor contributing to Carl's guitar style. He often could not afford new strings so "I'd slide along to where I'd had to tie a knot and push up on the string 'cause I couldn't jump over the knot. Maybe if I'd been wealthy and could've bought new strings I'd have slid down it and not developed the pushing up on the strings and I'd have sounded like everyone else."

Perkins finally decided to drive to Memphis to see Sam Phillips, although Sun was still a blues label by reputation. There were several unsuccessful visits before the band finally got past secretary Marion Keisker to audition. In

December 1954 Phillips finally got to hear *Movie Magg*, a novelty country song sung to a very fast beat. Carl says he was "told to go back and write another song and then return to Sam so I took him *Turn Around*." This was a classic hillbilly song in the Williams mold and by the end of December the two songs were on tape and a check was in the mail to Perkins at Box 513, Bemis, Tennessee. On January 25, 1955 a contract followed—it was for two years and gave Carl a two percent royalty.

On *Movie Magg* Carl plays fast runs on the treble strings in a style approaching his later rock numbers but on *Turn Around* he keeps a slow walking rhythm on the deadened bass strings while the lead is taken by Bill Cantrell on fiddle. At this time the country style forged by Cantrell, Claunch, Bud Deckelman, Charlie Feathers and Sam Phillips was still in a very early stage of experiment and only the Deckelman disc on Meteor had been issued. As a result, Cantrell's playing varies from the style of most of the other hillbilly releases. It had a higher pitch and more traditional feel than on Perkins' next release, *Let the Jukebox Keep on Playing*, issued amid a rush of hillbilly releases in early 1955 when Cantrell's style was more clearly defined.

Movie Magg and *Turn Around* were issued on Flip in February 1955 and positive deejay reaction was forthcoming from some quarters. The Perkins Brothers Band was back in the studio later that month for another session. Carl was paid ten dollars advance and given ninety-eight dollars by Phillips to buy some clothes, presumably stage clothes, for next month the band was on the road playing one-niters with Presley. By June the tour had been joined by Sun's latest acquisition, Johnny Cash, and the first show together was in Marianna, Arkansas. Often, the artists would play from the back of a truck to crowds varying from a few hundred down to a handful of onlookers who had nothing better to do. The admission charge was $1. In the '70s by contrast, the booking fee for Presley was usually in the vicinity of $100,000 plus 50% of the gate, and for Cash/Perkins approximately $40,000.

According to people who saw the show, $1 was a dream price as all three artists had strikingly new styles. Presley had sex appeal and Perkins had developed a wild stage act. Perkins sometimes topped the bill on account of his unfollowable stage act.

Phillips issued Carl's second record, his first on Sun, in September 1955. The songs had been recorded in February and once again they were aimed primarily at the country market. *Let the Jukebox Keep on Playing* has a powerful performance from Perkins singing and playing the bass strings of the guitar while Cantrell's fiddle is reinforced by the sympathetic steel guitar work of Stan Kesler. *Gone, Gone, Gone*, on the other hand, is primitive rockabilly, medium paced with searing guitar fill-ins, the rhythm accented by "Fluke" Holland's snare drum.

In November 1955 Presley's contract had been sold and Carl Perkins was next in line for promotion. That fall he made the first of many appearances on the Southern radio/stage show show circuit that linked the Louisiana Hayride with the Big D Jamboree in Dallas. When they finally appeared on the Opry in Nashville, a house rule prevented the use of anything other than a snare drum

Carl Perkins – boppin' the blues *Carl Perkins*

The Carl Perkins Band, 1955. Left to right: W. S. Holland, Clayton Perkins, Carl Perkins and Jay Perkins.

Perkins and Presley, 1957

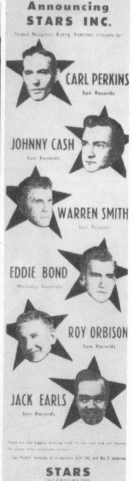

Announcing
STARS INC.

CARL PERKINS
Sun Records

JOHNNY CASH
Sun Records

WARREN SMITH
Sun Records

EDDIE BOND
Memory Records

ROY ORBISON
Sun Records

JACK EARLS
Sun Records

STARS
INCORPORATED

BOB NEAL
Manager

and brushes but this was to be one of the last occasions when Holland was to be restricted in this way.

In December, less than a month after Presley had gone, there was an abrupt change of policy at Sun and for almost a decade Carl Perkins veered away from country music to become a rock singer. "We had been playing country music because Sam did not want two artists doing colored music like Elvis but at this session he said to go right ahead and rock." It was December 19 and after a few trial runs the chosen A side was ready to be taped. It was a Perkins composition, *Honey Don't*, featuring a pronounced boogie rhythm played on the guitar and a heavily amplified string bass and drums. After it had been taped Carl asked Phillips to listen to a possible B side he had just written a few days before. It was about a boy, seen by Carl and Johnny Cash, at a Jackson dance who had been very careful not to let anyone tread on his new shoes. *Blue Suede Shoes* was the song and it was duly recorded in one take after a few trial runs and in the haphazard manner of genius a new sound was created. Bill Cantrell had a song called *Sure to Fall* "and Sam asked me what I thought about putting it out instead of one of the other sides. I said that I thought *Shoes* was best and *Honey Don't* a good second side. That little mistake cost me about $140,000. After that Quinton Claunch and I put our songs on the back of everything we could."

Judd Phillips recalls that by the time *Shoes* was taped a "relaxed session" was in progress and the liquor had been handed around. All the Perkins boys were strong drinkers and Carl's guitar had become appropriately fluid. Sam could sense the appeal of the *Shoes* theme as a symbol of the new teenage lifestyle and could hear sales potential jumping out of the grooves with the heavy backbeat and Carl's sharp, spluttering guitar solos which cut through the jumping rhythm. The record was released almost immediately on January 1, 1956 as a double 'A' sider and it was to set Perkins on the course of becoming one of the few poets of the rock 'n' roll era. It later got him a new contract with a 3% royalty.

Blue Suede Shoes not only topped *Cashbox*'s popular and country charts but by April 1956 it had topped the R&B charts too. This one record made rockabilly universally accepted. Presley's Sun records had laid down the basis for a new style, within the confines of country and blues songs, but Carl Perkins took things further by composing his own vehicles for the beat.

On the strength of *Blue Suede Shoes* Bob Neal and Judd Phillips put a special push behind Perkins on a national basis. He was booked on the big country shows, guested on the Webb Pierce television show as the house band and attained national television exposure. Further recording sessions followed on January 20 and March 22, 1956. The latter session lasted from 9:00 AM until noon and then the Perkins band took off by motorcade for the north where they were due to appear on the Ed Sullivan and Perry Como Shows. This would have represented the triumph of months of promotional work but Carl's car was involved in an accident in Delaware which slightly injured him and seriously hurt his brother Jay. Carl was forced to lay off for six months at a time when reputations were won and lost overnight.

Carl could see his hard work going for nothing. "I was a poor farm boy and with *Shoes* I felt that I had a chance but suddenly there I was in hospital." But, he added philosophically, "Elvis had the looks on me. The girls were going for him for more reasons than music. Elvis was hitting them with sideburns, flashy clothes and no ring on that finger. I had three kids. There was no way of keeping him from being the man in that music but I've never felt bitter, always felt lucky to be in the business. Most kids from my background never get to drive a new car."

By September Carl returned to work to find that he could still make a good living from hit records. *Boppin' the Blues*, recorded in January, had been released in May and found its way into the pop charts despite a lack of personal appearances. Another coupling of two country tracks, recorded at the same session, was scheduled for release in March but was limited to a DJ pressing.

These records may have gained Carl a foothold in the music business but the publicity had also widened the prospects for the Sun label, allowing Judd and Sam Phillips to move into the black and achieve national distribution for future releases. Finally, they had something they could sell on a national basis, even an international basis, so the brothers pulled out all of the stops. They were centrally located so they could get records into some stores more quickly. They could get product into Chicago, New York, Los Angeles or New Orleans while a competitor on one of the coasts might still have his product crated up halfway across the country. In addition, they took the risky and expensive step of giving away free records to deejays and distributors.

September 1956 saw another Perkins release, *I'm Sorry, I'm Not Sorry/Dixie Fried* and it had the heavy jukebox appeal, registering fairly good sales. The jogging rhythm laid down by brothers Clayton and Jay, backed up by the heavy bass drum effect, provided a platform for Perkins' guitar breaks and a raunchy honky-tonk lyric:

> Well on the outskirts of town, there's a little nightspot
> Dan dropped in about five o'clock
> Pulled off his coat, said "The night is short"
> Reached in his pocket and he flashed a quart
> Hollered, "Rave on, children, I'm with ya
> Rave on, cats," he cried
> "It's almost dawn and the cops are gone
> Let's all get Dixie Fried."

© *Hi-Lo Music Inc.*

The record, a product of the March session, had a marvellously raw edge to it, obviously influenced by the scenes which the Perkins brothers had witnessed at Saturday night dances. It was too soaked in the Southern honky-tonk tradition, however, for a pubescent rock 'n' roll audience. Most of them wanted to be Elvis's teddy bear and Carl's career sank to a lower level than Presley's from that point.

In 1957 Carl had three more releases and continued to be in demand on a minor scale, taking second billing to Johnny Cash on the Sun package tours put together from Bob Neal's office. His new material was quite varied but only sold averagely. *Matchbox* was an up tempo version of an old blues standard identified with Blind Lemon Jefferson, and it had Jerry Lee Lewis, just in from Louisiana, on piano. Lewis recorded a whole session with Carl in January 1957 but most of the recordings, which were of exceptional quality, had to wait fifteen years to get released. Instead, Phillips chose to issue a country ballad, *Forever Yours*, although the flip side was *That's Right*, another excellent up tempo honky-tonk song like *Dixie Fried*. It must have sold well in some rural areas with

Carl Perkins and Johnny Cash, 1956

The Canadian issue of
Carl's Sun album
(Quality V-1611)

Carl Perkins in "Jamboree"

lines like, *"When I find the cat that's been getting my sugar/It's gonna be rough when I catch that booger"* but it was not destined for huge success in the pop charts and was censored before release in England.

In December, Phillips tried rock again, issuing *Glad All Over*, a song that he managed to get into the Warner Bros. movie *Jamboree*, which also starred Jerry Lee Lewis, Fats Domino and some of the most truly forgettable artists ever to set foot upon a stage. Lewis was by now at the peak of his own short-lived popularity, unlike Carl who saw the label describe him as "The Rockin' Guitar Man," in case the public needed reminding. The ploy was a failure and his only other film appearances were in a 1958 release, *Hawaiian Boy*, produced by United Artists, and in some documentaries with Johnny Cash.

By 1958 Cash and Lewis had taken over from Perkins as Sun's headline artists and he began to feel that he was getting nowhere. The injury Jay had sustained in 1956 was becoming worse and the band worked less and less until June 1958 when it was temporarily disbanded. Clayton Perkins then sought relief in alcohol and was joined by Carl when Jay died a few months later.

Next, Carl's contract with Sun expired and he decided to go with Johnny Cash to Columbia on a more favorable deal. Columbia had previously recorded some rockabilly material with country artists but with Perkins they acquired a "name" act. Phillips was sure that he could groom singers as replacements but in fact this was virtually the end of the label's rockabilly era.

Perkins had been a national success but had never lost his basic country boy personality. Vocally similar to Hank Williams, he was probably more successful than anyone else, with the possible exception of Presley, in adapting the inflexions of black artists to his own style. Various vocal trademarks can be traced throughout his career—the slurred hillbilly pronunciation, the relaxed control of his timing, and the mumbled scat singing that accompanies guitar solos and fade-outs on so many of his recordings. *Her Love Rubbed Off*, released in the '70s, is notable in this respect, being virtually a collage of the things to be found in Perkins' other up tempo recordings. Similarly, recently issued Sun recordings reveal him to possess a penchant for self parody. In *Put Your Cat Clothes On* he develops the theme of *Blue Suede Shoes*, telling his young audience to dance and "pick your toenails up tomorrow." In *You Can Do No Wrong* you can "punch my nose, steal my clothes" even "scratch your name on my Cadillac," Jerry Lee Lewis is pounding out a relentless boogie in the background. It was a further development of the same theme.

The Perkins–Lewis team was one of the most exciting in rock history and was briefly reunited on records when Carl signed with Mercury Records in 1973 and contributed to Lewis's *"Southern Roots"* album. Before joining Mercury, Perkins had periods with Columbia (from 1958 until 1963), Decca, Dollie and then Columbia again. After he left Mercury in 1976 he formed his own label, Suede, and then moved briefly to Music Mill and M.M.I. before receiving the star relaunch in 1978 on Jet Records, the London-based label run by Don Arden.

His post Sun recordings have been varied, ranging from rock 'n' roll to country and pop and even an experiment with the modern rock band NRBQ in

1968. In general, his style has never lost the rockabilly and country influences with which it came to fruition.

Carl emerged in 1964 after half a decade of meaningless club appearances and personal problems, alleviated and enlivened by drink. He toured England with an embittered Chuck Berry who had just emerged from a prison term. He gained some reflected glory as one of the Beatles' idols and even had a minor hit with *Big Bad Blues* on English Brunswick, his first in Britain since 1956. He enjoyed another minor hit in England and Nashville with *Country Boy's Dream* on Dollie in 1968. He could probably have a fat living in England and Europe playing his old hits but he remains in the States.

He stayed with the Johnny Cash Show until relaunching his solo career with his sons in his band and Elvis's producer, Felton Jarvis, pulling for him. Today, Carl is as outwardly carefree about his career as he was in the beginning. "I figure I went from low to high to just about the middle. That's an advance isn't it?" He still wants another hit record, though. He nearly made it in 1959 when Columbia issued *Pointed Toe Shoes* which made the lower half of the Hot 100 and it was hoped that he could regain his popularity with another footwear hit or with a new style, as in *Sister Twister*.

Throughout the '60s Perkins continued to write prolifically, trying to interest everyone from Elvis to the Beatles in his new songs. Even during the early '60s when he was playing nightclubs in Las Vegas and professing that he was "Gonna buy me some clothes that'll be real loud/Take a trip down Sunset Strip with the Hollywood crowd" his songs were still basically country oriented. In 1968 he enjoyed a major country hit with *Restless* on Columbia, although he was unable to capitalize on this. His publishing company, Cedarwood, has managed to place a few of his songs and in 1971 Carl wrote the major part of the soundtrack for Robert Redford's cult biker movie, *Little Fauss and Big Halsy*. Certainly, as he says, he has moved to the middle of the ladder. He could yet reach a higher rung. Jet in England managed to push his *Old Blue Suedes Is Back* album into the charts with a television campaign but the album got lost in the shuffle in the States. Some of his later recordings have been good in their way but he will never reach the artistic heights he attained on his first and original Sun recordings.

His vocals, like Hank Williams', are full of sorrow, feeling or euphoria. He shares the same unaffected sincerity with his idol. As a guitarist he is never less than interesting, even on his poorest Sun track, *Your True Love*, on which the rhythm and vocal tracks have been speeded up to make him sound younger. Keeping the rhythm on the bass strings while singing and occasionally playing a boogie as on *Honey Don't*, Perkins takes off in his solos with a harmonic invention new to country guitarists. The closest parallels amongst those who preceded him are bluesman Arthur Crudup and country guitarists Arthur Smith and Merle Travis. Most country guitarists, apart from those in some bluegrass outfits, usually played a short variation on the melody during their solo space, letting the fiddle or steel guitar take the lead.

On some of the more up tempo country items such as *Movie Magg*, *Tennessee* or *Honky Tonk Girl* Carl plays a scat guitar style to match his vocals which skim above the rhythm. His solos on these recordings are almost within the country finger-picking style in contrast to his stronger rockabilly recordings. On discs such as *Blue Suede Shoes, Dixie Fried* or the 1958 Columbia recordings of *Where the Rio de Rosa Flows* and *That's Alright* we hear the fully developed rockabilly style.

Sam Phillips used amplification and reverberation to accentuate Perkins' harsh ringing tone. Once it would have sounded out of place in a country band; it would have drowned the piano, fiddle or bass but new recording balances were used for the dawn of the rockabilly era. Sometimes Phillips put the guitar's speaker in the washroom so that he could get the heavy over-amplified tone without obliterating every other sound in the little studio. Carl's 1968 recording of *Restless* for Columbia displays both the rockabilly legacy and his later development of that style, although the harshness has gone. On some Sun recordings, though, with the heavily accentuated backbeat, the ferocity of Carl's spluttering guitar solos is redolent of vintage post-War blues, the rockabilly equivalent of B. B. King or Pat Hare.

In all, during his four years with Sun, Perkins recorded thirty-nine sides, nine of which were singles (one not issued commercially) and the rest made up an EP, an LP and seventeen unissued recordings. At this point, everything he recorded for Sun has deservedly been issued.

February 4, 1969 was declared "Carl Perkins Day" in Jackson and in May 1974 the Memphis Music Award for services to the city was presented to Carl by Sam Phillips. Carl has received other accolades, which are partly due to his success as a songwriter with Johnny Cash, but mostly due to the reputation he gained with Sun. Certainly, if anyone ever embodied the Sun sound it was Carl Perkins in 1956 and it was through Sun that he exerted his greatest influence. His jumping solos were echoed in hundreds of rockabilly discs issued between 1956 and 1958, from those of Buddy Holly to James Burton playing guitar with Ricky Nelson. Burton, in fact, played guitar on Perkins' 1964 recording of *The Monkeyshine* on Decca, and Nelson has said of his earliest recordings, "I used to listen to the radio and longed to be a recording artist. I wanted to be Carl Perkins."

Nelson was one of the first to adopt Carl's style, but there have been many others over the years. In 1964 the Beatles recorded four of Carl's songs and George Harrison has credited Carl with being a big influence. John Fogerty and Credence Clearwater Revival had many hits during the late '60s with records that were vocally reminiscent of Little Richard with the guitar playing straight out of Carl's book. It's unfortunate that the Carl Perkins sound, now thoroughly integrated into the melting pot of rock, has become more influential than the name of its originator.

"We Called It 'Rockabilly'"

So I took my guitar, picks 'n' all
Bid farewell to my overall
Split for Memphis, where they say y'all
And them swinging cats are havin' a ball.

One of the most popular novelty songs to emerge from the rock 'n' roll era was *The All American Boy*, recorded for Fraternity by Bobby Bare under the name "Bill Parsons" in 1958. It was not the only record to make light of the rags to riches saga which rock 'n' roll could provide. Comedian Stan Freberg made an album of send-ups, including the classic *Payola Roll Blues*, on Capitol. It seemed that almost any boy with the nerve to get up there and sing could make it provided that he had a managerial star-maker like Presley's Col. Parker. Carl Perkins in *Hambone* cries, "Hey there Colonel with the big cigar/how's about you makin' me a big star?"

At one time it seemed that you only had to mention Presley in a song to guarantee a million seller and these songs, often written by country artists, recognized where the record sales lay but also pointed out the impermanence of star status. They centered around an exaggerated character based largely on Presley and the other rockabillies who came out of Memphis in the mid '50s. In fact, Memphis had become the focal point of white rock 'n' roll after Presley's and Perkins' success.

Only a few major artists in this new style were actually born and raised in Memphis—Eddie Bond and Johnny Burnette, for example—but the city did become the focal point for dozens of country boys from rural Tennessee, the immediate Delta area and, eventually, from all over the South. They were usually in their late teens or early twenties and they came, guitar in hand, looking for overnight success. Their sound was rockabilly. If they had emerged as musicians in 1950, rather than 1955, they would almost certainly have channeled their talent into straight country music but now Memphis had Presley, it had Carl Perkins and it had the Sun label with its exciting new music.

This is not to say that the new style remained peculiar to Memphis or that it originated with Sun Records. Sun crystalized the sound in its best known form but the origins are embedded deep in the history of post-War country music and down home blues, what Mississippians call the "cottonpatch blues." Carl

60

Perkins says that "all we did was take country music and give it a colored beat," and the country audience had been partially introduced to this during the previous decade with "honky-tonk" and "country boogie." Artists playing these brands of music in Memphis, such as Malcolm Yelvington and Charlie Feathers, made a fairly smooth transition but none of them admitted that the beat had its origins in black music and because of this, in a sense, it did not. Country boogie and honky tonk music remained within the framework of the development of country music, which has always been fed by outside influences.

The country boogie idiom was an offshoot of the boogie woogie craze that swept New York in the early '40s and then extended to country music. The Delmore Brothers, Arthur Smith and Merle Travis were among the first artists to record in this new style in 1945. The Delmores had *Hillbilly Boogie* on King and Smith had his hugely influential *Guitar Boogie* on Super Disc. Travis, from Muhlenberg Co., Kentucky, is almost worth a book by himself. He took his jumping, finger picking guitar style to California after the War and his Capitol recordings inspired guitarists everywhere. He wrote *Sixteen Tons, Smoke, Smoke, Smoke That Cigarette* and had a slew of hits but his guitar playing made his records stand out. He also claims to be the inventor of the first solid bodied electric guitar even though he has hardly played one. All these recordings established the framework for boogie licks on country records and innumerable country recordings since the mid '40s have used them. Jack Guthrie enjoyed a hit in 1947 with *Oakie Boogie* on Capitol and the trend cluminated in a series of recordings by Tennessee Ernie Ford in the wake of his successful *Smokey Mountain Boogie*, also on Capitol in 1949. Red Foley, Hank Snow, Webb Pierce, Moon Mullican, Hank Thompson, the York Brothers, Merrill Moore and the young Bill Haley all contributed to the perpetuation of the boogie beat.

Tennessee Ernie Ford's success carried him away from his first love of gospel music and away from the country radio shows he had played for over a decade. He became a prominent show business personality and this may have encouraged Capitol to pick up on Merrill E. Moore, a singer and pianist from Iowa who had moved to California. Moore recorded many country boogie tunes between 1952 and 1958 featuring his forceful piano in front of a fast rhythm section. Sales of his records inspired small companies in a dozen places throughout the country to issue similar material.

In Philadelphia, western swing artist Bill Haley, who had recorded in 1944 with the Downhomers on Vogue, left the Cowboy and Keystone labels and began making country boogies for Dave Miller's Holiday Records, a subsidiary of Essex. *Rocket 88* and *Sundown Boogie* and other similar titles were issued in 1951 before the renowned saxophone of the late Rudi Pompilli fronted the band. In 1952 Haley's group changed their name from the Saddlemen to the Comets, as the influence of the R&B bands became more pronounced in their music. Previously, they had used strong rhythms and a slapped bass sound and among the early recordings was *Icy Heart*, on Essex, very reminiscent of Hank Williams. Haley, from Michigan, was working as music director of WPWA

(Chester, Pennsylvania) and was also familiar with jazz and other styles. It is significant that before signing with Essex Haley had been touring the south and had been inspired not only by Hank Williams, whom he met in Shreveport, but also by the R&B singers in New Orleans, particularly by Joe Turner who, with Pete Johnson, had been responsible for taking boogie woogie to the Café Society in New York in 1938, thereby starting the whole craze.

It is noticeable that the vocal strength of singers such as Tennessee Ernie Ford and Merrill Moore was not great. It was really the boogie rhythms that led to their popularity and even the words of the songs were often about the music itself. This was a tendency that became more pronounced in later years. Many country bands played boogie-woogie during the early '50s, often combining it with other styles, such as Hank Williams' hillbilly style. It was probably this fusion that led to the development of Sam Phillips' type of rock 'n' roll— rockabilly.

Phillips was not alone in searching for the elusive white singer who could channel the energy and meaning of the blues into a marketable style. In the north, Alan Freed, Bill Randle and other white R&B jocks looked for much the same thing, encouraging the emergent beat of Bill Haley's brand of white rock & roll as the medium through which they could satisfy an increasing demand by white audiences for rhythm music. Phillips had recorded R&B and it had sold, just as the New Orleans R&B from Cosimo Matassa's studio had sold but it was selling to a primarily black audience. Phillips needed the young white market, as this was where the growth potential in record sales rested in an era of increased teenage affluence. Many young white kids tuned into black radio stations in the hope of hearing beat music and the initial success of Bill Haley confirmed that there was a demand for something different. Despite the purifying process that Haley's records were subjected to before they were allowed on the market, his band did retain the essential driving beat that was eminently danceable. In Cincinnati, King Records had hits by Boyd Bennett and His Rockets in the Haley mold. This meant teen-oriented lyrics, a steady back beat and riffing sax section. It would not have been beyond the scope of the Sun studio to produce this sound immediately, as Hardrock Gunter's 1954 session shows, but Phillips wanted the conviction to go with the music. He wanted rock 'n' roll on his own terms and he got it.

It is difficult to know when the term "rockabilly" or "rock-a-billy" was first used to describe the various types of up tempo country music but record company personnel were using it in 1955 as a means of describing the new phenomenon they were recording. Before this, however, many Southern deejays had used the word to convey the notion of rocking a hillbilly song. The word "rock" had been increasingly accepted into the country vocabulary, especially when it began to lose its original sexual connotation.

By 1955, the words "rock 'n' roll", first used in country song by Buddy Jones in 1940 (*Rockin' Rollin' Mama*), had taken on accepted associations beyond their original, purely sexual ones. They now related to up tempo music with a dance beat, honky-tonking, or just having a good time. Examples of this occur in Bill Haley's recording of *Rock the Joint* on Essex Records, and Joe Almond and His Hillbilly Rockers' *Gonna Roll and Rock* on Trumpet. These records use "rocking" as the opposite of "having the blues" and these usages are reflected in primitive rockabilly lyrics.

Throughout 1955 the word rockabilly became more widely used. It appeared in the review section of the trade weeklies, *Billboard* and *Cashbox*, and by June 1956, just two months after the success of *Blue Suede Shoes*, the word reached England. James Asman, writing in *Record Mirror*, reviewed Johnny Carroll's *Wild, Wild Women* on Decca under the category of "rock-billies" music by "an eighteen-year-old Texan who puts his back into this wild, pulsating corn." It is amazing that such a raw disc as Carroll's could be termed "corn" when the pop charts were full of such excruciating banalities. The *Billboard* reviewers were closer to the mark, though, when they reviewed Sun recordings. Carl Perkins, Slim Rhodes, Billy Riley, Malcolm Yelvington, the Miller Sisters, Warren Smith and Jerry Lee Lewis were all described as "rockabilly." Charlie Rich's first record was dubbed "frantic rockabilly chanting," but so was another record by Rosco Gordon. Ray Smith's *You Made a Hit* becomes a "good rockabilly blues," while Sonny Burgess received adjectives like "wild," "screaming," "driving" and "crazy." The slower rockers were dubbed "rockaballads." England was still finding the concept hard to grasp and *Jazz Journal* called New Orleans R&B star Smiley Lewis "rockabilly." Pulp writer Harlan Ellison used the word as a title for a book based loosely on Presley's saga. The real meaning was becoming obscured.

There is no doubt that the fusion of rock 'n' roll with hillbilly music was the basic element of a rockabilly record and groups began to appear with such names as Bill Flagg's Rockabillies, Bob and the Rockabillys and songs like *Rockabilly Hop, Rockabilly Boogie* and *Rockabilly Rhythm*. Jerry Lee Lewis is an example of an artist who recorded both country and rock without being basically a rockabilly singer and the issue has become clouded by the use of the term "country rock" for music without the essential rawness of

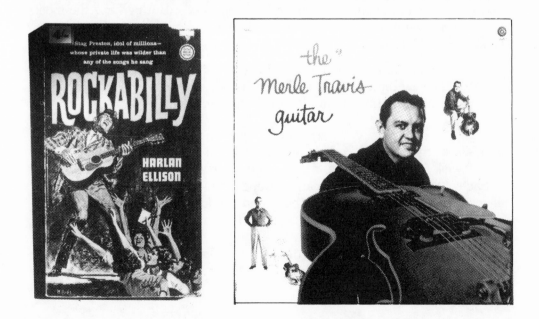

rockabilly. Many other pianists from Merrill Moore and Roy Hall to Charlie Rich and Mickey Gilley are best described as country rock rather than rockabilly.

The rockabilly style contains four basic elements. The first is that the vocalists usually had a background in country music because they were predominantly white and Southern. This is even true of singers who had not recorded previously in a honky-tonk or country boogie style. Bill Flagg, for instance, whose *Go Cat Go*, on Tetra, is an extremely simple and basic early example of the style.

The white Southerness is a common feature but added to it are three other factors which vary in importance from one recording to another and within the style of each artist. One is the use of blues rhythms reinforced by the use of blues structured songs or by the actual recording of blues songs in their entirety. Presley provides the most notable example of this.

Another vital ingredient was the pattern of the instrumental solos. The rhythm on most rockabilly records was supplied by the string bass, acoustic guitar (usually played by the singer) and, in some cases, drums. Electric or steel guitars took the solos and the piano was sometimes in evidence. What made rockabilly fascinating was its compulsive rhythm with the accent on the second and fourth beats, usually achieved without the use of a heavy drummer. Other instruments used in the early days were the fiddle and, later, the saxophone when artists had designs on a hit record. The Sun recording of *Red Headed Woman* by Sonny Burgess even has the addition of trumpeter Richard Nance.

Finally, there were the songs themselves. Rockabilly, like rock 'n' roll, was primarily a "sound" and lyrics were of secondary importance. Nevertheless, there was an identifiable lyrical pattern. Out of the honky-tonk and boogie songs came early tributes to fast living, exemplified by Perkins in *Dixie Fried* but other themes developed. From R&B came the reworking of old blues choruses and a use of terms derived from black culture. Allied to this were themes designed to appeal to the newly created teenage market. Catch phrases appeared, like Haley's *Rock Around the Clock* or Presley's *All Shook Up* and there was a boom in the sales of *Blue Suede Shoes*. But perhaps the most typical lyrics were those which celebrated the music itself. On *Get With It*, Charlie Feathers sang:

> Well, you pick the tune, and you slap the bass
> I'll play the rhythm and I'll set the pace
> But we gotta get with it, got no time to waste

> © *Meteor Publishing*

In a similar mood, Carl Perkins announced "All my friends are bopping the blues" while Warren Smith and Jerry Lee Lewis did the *Ubangi Stomp*.

Each of these four elements can be found in the Sun rockabilly releases. Sun developed a balance between them and in doing so made way for the acceptance of a typical rockabilly style, if there could, in fact, be a norm in a music so diverse.

Occasionally black singers attempted the rockabilly style. G. L. Crockett's *Look Out Mabel*, on Chief Records, shows a profound rockabilly influence and

Roy Brown was encouraged by Imperial Records to record in this style in the mid '50s. The same influence crops up on the Nashville recordings of Arthur Gunter for Excello and Tarheel Slim's *Number Nine Train* on Fury Records also has the Memphis feel. The country tradition normally prevailed, however, and its grip was strengthened by a need to aim at both the country and pop charts for high sales. In the mid '50s the country and blues markets overlapped even less frequently than today and very few rockabilly records entered the R&B charts. It was for this reason that Sam and Judd Phillips worked so long to find an artist like Presley who could take R&B into white homes. Judd recalls, "In the early days when I was working at peddling Sun records out of the back of a car, even then it occurred to me that people were really digging the music that was on our R&B records, the music that the black people were putting down. But there was so much prejudice and division that they couldn't idolize the artist that was delivering the song. Elvis Presley was just what we needed at that time."

The Sun Sound

Most singers who recorded rockabilly for Sun are also properly described as country or rock 'n' roll artists. There could be a world of difference between a young singer trying to emulate Presley and an older, established country musician who merely played hillbilly rock 'n' roll because it was in style. The fact that they used the Sun sound at some point makes them both rockabilly artists. It was the recording methods employed by Sam Phillips that ultimately set Sun records apart. If there was a "Memphis synthesis" in the blues scene of the early '50s, a rockabilly sound followed to become not only the basis of much white rock 'n' roll but a continuing influence on the city's musical development.

The "Sun Sound" is usually identified with rockabilly music but, in fact, elements of it are found in the entire range of recordings made at 706 Union Avenue. Sam always wanted that blues feel.

Initially, Phillips only had five microphones and a single-track, mono-input board, through which the pronounced raw edges of the blues recordings could be retained. Blues should always be recorded for its feeling rather than technical quality and it was Phillips' experience in capturing the blues feel that helped him so greatly in conceptualizing how white rock 'n' roll should sound. The artists had to really mean it.

The studio itself was often described as a "hole in the wall," being roughly thirty by eighteen feet, leading at one end into a small control room and shipping room and at the other into the front office guarded by secretary Marion Keisker. In such a confined space spontaneous rockabilly sounds could be captured just as well as intimate blues.

Presley and Perkins had a positive feeling for the blues but many of their contemporaries did not and Phillips would use his knowledge to modify their hillbilly influences and produce something with which most of them could identify. He rarely had a predetermined idea about how a song should be performed and he is at pains to point out that he never told white men to sing like blacks. "I was trying to establish an identity. Each singer had to have feel and fervor in his music. Can I touch you in some way or another? If it's there it will come out. I'm no genius but I wanted to give my people the freedom to express themselves. Often they played what they thought I wanted to hear at first. I had to get past that."

This made for long informal recording sessions. Scotty Moore says, "We played entirely by ear and feel was the important thing to us." This made the choice of the right song very difficult and many takes were sometimes needed to achieve the desired result.

As we have noted, Phillips' main priority was to capture a resonant bass sound, which was often lost on the appalling surface quality of his early 45 rpm pressings. He used an amplified string bass and drums. The bass strings were often slapped with the hand or a drumstick to set the pace and the guitar solos were allowed to cut through in sharp contrast, emphasizing the clear, ringing quality of the early electric Fender, Gibson and Les Paul guitars. The final balance was usually performed for direct taping as Phillips had neither the equipment nor the inclination to remix, splice or overdub.

Singer Sonny Burgess found that "Sam seemed to care little about the sound you made so long as you got the feel. I like country music but also rock, and we cut a lot of Little Walter, Smiley Lewis annd other R&B numbers that I thought turned out real well." Phillips felt spontaneity to be more important than instrumental brilliance and the only device used to enhance recordings, apart from a new studio ceiling with improved acoustics, was echo. Scotty Moore was one of the first country guitarists to use the echo chamber as an aid and Phillips was quick to adapt this for vocalists too. Vocal echo was actually quite common in country music, Eddy Arnold used it on his hit *Cattle Call* as did Slim Whitman on almost all of his Imperial recordings. Presley, however, was the first white singer to be recorded at Sun with tape echo and he became so successful that the effect was to be used continually for the next few years. Malcolm Yelvington was the next artist to record after Presley made *That's All Right* and he remembers being introduced to echo by Phillips who stressed his liking for the eerie, faraway sound. "Sam took trouble to explain to me what he could do to my voice and at which points he wanted to raise it." There was also a more practical reason, "Echo was a good way to cover up the bad places in your voice."

The Sun Artists

Each of the rockabilly singers who recorded for Sun had a slightly different background and approach. Some took to it naturally, others were pressured into it but all of them can be seen as having contributed something to the composite style. Initially, honky tonk bands like Malcolm Yelvington's Star Rhythm Boys adapted best to rockabilly as a musical form, although not to Presley's method of performing it on stage. The Star Rhythm Boys employed a honky tonk hillbilly sound, using acoustic bass and guitar, electric guitar, steel guitar and piano. They were aware of some R&B tunes but always gave them the hillbilly treatment.

They had three sessions with Sun, in 1954, 1956 and 1958 but only two singles were released. They illustrate the musical transition in Memphis from what was essentially up tempo western swing through to countrified pop. Yelvington's partner, Reece Fleming, made an even greater jump, having recorded pre-War for RCA-Bluebird in the duo, Reece and Raspus. Yelvington was most interested in country music, especially the hillbilly style. "Of course that was the popular music around here then. It was very different from bluegrass or country and western. Rockabilly, I didn't care for at first but at that time it was the only thing going. Country was at an all time low. I wanted to record like Hank Williams or Moon Mullican but Sam wanted something with a beat to it. So we turned up at the studio at the time he said, 'cause when Sam said to come, you went if you were interested in doing anything in music. We were going through some material that we had and couldn't come up with anything that Sam wanted to record. I said to the boys, 'Let's try *Wine Spo-Dee-O-Dee* we don't even have to rehearse that one, we play it every week.' So he was sitting in the control room there and my lead man, Gordon Mashburn, he took off on it and I started to sing. Sam poked his head around the door and said, 'Where'd you get that one?' and I told him, 'Man, we've been doing that thing for a long time.' It was first done by a fella the name of Stick McGhee and then I think Lionel Hampton did it. I was the first white artist to record it. Sam said, 'Let's cut that, it sounds good.' So we did but it took a lot of takes to get it like Sam wanted. He was most particular about the overall sound."

Yelvington was actually not the first country artist to record *Wine Spo-Dee-O-Dee* but he was typical of many Southern hillbilly singers of the rock 'n' roll era who caught the ear of record company executives at the time when they were desperately trying to adapt themselves to new trends, changing up tempo jump tunes into a form of rock 'n' roll. The singers themselves were usually glad to try this new style because of the sinking popularity of straight country music. A few months after the Yelvington session, Luke McDaniel arrived for an audition. He had recorded for Trumpet and King in the old style and later made some rockabilly records for Big Howdy Records in Angie, Louisiana, but the Sun test did not reveal the approach that Phillips sought. There were continual interjections from the control booth asking to "hear that one again" or inquiring whether McDaniel could "get a beat going there." As it happened, he couldn't and the session ended in failure. This is interesting in view of the fact that McDaniel was one of the more expressive and bluesy hillbilly singers of the time. At a later session McDaniel did find "the sound" and the unissued *Uh Babe* is fine rockabilly.

Most hillbilly singers had little contact with the blues but Phillips could usually modify their style to suit the sound he heard in his head. In May 1956 the Yelvington band skipped work again for a midweek session. Phillips recorded them in full rockabilly style, choosing Yelvington's own novelty song *Rockin' with My Baby* for release. On the flip, the bluesy *It's Me Baby* captured the feeling and phrasing that had eluded McDaniel. A drum was used to accentuate the hillbilly rhythm and an accidental mumbling effect was achieved when Yelvington removed his false teeth for comfort.

In between the two Sun dates Yelvington recorded for Phillips' rivals at Meteor under the pseudonym of Mac and Jake and The Esquire Trio. *A Gal Named Joe* was a relaxed honky-tonk tune with a rockabilly leaning, clearly showing the origins of the group's sound.

Another new convert to rockabilly was Jack Earls, a baker living in West Memphis, who made some of the most primitive rockabilly music on Sun. Earls had his own band but he was backed on the Sun sessions by Bill Black, Luther Perkins and Billy Riley. His coarse, untutored vocal style was very effective on the faster numbers such as *Slow Down* or *Sign on the Dotted Line* and *Let's Bop*. Earls' style was decidedly wild on occasion but Phillips did not persevere. Probably, the poor sales on *Slow Down* convinced him that Earls' voice contained weaknesses that no amount of echo could disguise. Earls was rediscovered in the '70s and made some more recordings which showed that his voice had altered remarkably little with the passing of almost twenty years.

Ray Harris was another fairly limited vocalist who made up for it with boundless enthusiasm. Bill Cantrell recalls Ray Harris in 1956: "Ray wanted to be another Elvis. He couldn't sing and he wasn't good to look at but he didn't care. Man, he was crazy. You would go to visit him and hear him practising there on Ogden from two blocks away. He would open the door wearing nothing but his overalls and dripping with sweat. He had an old portable tape recorder and he'd go back to singing and playing and sweating. In the studio he would throw himself around with his arms going like windmills. That record *Come On Little Mama* was a triumph for the guitar man Wayne Powers and drummer Joe Riesenthal. They had to keep up with the guy." *Billboard* reviewed *Come On Little Mama*, describing Harris's vocal as "excitable."

Harris later gave up singing and became a producer and studio owner, in and out of partnership with Sam Phillips.

The exceptionally raw Harris and Earls records were issued in the fall of 1956 and this was also the time that Hardrock Gunter made his second appearance on Sun. He recorded a duet with fellow deejay Sonny "Buddy" Durham in the studio of WWVA (Wheeling, West Virginia). They called themselves The Rhythm Rockers and issued *Jukebox Help Me Find My Baby*, which had previously been available on Cross Country Records. Sam leased the song, edited it down slightly and put it out on Sun. The novelty flip side, *Fiddle Bop*, was left alone. Phillips did not usually lease or buy tapes because he had enough hopefuls seeking auditions. It was in this way that one of the most promising young hopefuls, Warren Smith, came to his attention in 1956.

Smith was considerably younger than Gunter or Yelvington, had a better voice than either Harris or Earls and possessed Presleyish good looks. With such material Phillips was able to develop a full-bodied rockabilly sound and image, even though Smith had not encountered the style until his arrival in Memphis a few months before. He says, "I was born in an out of the way part of Mississippi and had always lived in the country. I came to Memphis and began to look for a job in music. I was always a singer and wanted to get into the business. I took some jobs around town and then I met up with Clyde Leoppard." He became vocalist with Leoppard at the Cotton Club and it was there that Phillips first witnessed his act in February 1956.

Smith was summoned to Union Avenue to cut demo tapes and some have survived. They display a preference for country music but Smith's voice is equal to the new demands being made upon it. Songs like *Savin' It All for You* and *The Day After Heartbreak* feature support from the Leoppard band who were also on the first recording chosen for release, the Johnny Cash composition *Rock 'n' Roll Ruby*, on which Smith sounds at ease with the fast hillbilly piano of Smokey Joe and the rock guitar of Buddy Holobaugh. He is equally relaxed on the flip side, *I'd Rather Be Safe Than Sorry*, in the company of steel guitarist Stan Kesler and his voice takes on the whine of Hank Williams on the high notes. Smith possessed a wider vocal range than most of his contemporaries and despite his aptitude for rockabilly he always saw himself making an impact on the Nashville country scene.

Rock 'n' Roll Ruby reportedly registered local sales of almost half a million and Phillips signed him to a three year contract. Until then only Presley, Perkins and Cash had moved Phillips to exceed the more usual one year term but from 1956, as the competition for artists became more severe, Phillips offered more and more three year contracts. A union dispute prevented Leoppard turning professional with Smith, although Smokey Joe gained himself a one year contract.

Joe's disc was issued before Smith's but Joe never saw a follow-up hit the market. Smith went back to the studio to cut his second release, *Ubangi Stomp*, which was backed with an old folk tune, *Black Jack David*, which, as *Gypsy Davy* or *The Gypsy Lad* has its origins in an English ballad from the sixteenth century. It was made with a new band, Al Hopson, Marcus van Story

Sonny Burgess

Malcom Yelvington and the Star Rhythm Boys. Left to right: Miles Winn, Gordon Mashburn, Yelvington, Reece Fleming and Jake Ryles.

Billy Riley

Warren Smith and Billy Riley

Louisiana Hayride, 1955. Left to right: Luke McDaniel, Joe Clay and Elvis

Warren Smith

and former Louisiana Hayride drummer, Jimmy Lott. In April 1957 they combined again to record a Roy Orbison song, *So Long I'm Gone*. This provided a second country hit and became Smith's only entry in *Billboard*'s pop charts. Sales of this medium-paced rocker were helped by a frantic flipside, *Miss Froggie,* an adaptation of a traditional blues theme, belted out with real fervor and highlighted by a dazzling guitar solo from Al Hopson. The follow-up, *Got Love If You Want It,* was taken at a similar pace, although it had been written and recorded by bluesman Slim Harpo in a more restrained style. It failed to capitalize upon the previous successes, however, and as a result Smith was allowed to turn back to country music for his next single. When *Goodbye Mr. Love* also failed to hit the heights Smith moved to Hollywood in 1959. He says, "I wanted country music to be my career and I was lucky to make it with Liberty right away and would not have missed it, but I enjoyed the days at Sun." He left behind a wealth of unissued recordings, none of which were issued until the '70s, despite his success on Liberty.

According to bassist Marcus van Story, Smith's enjoyment of the touring days was marred when Jerry Lee Lewis emerged as headliner on the Sun show. "There was a clash of personalities, I guess. Touring was a real hectic thing to do again and again, after all. Anyway, it ended with Jerry Lee playing all his own discs on the jukeboxes whenever we stopped over and he did this over and over again. Warren would retaliate by going to the local record store and buying up dozens of Lewis discs. He would ceremoniously smash each one of them right there in the store."

Smith appeared to be on the verge of a breakthrough in 1956 and then things went wrong. The same situation overtook Billy Lee Riley, perhaps the most promising of all Sam Phillips' protégés for he played bass, harmonica, guitar and drums and was gifted with clean-cut good looks, accentuated by the high cheekbones of his Indian ancestry. Looks were becoming important but Riley attributes his failure, and that of other Sun artists, "to the distribution of Sun discs. They sent out a batch of discs altogether and when there was a Perkins release, a Cash release and later Jerry Lee Lewis, the deejays didn't want to be bothered with the rest of the bunch. The public could only afford so many at one time, anyway."

Riley's first release was not typical. *Rock With Me Baby* had a restrained country-oriented sound, betraying influences gained during a childhood in rural Arkansas. The other side, *Trouble Bound*, was an atmospheric country blues.

Riley told the *Memphis Press Scimitar* in 1961 that he had always admired Memphis and that he came there to record after forming a hillbilly band in the army. The master of his first recording was made from a rough tape cut in the garage of country band leader Slim Wallace on Fernwood Drive in Memphis. Supervised by Jack Clement, it was intended to be the first release on the new Fernwood label but Clement found that "Riley was doing country but he was one of these rockabilly types, he had a beat. Fernwood had an old Magnacord tape machine we bought from deejay Sleepy Eyed John, but no real studio then so we rented the studio at WMPS and recorded there. Billy played guitar, bass and drums and we dubbed each track onto the others. We were going to make it the first on Fernwood but I took it to Sam to do the final mastering and he called me up one day, said he liked it and we worked on a lease deal."

Phillips also recognized Clement's talent as a producer, for this was probably the first Memphis recording to be pieced together, or *produced* in the modern sense. By late 1955 both Riley and Clement were on the Sun payroll, Clement at ninety dollars a week. The association was fruitful—Riley's presence enhanced many recordings, including those of Sonny Burgess and Jerry Lee Lewis and he had some solo success too. Clement started taking over engineering and production duties and auditioned a lot of the good ol' boys waiting outside the door.

Rock With Me Baby sold "like yesterday's hot cakes," according to Billy Riley. Success came with *Flying Saucers Rock 'n' Roll*, a fast rocker with Jerry Lee Lewis on piano and topical novelty lyrics. Released in January 1957, in the wake of the Buchanan and Goodman's *Flying Saucer* record in September 1956, it proved very popular in the mid-South and Riley was booked on the one-niter circuit, developing one of the wildest stage acts in the area.

He gained his nickname "Red Hot" Riley after his biggest hit, an adaptation of Billy "The Kid" Emerson's jump blues. It featured the rasping, red-hot larynx style heard on *Flying Saucers*. The song, *Red Hot*, featured Jerry Lee Lewis on piano again and it led to a tour of Canada with Chuck Berry's package show. Unfortunately, Jerry Lee Lewis began to have monster hits at the time and promotion for *Red Hot* was limited.

Riley's sound, although based on the rockabilly sounds of Carl Perkins, Warren Smith and Elvis Presley, often placed more emphasis on the speed of the rasping vocal delivery, developed from impersonations of Little Richard, and the harshness of the guitar and drums. Another departure was the use, from the third disc on, of a saxophonist to augment the sound of his backup group, the Little Green Men. The first sax man was Martin Willis and he was followed by Ace Cannon. Both went on to work for Hi Records and the Bill Black Combo while continuing to do session work with Riley. Others in the group were Roland Janes, Jimmy van Eaton, Marvin Pepper and Jimmy Wilson, who took over the piano stool from Jerry Lee Lewis. They became the next Sun houseband, appearing on many recordings made in Memphis during the '50s and '60s. They also appeared on discs that Riley made under pseudonyms, such as the Rockin' Stockin's, who made a Christmas record, pressed on festive red vinyl.

Riley eventually lost his rockabilly influence but remained an important part of the Memphis scene for some time before moving to Nashville. His versatility led to a series of soul and funky country recordings and they were preceded by a variety of pop records in many diverse styles. He even made a blues in 1960 for his own Rita label under the pseudonym of Lightnin' Leon. Such releases have had little impact and Riley still looks toward the future. "I have made a lot of mistakes but I guess sooner or later I will be lucky. Right now I am feeling at the start of a lucky phase. I sold out of Rita just before we had a big hit, I was cheated by developments at Sun. I sold a lot of good songs when I was drunk or fed up and a lot of masters of good songs too. There have been so many times I've needed to do that and I just lost count. There must be a dozen of my records I don't even know about because I moved on or sold them to someone I didn't know, or because the company released them under another name. I even did a backing track for Bo Diddley once."

If Sonny Burgess had stayed in the professional music scene he might have been able to tell a very similar story. His career at Sun closely followed the pattern of Billy Riley's.

Burgess also came from rural Arkansas and came to Memphis because of the growing reputation of Sun. He auditioned with drummer Bobby Crafford and their group, the Pacers, midway through 1955. He followed a familiar musical path in his youth, growing up on country music but by 1956 he was starting to appreciate R&B and this showed in his vocal and guitar style. Phillips found it an easy task to attach the rockabilly tag to Burgess's recordings, encouraging him to copy the guitar licks off Junior Parker's records and to coarsen his voice. This is demonstrated on both the rockabilly sides that were issued and the many demos of Chicago blues that remained in the vaults. Burgess tried his hand with many blues hits including *One Night, Fannie Brown* and *So Glad You're Mine*. Burgess confirmed, "Yes, I really liked R&B, Fats Domino, Jimmy Reed, Muddy Waters. I didn't go too much for B. B. King, though."

Burgess's first record was *Red Headed Woman* backed with *We Wanna Boogie* and the wild beat obliterates any tuneful aspects the songs may have had while the piano and guitar solos are also a little ragged. The vocal was powerful if somewhat incoherent and the takes chosen for release were out of tune and off key but they have the marvellous spontaneous dance rhythms that Phillips sought. Burgess says, "That disc sold ninety thousand but then came *Restless* and that looked set to be a monster hit. Then after about one month it quit selling and I don't know why. Maybe the lack of money that Sam used to promote it, or maybe it just wasn't that good."

The record was certainly good, as were the others he made for Sun. Jack Clement spent many hours with Burgess, recognizing his talent but lamenting that "Burgess just didn't fit into a groove that we could sell records with." *Ain't Got a Thing* is particularly fine rockabilly music of controlled exuberance. The group also applied great energy to their interpretation of the hillbilly standard *My Bucket's Got a Hole in It*. An instrumental with harmonica was also issued, named *Thunderbird* after the wine that flowed during the session but it did not sell. Burgess was unable to come up with another hit and his final disc for Phillips was issued in 1959 on the new subsidiary label, Phillips International. The backing was provided by the Cliff Thomas group with Ed Thomas on piano. The wild piano style, together with the vocal, chorus and guitar solos, gave the impression, as did all of Burgess's rockers, of loosely organized chaos. In 1960 Burgess began to drift away from rock, back to country music and he joined Conway Twitty, then a pop artist, on a tour of Canada.

Like most Sun artists, Burgess undertook many exhaustive tours during his contract, usually to support Johnny Cash. "The arrangement was," he explains, "that we would get together and drive to some point where we would meet up with the rest of the guys, usually Waco, Texas. From there we traveled the entire western part of the country, always by car. When we were not on the road, we stayed around Newport, Arkansas, which was my home. I guess that if we had moved to Memphis we might have been more successful, you know, been around at the right time." Modest in dismissing his contribution to the Sun sound and to the rockabilly style, Burgess is remembered with affection by other artists as one of the more flashy characters around town in the mid '50s, buying clothes at the favorite haunt of local rockabilly and blues musicians, Lansky's on Beale Street.

Roy Orbison went on many tours with Burgess and remembers one show in Albuquerque, "Sonny was traveling with John Cash because his car had broken down. We had to leave a lot of gear behind and the show was a complete disaster because the band did not know what we were doing. Sonny at least created a diversion with his appearance. He had died his hair red, had a Fender guitar with red shoes along with a red suit but even that didn't save him. He came to the car afterward and said, 'Man, they'll always remember us in Albuquerque as the Wink Wildcat and the Red Clown.'" Burgess had bought his red suit from Lansky's where, he recalls, "I ran into Elvis one day and he was kinda hot at the time and could've walked right past me but he seemed glad to see a familiar face and stopped to talk." Presley had almost grown up there.

Billy Riley was another singer to use Lansky's. "I ordered my first set of stage suits for the band from there," he remembers with some displeasure. "They were green. The band was mobbed on the first night we wore them and they were torn to shreds. Cost me a lot of money." This type of occurence made business brisk for Lansky's in the mid '50s. In those days the famous blues area of Beale was already in decline and has now sadly lost its character in an urban development scheme. It was a gathering point for many singers and contributed to the lifestyle of many rockabilly artists. It was here that Presley would come to watch the blues artists, such as B. B. King, and Jack Clement recalls that the "only rival as a meeting place was Taylor's Café, next to the Sun studio. That was where all the guys did their writing and talking and that was where the Sun sound was really born."

A regular at both haunts was Hayden Thompson, who on the strength of one good rockabilly disc, a remake of Junior Parker's *Love My Baby*, acquired all the mannerisms associated with Presley. The guitarist on that record, Roland Janes, says, "Billy Riley and Hayden Thompson would do a finale when on tour which involved Thompson cutting up like Presley and Riley acting like Little Richard. It was incredible to watch." Thompson eventually quietened down and became a country singer with Kapp Records, having recorded some more rockabilly for Profile and collaborated with Rosco Gordon to write *Cheese and Crackers*. In the fall of 1958 Gordon became the only black artist to record rockabilly for Sun when *Sally Jo* with Roland Janes and Jimmy van Eaton was issued.

Another artist with more to show for his rockabilly days than most but with less feeling for the sound was Roy Orbison, who had auditioned for Sam Phillips in March 1956 with a dub of a song called *Ooby Dooby*. As Malcolm Yelvington, present at the time, says, "It was the silliest thing I ever heard, but it went. It was

Conway Twitty

The Lansky brothers at their shop on Beale Street

The Teen Kings. Left to right: back row, Billy Par Ellis, James Morrow and Jack Kennelly; front row, Roy Orbison and Johnny "Peanuts" Wilson

Conway Twitty with Bob Neal

Johnny Carroll

a hit." During the summer of 1956 the record sold nearly half a million copies and made number 59 in the *Billboard* Hot 100 by June. This was the highest position attained by any Sun artist during the rockabilly era with the notable exceptions of the big three, Perkins, Cash and Lewis. *Ooby Dooby* was covered by other singers but it was the overall sound and approach that sold the record, rather than the vocalist or the song itself. Orbison's high voice is well suited to the tearful ballad style that he later adopted but not quite raw enough for rockabilly. His guitar work on his Sun recordings was, like the instrumental support of his backing group, the Teen Kings, pure rockabilly. His vocal style stood out because it rode high above the beat, like that of fellow Texan Buddy Holly, who made some excellent rockabilly in Nashville in mid 1956.

Orbison began his recording career, like Holly, in Clovis, New Mexico, where he cut *Ooby Dooby* and *Tryin' to Get to You* for Norman Petty's Je-Wel label. The record had a very limited distribution and Orbison quickly recut the demo for Columbia Records. It was turned down by that label's Dallas office but they promptly had their own artist, Sid King, record the song and his version was released before Orbison had a chance to offer the tape elsewhere. The Je-Wel cut of *Tryin' to Get to You* was acquired by Imperial at about the same time and issued as the flip side of a record by Weldon Rogers and credited to Rogers.

Faced with these set-backs, Orbison decided to send the tapes to Sun and was immediately sent for to re-record them, despite the existence of the Columbia version. This was in March 1956, about a year after Orbison began to play rockabilly, and he recalls, "I had a TV show in Odessa, Texas, and we played mainly country music. But after Presley came through town for a show in late 1954 I began to notice the rhythm music. I had heard groups like the Clovers and their hits like *One Mint Julep*, all based on seventh chords, and I really didn't like them but at a New Year's Eve Dance in 1954 we had to play through the actual time of midnight and when someone requested *Shake, Rattle and Roll* we struck up on it but we had nearly ten minutes to go to the hour so we kept playing the same song. By the time we were finished I was fully converted. I think it's a matter of instruments that defined whether you were playing country or rock. We just got ourselves a drummer."

Orbison does not like his early recordings but is very interested in the development of rock music and took time out to explain all the details of his early career. During 1957 his dislike of rockabilly rose to the surface but he persevered with Phillips' requests, explaining that, "I was writing more ballads then, but I didn't bother to ask Sam to release them. He was the boss and there was no arguing. I made some demos of things like *Claudette* but that was about it. I would never have made it big with Sun. They just did not have the ways to get into the audience I wanted to go for." Jack Clement reinforces this, saying, "The first artist Sam gave me to record was Roy Orbison. I recorded *Rockhouse* with Roy and it was good but Roy was not into what the Sun studio was capable of back then."

In 1958 Orbison made a deal with Sun to buy back his contract in return for the composer's rights on his songs. The biggest one, *Ooby Dooby*, was excluded from this because it had been written by Wade Moore and Dick Penner who had followed Orbison to Memphis the year after the record was released. They had been colleagues of Orbison at North Texas State University in Denton during 1955 when Orbison was studying geology.

Dick Penner says, "I began playing guitar when I was sixteen and then when I was eighteen I joined the staff of the 'Big D Jamboree' in Dallas. I can remember one day when Elvis Presley, Scotty and Bill were to be the star attractions on the show. They were about half an hour late but it was a great thrill for the audience and for me when they did show up. I had no thoughts then that I would record for Sun myself. I met Wade Moore at University in January 1955. He was from Amarillo, Texas, and we wrote *Ooby Dooby* in February, I believe. We sang together through the college days and then, at the end of 1956, we took some songs to Memphis. *Bop, Bop Baby* was released and got good reviews in *Cashbox* and so did my solo disc, *Cindy Lou*. I promoted that on 'American Bandstand' in June 1958 but then I went into the Army and nothing came of it. The only song that was successful was the one we didn't record, *Ooby Dooby*, but then I still get the royalty checks."

Penner is now professor of English at the University of Tennessee in Knoxville and is embarrassed by the lyrics of his best known song. "Hey, baby, jump over here/when you do the Ooby Dooby I just gotta be near." Great for dancing, though.

Johnny Carroll was from Memphis. His demo tape was auditioned and accepted, possibly because one of his recordings was the title song to the movie, *Rock Baby, Rock It*. *That's the Way I Love* was recorded in June 1957 in Fort Worth, Texas, and was released on Phillips International. It did not sell and Carroll is better known for his Decca recordings, such as *Hot Rock*. Although the Decca sides had the ingredients of slapped bass, driving rhythm and enthusiastic vocals they lack the overall sound of the Sun product from this period and appear somewhat contrived. The Fort Worth recordings were more solid and Carroll belonged to a pool of Fort Worth musicians who helped each other record for whatever label would take them. Mac Curtis, Groovey Joe Poovey and Gene Summers were among the group. Carroll's Phillips International recording has additional interest because country star George Jones is the guitarist.

Conway Twitty is a country star from a later period, who came to Memphis from Helena, Arkansas, to record for Sun with his group, the Rockhousers. This was 1955 and Twitty was known under his real name, Harold Jenkins. He had friends in Memphis, notably steel guitarist John Hughey and drummer Jack Nance, both of whom played in Twitty's first band, the Arkansas Wood Choppers back in Helena. Sam Phillips taped three songs but they were not issued, although they were good rockabilly performances. Again, Jack Clement recalls putting in a lot of time with Twitty, "He never did do anything that sounded much like a record, though," was the verdict.

Twitty was not the only singer to be spurned by Sun, only to find success elsewhere. Gene Simmons, for example, had one rockabilly issue on Sun but in 1964 topped the national charts with *Haunted House*, on Hi, a cover version of an R&B hit. Cliff Gleaves also achieved some limited success on Summer Records but his fine demonstration tape of *Love Is My Business* was left unissued by Sun. This also happened to various other recognized rockabilly artists, including Teddy Reidel, Dean Beard and Curtis Hobeck.

The reasons why so many fine singers were turned down are varied. Judd Phillips may have turned them down, feeling that he had enough to work with. Sam was interested in anyone who could produce a hit sound but Judd had to promote them and he would not touch an artist unless he felt that they had some feature of musical style or personality which could be used to build an image. This certainly did not prevent the no-hopers from knocking on the door and some of them got onto records, if only briefly.

Sun had a policy never to take much notice of unsolicited demo tapes. When New Yorker Hank Davis, an aspiring rockabilly singer on Stacy, went to Sun in June 1960 he found "piles and piles of demos that had never been played. There was a seven foot high pyramid of tapes in one corner, among them the original tape of Bill Anderson's *City Lights* that later came out on TNT and started his tremendously successful career." It has often been rumored that in this way Sun lost the chance to record the likes of Eddie Cochran, Buddy Holly and Johnny Rivers. We will never know for sure but Sam Phillips had faith in the personal audition system. Barbara Barnes, who worked in Sam's office explains this, "Potential artists or writers plugging their songs had to see Sam or his A&R men, Jack Clement and Bill Justis. Telephone calls from strangers were not returned. Sun did not have scouts and did not steal artists from other labels. Tapes and lead sheets arriving by first class mail had an uncertain further destination. Anything sent by registered mail was refused. Sam felt that if Elvis and the others had been discovered from walk-in auditions, it was a workable system and worth keeping. The only way to get an audition was to hang around until someone finally agreed to listen."

Another factor is that as Sun's success developed, less was left to chance. The high standard of so many Sun recordings is due to the session musicians gathered around 706 Union Avenue. Jack Clement testifies to their importance. "There are a lot of influential people that nobody ever gets to hear about, like guitarist Roland Janes and also Jimmy van Eaton who was drummer on a lot of stuff. The sound that became magic to a lot of people was partly due to him, it was so funky but at the same time it captured the fun. It's hard to say who was ultimately responsible, everyone was doing their thing and it all came together at Sun."

The Memphis Scene

In the mid '50s Memphis witnessed the growth of several other record companies, mostly producing rockabilly after the example of Sun. Some, like Hi, formed in 1956 by Bill Cantrell, Quinton Claunch and Ray Harris, with capital supplied by Joe Cuoghi, went on to become important independents. Many others were short-lived. Sun began by catering to the local market and then branched out nationally but most of the new labels remained small-time and had to lease occasional hits to a larger company.

Many of the smaller labels were owned by singers themselves, as were many of the publishing concerns. This trend had started during the blues boom of the early '50s. B. B. King, for example, participated in the Blues Boy label. In contrast to Hi, there were several one-record labels such as F&L, formed by Harmonica Frank and Larry Kennon to issue their own recordings. Billy Riley and Roland Janes were more deeply involved, having a part in Rita, Nita and Mojo Records. Rita came up with a national hit by Harold Dorman, *Mountain of Love*. Most of the smaller companies did not have any hits and it was not necessarily a passport to riches if they did. Distributors and one stops were notoriously slow in paying bills to one-hit record companies and the profits were often tied up in uncollectable receivables.

Many companies seem to have been started on a whim by people who thought that anything connected with the record business automatically made money. Aaron Records in West Memphis, for example, issued two good Sun-styled rockabilly discs in the late '50s and then disappeared. Like Nita, it was owned by a businessman in West Memphis who, according to Billy Riley, named his labels after Presley's middle name and his current girlfriend, Anita.

Other record labels which produced some rockabilly included Peak, Moon, Memphis and Erwin. Hoyt Johnson recorded for Erwin, issuing *Eanie Meanie Minie Mo*. He later wrote Johnny Cash's Sun hit *You're the Nearest Thing to Heaven* and recorded in a Cash-styled country vein for both Erwin and Jim Stewart's Satellite label. Stewart's first label, Jaxon was run during 1958 from his garage in the suburb of Arlington and distributed through his store on McLemore Avenue. Promotion was handled through KWEM, where Stewart formerly worked as a disc jockey and fiddle player. The first releases on Jaxon by the Jimmy Martin Combo and Carl Mann sold slowly and after only five issues the label changed its name to Satellite. For a time, country and rockabilly issues continued from artists like Don Willis, whose *Boppin' High School Baby* got no further than promo sampling. A similar fate befell Ray Scott, who had written Billy Riley's first hit, *Flyin' Saucers Rock 'n' Roll*.

The list of these small labels is virtually endless, although a few gained some momentum. In 1954 Bill Biggs and Red Mathis set up the OJ label as a country pop venture under the direction of Bill Cantrell. The main artist was Memphis deejay Wink Martindale, although there were later experiments with R&B. More successful, however, was Fernwood, run by truck driver and country musician Slim Wallace. Between 1956 and 1958 with the help of Jack Clement, Scotty Moore and lawyer Bob Buckalaugh, he intermittently operated the Fernwood, Whirlaway, Boot Heel and S&W labels, gaining some success in the '60s with Ace Cannon but achieving only one monster hit in 1959 with *Tragedy*, recorded by Thomas Wayne, brother of Johnny Cash's guitarist Luther Perkins.

Wallace's original partner, Jack Clement had "left Sun in 1959 and started up Summer Records—Summer hits, summer not, hope you like the ones we got. We used to send out promotional poems with every disc and different ones to the distributors like, 'Summer comes, autumn follers, you owe us 187 dollars.'" Despite the inspired sloganry, Summer Records sank without a trace.

Sun's main local competitor since the beginning had been Lester Bihari's Meteor label. They had enjoyed success with their very first record, Elmore James' *I Believe*, but thereafter they only seemed to enjoy local sales, apart from Bud Deckelman's country hit, *Daydreamin'*. Meteor reinforced, or mirrored, Sun's development. Established at the same time, its choice of blues, hillbilly and rockabilly issues was greatly influenced by its rival's output.

In 1955 Malcolm Yelvington was introduced to Les Bihari and after *A Gal Named Joe* several white rock 'n' roll discs were issued to jump on the rockabilly bandwagon. Junior Thompson, Wayne McGinnis, "Mason-Dixon," Bill Bowen, Jimmy Lamberth and Charlie Feathers were responsible for a variety of rockabilly records usually based on the Sun sound and Sun artists were used whenever possible.

Brad Suggs left Slim Rhodes' Band for one disc, *Bop, Baby Bop*, and Charlie Feathers came up with a very superior style developed from his hillbilly recordings. The first for Meteor was issued as Jess Hooper, while the next, *Tongue Tied Jill*, introduced the peculiar rhythm and high pitched mumbled vocal which characterized Feathers' '50s recordings. In 1968 he recorded the rockabilly recreation, *Stutterin' Cindy* on Philwood, produced by Tom Phillips, Sam's younger brother. Feathers' influence seems to have been quite pervasive in Memphis and his songs were recorded by other artists, Tommy Tucker's *Lovin' Lil*, on Hi, for example. Junior Thompson's entire style was largely derived from Feathers, as his unissued tape of *Who's That Knockin'* in the Sun vaults shows. He also recorded Roy Orbison's *Ooby Dooby* without success.

Feathers was signed to King in 1956 and recorded two excellent rockabilly sessions, one in Cincinnati in February 1956 and another in Nashville in January 1957, with vocal support from Johnny Bragg and the Marigolds. Feathers was unlucky. Most contemporaries share an enthusiasm for his music, agreeing with Malcolm Yelvington that "Charlie's style could have caught on in a big way but he didn't have the stage appeal of Presley." Today, Feathers alternates playing country bars around Memphis with racing cars at local meetings and organizing softball games. He is a little bemused, and a little taken, with the interest that is accorded him. It is noticeable that his current repertoire, which includes *Steamroller Blues*, *Proud Mary* and *Help Me Make It Through the Night* is still performed in his own style and even rock standards such as *Good Rockin' Tonight*, *Tear It Up* and *Blue Suede Shoes* take on fresh emphasis. Feathers says, "It's no use to go thumping that beat, you've gotta play around it. I like most music but those old country and rock songs get to me most. I try to bring out a little of that feel into my songs. The blues, man, when you take that out of country you ain't got no more country music."

Another of Feathers' contemporaries still plays regularly in Memphis. Eddie Bond is an artist who, for one reason or another, has usually traveled in different circles. Born and raised in Memphis, Bond began, as did so many others, with country music gaining a contract with Mercury Records in 1956 and almost gaining a hit with *Rockin' Daddy*. Once again, he did not have the personality and good management to effect a breakthrough into national rock 'n' roll and has remained in Memphis as a deejay, television personality and small-time record label owner. He has appeared on over twenty labels, including his own such as Tab, Millionaire and Diplomat, and is a familiar name in the city, standing for sheriff in 1974.

"I began by leasing tapes to Ekko in Hollywood and before that I worked on the Louisiana Hayride with Elvis and Johnny Horton. The Ekko sides were dubbed with West Coast musicians but they didn't do anything anyway so I decided to cut some rockabilly. We added a drummer to our group, the Stompers, and auditioned for Sam Phillips. I had always listened to country music but we did rock then because it was the coming trend. It was hot. Now, Sun had a unique thing with rock 'n' roll, rockabilly, what ever you might call it; we called it rockabilly back then. Sam got a real full sound but he told me that my voice was too mediocre and I couldn't make it. Later he had to change his mind and we did record a lot of country and gospel things but in '56 I was rejected. That was when I went with Mercury and we had a hit."

Bond's voice actually copes quite well with the strenuous demands of rockabilly, although it is better suited to country material. It was really the instrumentation on records such as *Boppin' Bonnie*, on Mercury, or *Monkey and the Baboon*, on Diplomat, that made them such excellent records. The Bond sound was right in the Memphis tradition. His only black influences seem to have come second hand through the recordings of Presley and his lack of blues phrasing is noticeable. The personnel on many of his sessions includes some of today's top Nashville session musicians, Chip Young, Hank Garland, James Wilson and John Hughey, for example. Hughey, one of the best steel guitarists in Memphis, was still with Bond when his sessions with Phillips finally materialized in 1962. The songs recorded at that time include a remake of *Rockin' Daddy*, although only the gospel sessions were used for an album.

The Ekko label that Bond mentioned had a Memphis office at one time on

North Cleveland Avenue and took steps toward rivaling Sun. Little came of this except several good records, including *Guilty Conscience* by Eddie and Hank Cochran.

It is obvious, therefore, that sustained success was almost the sole property of Sam Phillips and Sun Records. How did Sam handle the rapid growth of his business?

When Sun's distribution was expanded Sam also built up the Hi-Lo and Knox publishing concerns and signed a deal with Hill & Range for European rights. Artists such as Cash, Orbison and Perkins wrote most of their own material and some of the earlier songwriting teams such as Stan Kesler, Quinton Claunch and Bill Cantrell were successful in adapting to the new style. To his credit, Phillips did not usually subscribe to the once accepted practice of claiming part of the composer royalty. He also signed a deal with London Records for international representation in most countries.

This period of general prosperity and great activity did not come without its problems, however, and many artists have gone on record as saying that they left Sun because of low royalties. Roy Orbison expands on this, "To be honest about Sam Phillips he paid a smaller royalty than anyone else, which, coupled with the fact that nobody told me I should be collecting composer's royalties from BMI, meant that I was losing money coming and going. That was the main reason I left Sun after two years."

It is an inescapable fact that most of Sun's artists recall Phillips' reluctance to spend money but many agree that it was just part of his nature. Carl Perkins jumped at the chance to move to a major label but later admitted, "It didn't take long to learn that being on a major wasn't all that we had imagined. Sam was probably the straightest man we ever dealt with." Phillips himself had this to say,

Charlie Feathers and his Musical Warriors. Left to right: Jody Chastain, Charlie Feathers, Jerry Huffman.

Eddie Bond

"I was trying to be a businessman to the best of my ability. I made sure everyone got exactly what was coming to them."

Barbara Barnes, whose job it was at one time, insists that details of recording sessions were lodged with the AFM and their files show that union rates were paid. In the early '50s this was $15 per session, but by the early '60s it had risen to $45. Top artists received more, of course. Johnny Cash started at $82 per session and went up to $165 per session. Carl Perkins received $200 for himself per session, with the same for his band.

Any criticism of Phillips should be seen in the context of the strained finances of the little independent labels. There was no reward for endeavor alone. Not even success was good enough unless it could be followed with more successes. Many labels settled for a lower profile, catering for a specific local market and this did not allow for extravagance.

At the height of the rockabilly boom, Sun had become an exception and Sonny Burgess remembers, "Back in 1956 Sun was the biggest label here for miles, the whole mid-South. They were much bigger even than RCA Victor." Bill Fitzgerald, manager of the Music Sales One Stop in Memphis, adds that, "Sun sold more Carl Perkins, Billy Riley, Warren Smith and Roy Orbison records here in the mid-South than they did Johnny Cash, Jerry Lee Lewis or even Elvis Presley. But nationally that wasn't so. I was not responsible for selling Sun in the northeast or the midwest and I believe those artists sold well there. My area was the whole south and west coast and within that area the top selling districts were Memphis, Dallas, New Orleans, Atlanta, San Francisco, Chicago and St. Louis in that order. I sold 80% to juke box operators until 1957 when radio programming of Top 40 shows came in. Then the record stores took a wider stock and that market opened out more but one way or another we surely moved a lot of Sun product in those years."

Records had to be packed for shipping, of course, and promo samples had to be mailed. Most Sun artists helped with these chores in the early days. "It was a kind of a small operation," as Roy Orbison said. By the end of the rockabilly era, however, the sales volume was such that Sam Phillips' days of financial instability had gone. Instead, he was faced with other problems such as the need to maintain success, to ward off the I.R.S. and to keep an eye on business colleagues who were not quite so frugal in their lifestyles as himself.

Roots & Branches

Most small companies in the South recording blues or hillbilly music tended to veer toward rock 'n' roll in the mid '50s. In Jackson, Mississippi, Lillian McMurray ran Trumpet and Globe in competition with Delta and later, Johnny Vincent's Champion and Ace labels. In Louisiana there was the added presence of cajun music and the best-known label in the area was probably Goldband.

Goldband was formed by hillbilly singer Eddie Shuler in Lake Charles, Louisiana, as an outlet for recordings by his own Reveliers. The label was expanded in 1952 to concentrate on cajun artists and later blues and rockabilly. The main artists in the rockabilly style were Ray Vict, Larry Hart and Al Ferrier whose *No No Baby* appeared in late 1954. The sound of Ferrier and His Bopping Billies is interesting, being similar to that of Carl Perkins, and three singles were issued showing the transition from hillbilly to rockabilly as the rhythm strengthened and the electric guitar came to the fore.

Ferrier was not the only artist to be making rockabilly records outside Memphis. Norman Petty's studio in Clovis, New Mexico, was the launching pad for the careers of Buddy Holly, Roy Orbison, Waylon Jennings and Buddy Knox. Other important Southern recording centers were Houston, Shreveport, Dallas, Beaumont and San Antonio. Shreveport was the home of Stan Lewis who distributed Sun and recorded his own artists. Shelby Singelton, who later bought the Sun catalog, operated from there in the late '50s. Beaumont was mainly important as the home of Jack Clement and Bill Hall who were successful in the '60s, following the success of Starday and D in the '50s.

Other important local centers included New Orleans, Atlanta and further west Lee Hazelwood worked out of Phoenix, Arizona. Kansas City was the home of Westport Records who turned out countrified rockabilly discs by Alvis Wayne and Lee Finn. Cincinnati had King Records and smaller concerns such as Lee and Lucky Records. In California Crest Sage and Sims recorded rockabilly while a future country star, Alvis "Buck" Owens dabbled in rockabilly on the Pep label, recording songs like *Hot Dog* and *Rhythm and Booze,* which were really very good.

A small town like Hammond, Indiana, supported the Mar-Vel and Glenn labels, owned by Harry Glenn. Important, though obscure, rockabilly records were made throughout the States in the most unlikely places, even Hawaii and Alaska.

Many West Coast and New York labels went for leasing rockabilly from Southern sources. Music by Patt Cupp and Don Cole appeared on RPM. Jimmy Lloyd (actually hillbilly singer Jimmie Logsdon) and Buddy Knox recorded for Roulette, as did Rockin' Ronnie Hawkins who had earlier tried to make it in Memphis. In fact, Roy Orbison had witnessed Hawkins' earliest stage performance with some displeasure. "I played the University of Arkansas and they said there was a young man who wanted to sing on the show, so I said he should go up on the stage but when he got up there he played all my numbers— before me! I couldn't believe it. So I went right ahead anyway and sang them over again. Later we were sitting in front of someone's house in an auto with a couple of girls and Ronnie said, 'I sure do want to get into the business. Can you recommend something I could record?' So I sung him a little snatch of *Mary Lou*. A few weeks after that I was standing on Union Avenue when a truck pulled up with Ronnie Hawkins and all his gear in it. He said he was hitting the road, going to Canada. In fact, he also got in with Roulette and before I knew it I was hearing him on the radio singing *Mary Lou*. That hit before I ever did have a big hit."

Many other Northern labels sent scouts into the South looking for talent. Carlton used Lelan Rogers and they came up with Jessie Lee Turner and had several southern hits to go with those by Jack Scott. ABC also purchased masters by Scott and issued some titles by Bobby Lee Trammell, a Memphis artist.

These examples give some indication of the pervasive nature of the rockabilly boom and the fortunes of country music serve to underline this. Recording in Nashville underwent many changes at this time—changes that ultimately laid the foundations for the country-pop Nashville sound of the 1960s.

In the climate of the mid '50s, when sales of country records had been checked, rockabilly was the natural compromise for the industry. Most rockabilly singers were just good ol' boys at heart anyway. There was a very real distinction between rockabilly and honky-tonk music, though. Many rockabilly singers saw themselves as working in something other than country music. Rockabilly *was* different; it was more than Nashville's attempt to produce rock 'n' roll on its own terms but at the same time rockabilly *was* the Southerners' rock 'n' roll.

The fact that rockabilly developed from honky-tonk music tends to obscure the fact that there was a clear difference in attitude between those artists who just made rockabilly music with no real aspirations to become a rock star and those who tried consciously to forge an image in the new style. The ground rules for the latter had been laid by Presley when he strutted onto the Dorsey show and a thousand stages across the country. Malcolm Yelvington, for example, made good rockabilly records and was a good honky-tonk singer but he stood no chance of being marketed in the same way that Presley and, to a lesser extent, Carl Perkins, could be marketed.

The period of transition from the time of Presley's first recordings in mid 1954 to the joint success of Perkins' *Blue Suede Shoes* and Presley's *Heartbreak*

Hotel in the first few months of 1956 is one of some confusion. Established country musicians and newcomers alike came to achieve the sound, using a heavily amplified string bass and a light acoustic beat, before a dependence on a drummer emerged. It is important to distinguish between the influence of Presley's early music and the influence of his image, which came much later. For the first two years of his career, Presley was only known regionally in the mid-South and his phenomenal success in later years has tended to obscure the fact that the "Presley image" took a long time to permeate through to most musicians.

The phasing of country music through an essentially acoustic period to another period characterized by the drumbeat and the new image was illustrated in Sun's music and echoed elsewhere. Meteor mirrored Sun and in Beaumont, Texas, Starday provides another example. Formed in late 1952 by "Pappy" Dailey and Jack Starnes Starday quickly assembled an impressive roster of hillbilly artists. They also made gestures toward rockabilly with the excellent recordings of Sonny Fisher who came from Tyler, Texas, and was discovered at Jack Starnes' Cozy Corner nightclub. In 1955 he wrote and recorded *Rockin' Daddy*, over a year before Eddie Bond picked up on the song. Fisher had started out as a hillbilly singer in 1950 but on *Rockin' Daddy* and other recordings he made we can hear some of the best and most primitive early rockabilly records. The lead guitarist, Joey Long, whatever his stylistic influences, succeeded in producing music with perhaps greater affinity for the down home blues tradition than even Carl Perkins.

In general, Starday stuck with hillbilly releases in 1955 but in 1956 they launched an onslaught on the rockbilly market. In May and June came a dozen or more releases and among them were *Rock It* by country star George Jones, recording as "Thumper" Jones, cajun singer Link Davis, deejay Bill Mack, western swing veteran Leon Payne working under the alias of "Rock Rogers" and Rudy Grayzell whose *Ducktail* proved to be the best seller of them all. By now Don Pierce had taken over promotion of the label and a lease deal was arranged whereby Mercury gained the rights to Starday recordings and Pierce took control of all country and rockabilly product on both labels together with the Starday subsidiary, Dixie. Sides by Sleepy LaBeef and Rudy Grayzell were leased to Mercury with some success and Pierce soon busied himself recording in Nashville.

Rockabilly records on Mercury again display a marked change over a short period, from the acoustic influences of such artists as Billy Wallace, Curtis Gordon and Roy Moss to the post-1956 music of Eddie Bond, Conway Twitty and Jimmy Edwards. The latter enjoyed a hit with *Love Bug Crawl*, a rock number which featured a prominent piano and is in marked contrast to the adapted hillbilly and blues of Roy Moss and Billy Wallace. It was Wallace's style in particular, played primarily on acoustic instruments, that sounded increasingly out of place by the end of 1957 when the rockabilly style was losing its rawness and individuality. The flirtation of Mercury and Starday with rockabilly was a result of circumstances and economics. Starday later moved to Nashville and switched to bluegrass and gospel music while George Jones stayed on Mercury to become one of the leading country stars of the '50s and '60s.

This is not to say that rockabilly was unpopular with country artists. Many took to it as a natural development of their up tempo songs, just as Malcolm Yelvington and Slim Rhodes had been able to do in Memphis. The style failed to impress such institutions as the Grand Ol' Opry, where drums were still not allowed on stage and Presley flopped mightily on his first appearance in 1955. There was, however, a major change in the character of country output from each major record label in Nashville. Sam Phillips recognized that rockabilly was accused by many of killing country music. His reply was, "I wasn't out to destroy country music. I had been raised on the Grand Ol' Opry but country had become stereotyped. I told Opry manager Jim Denny that, and he said that if it changed it would lose its appeal. I replied that anyone attempting to block progress was headed for trouble."

Before long, the record labels started to show radio the way and Ferlin Husky, Johnny Bond and George Hamilton all approximated a rockabilly beat by hotting up the guitar work and strengthening the rhythm. Decca even had their top country star, Webb Pierce, work in the new style together with Autry Inman, Red Sovine, and Roy Hall who covered such songs as *All By Myself* and *Blue Suede Shoes*.

Two of the largest record labels, operating from both the West Coast and Nashville, M-G-M and Capitol, also recorded rockabilly artists in both locations. M-G-M dubbed some hot guitar onto some Hank Williams recordings, making him into a posthumous rock 'n' roll artist with *Roly Poly*. Williams' influence was still so pervasive that the sound so easily achieved by doctoring his tapes must have eased the conscience of many hillbilly singers who had turned to rock. Hank did not sound as bad with a hot guitar as he did with strings, an effect which some have likened to painting a mustache on the Mona Lisa. Bud Deckelman, Buck Griffin and Andy Starr all recorded for M-G-M in a rockabilly vein and Capitol brought the diverse country sounds of Skeets McDonald, Jimmy Heap and Gene Vincent into line with the influence exerted by Presley and Perkins.

Ken Nelson, Capitol's A&R boss in Nashville, recalls, "We were going on in the same old vein because people thought that rock was a passing phase but I was traveling around and I could see that this was not so. I soon became bound and determined that I was going to get some rock 'n' roll acts, so that's what I did."

RCA Victor, of course, had Presley and they really did not need anyone else to keep their presses busy but they persevered for a while with other rock acts such as Janis Martin, Milton Allen and Joe Clay and even began a subsidiary label, Vik, as an experiment to place this kind of artist but it finally became clear that they had the one and only superstar of the genre.

Another company to take a great interest in the new style was Columbia. In the early '50s, Mitch Miller, goateed head of A&R, experimented by placing country songs with pop singers such as Tony Bennett, Frankie Laine and Guy Mitchell. The results were successful and Columbia went on to adapt the style of certain other artists to an approximation of rockabilly. In their Dallas studio, local artist Sid King recorded rockabilly with his Five Strings, providing a western swing-tinged sound that probably did well in the local market but in Nashville there were three better known musicians involved.

In the case of Onie Wheeler it is fair to say that a unique interpretation of the music was involved, for the harmonica and bass player who spent many years working with Roy Acuff, had first recorded in 1953 and thereafter with Okeh, Columbia, Sun and a host of other labels. He was always instantly recognizable. In 1957, his last year with Columbia before briefly joining Sun, Wheeler had a major success with *Onie's Bop*, a novelty song with a pounding bass rhythm and a guitar solo that owed much to Carl Perkins. Wheeler says, "Well, you know, I liked that sound but it came quite naturally—I'd used drums since 1953 but not the heavy off-beat. Presley and his boys, Scotty and Bill, they used to play with me on tour in 1954 and that's the way I liked him to sound. The heavier type of rockabilly just came natural to him just as my kind was to me. I'm not against changing my style but at Columbia it just happened. At Sun I couldn't get on with Jack Clement's methods and Columbia was wholly more professional, I thought." In response, Clement maintains that it was the freedom to work all night that made Sun rockabilly better than that of any major label.

Johnny Horton, who found popular acclaim with *The Battle of New Orleans* and an early death in an auto accident in 1960, employed a style during the mid '50s that was similar to Onie Wheeler. He retained predominantly acoustic

Distant shades of rockabilly on this 1958 album from Skeets McDonald.

Onie Wheeler

Almost the first rockabilly anthology: Ferlin Husky, Sonny James, Tommy Sands and Gene Vincent (Capitol, 1957)

instrumentation, except for the lead guitar, and strengthened hillbilly rhythms. His recording of *Honky Tonk Hardwood Floor* has a strong growling electric guitar figure throughout. Horton had previously worked for the Louisiana Hayride and adapted very successfully to rockabilly.

This was also true of Columbia's best selling country artist of 1957, Marty Robbins. Beginning in 1952 with country ballads, Robbins progressed to reach the country pop audience in 1957 when he won virtually all the country & western poll awards with hits like *White Sport Coat*. Before this, however, he had been responsible for many fine rockabilly songs including *Mean Mama Blues, I Can't Quit* and *That's All Right* which epitomized the mixture of Memphis and Nashville influences.

In southwestern Louisiana and east Texas the rockabilly sound even permeated the local country style, Cajun music, a distortion of the name "Acadian," which belonged to the French settlers who came from Nova Scotia to Louisiana in the eighteenth century. Cajun is essentially accordion music, played to provide a swirling rhythm, while the fiddle provides the lead instrumentation. The lyrics show their French origin and it is essentially good time dance music. As such, it suited outside influences and rockabilly was easily assimilated into the music. Cajun rockabilly recordings, such as *Louisiana Man* by Rusty and Doug Kershaw on Hickory Records, were fine examples of this compelling mixture of styles.

The leading Cajun recording studios were run by Eddie Shuler at Goldband and Jay Miller in Crowley, Louisiana, where rockabilly music was performed by Rocket Morgan and others on the Zynn, Feature and Rocko labels. Cajun-rockabilly was also recorded by Starday and the labels owned by George Khoury but it was Goldband who had the biggest hit in this style with Cleveland Crochet's *Sugar Bee*, which made the national charts. The infectious bopping rhythms of *Sugar Bee* were part of a small boom in such recordings which developed into a genre known as swamp pop.

If Cajun and country labels allowed themselves to be influenced by rockabilly music then so did several blues labels. The popularity of the style induced Ernie Young's Nashville-based Excello label to issue Al Ferrier's *Hey Baby* and on the west coast RPM issued rockabilly by Don Cole and Patt Cupp. Savoy in Newark, New Jersey, enticed Werly Fairburn away from Trumpet, Capitol and Columbia to record three rockabilly singles and even Chess in Chicago purchased exciting Sun imitations. Bobby Cisco's *Go Go Go* and Billy Barrix's *Cool Off Baby* came from Stan Lewis in Shreveport, as did the successful Bobby Charles recordings. Even the early work of Chuck Berry had a rockabilly influence. Dale Hawkins had great success on Checker with more Shreveport recordings and United, another Chicago blues label, picked up John Hampton's *Shadow Blues*.

The reaction of Imperial in Hollywood was of similar significance. Following their success with Fats Domino and others in the rock market and with Slim Whitman in country they branched out in 1957 to sign artists who could sing rockabilly. There was a marked Sun influence in the Imperial sound of the late country artist Bob Luman. Working in the Shreveport area, he recorded the

Billy Emerson blues, previously recorded by Billy Riley, *Red Hot*. He also recorded *Red Cadillac and a Black Mustache*, which Warren Smith in turn took from him. Weldon Rogers' *So Long, Good Luck and Goodbye* was issued with the previously mentioned Roy Orbison ballad on the flip side and Imperial later went on to record a session with Sun artist Ray Smith.

Imperial also had the second most important artist of the era, Ricky Nelson. He was not a rockabilly singer but he wanted to be one. He was a pop idol, vastly superior to most, whose recordings introduced more people to rockabilly than anyone else, with the exception of Presley. This was not due to his singing voice but more to the backup sounds provided by bassist James Kirkland, drummer Richie Frost and, in particular, guitarist James Burton, freshly arrived from the Louisiana Hayride. Nelson and his band attempted to copy the Sun sound and Nelson himself is on record as saying "I wanted to be Carl Perkins." Perhaps his best rockabilly recording was *Waitin' in School*, written by Johnny and Dorsey Burnette from Memphis.

Another singer who brought rockabilly into the mainstream of rock 'n' roll was Sanford Clark with a singing voice remarkably similar to, though better than, Nelson. Both artists have recently returned to country music. Clark began in Phoenix, Arizona, where he met Lee Hazlewood at WTYL and they worked on a song called *The Fool*, a slow rockabilly song released on Hazlewood's MCI label before being sold to Dot in 1957. The record featured Al Casey, who also worked with Viv Records in Phoenix and later returned to country music on the west coast.

The year 1957 also saw the Everly Brothers break into rock 'n' roll with a sound that owed something to rockabilly, and Buddy Knox scored heavily with *Party Doll* on Roulette, another song with a heavy leaning toward rockabilly. Perhaps the best example of a rock singer who had previously recorded in the country and rockabilly fields was Buddy Holly. He began by performing pure country music over KDAV in Lubbock, Texas, and, as in the case of Roy Orbison, reputedly changed his direction after seeing Presley perform. Holly's Decca recordings from 1956 are almost totally derivative of the Sun sound and two titles from these sessions stand out. *Midnight Shift* has risqué lyrics and a guitar solo in the Perkins mold and *Ollie Vee*, who significantly "comes from Memphis."

There were others from Memphis, including Johnny and Dorsey Burnette. They tried to get on Sun but eventually recorded for other companies in the Sun rockabilly style. The brothers formed their Rock 'n' Roll Trio with Paul Burlison in Memphis in 1955 and after an appearance on the Ted Mack Amateur Hour they landed a contract with Coral Records in New York. The excellent *Tear It Up* and subsequent singles failed to make a major dent in the charts and the Trio split up. Johnny and Dorsey later patched over their differences on the west coast and began peddling songs. They sold some to Jerry Lee Lewis as well as Ricky Nelson. Johnny later went on to find fame and fortune with Liberty Records before his death in a boating accident in 1964. Dorsey had varying degrees of success with country music, before his death in August 1979.

The Burnettes' recordings also marked the decline of rockabilly from a potent, exciting, raw, feverish sound in 1956 to the blander style right within the pop mainstream by 1958. By that time Tin Pan Alley had fought back and the balance of power in creating hit sounds shifted back to the more traditional centers such as New York.

In the decline of rockabilly, as in its growth, Elvis Presley played a part. Many singers had been manufactured in his image although others had come to rock independent of his influence. By 1958, however, his stature had assumed truly enigmatic proportions and whatever he did became a basis for future styles. During 1957 and 1958 he recorded an increasing number of rock ballads with the Jordanaires and rockabilly was forgotten in the rush to copy the new Presley sound, especially when the King was temporarily dethroned by the draft. Presley imitator Ral Donner even went so far as to record in Memphis, possibly seeking inspiration for the perfect cover version.

The loss of the primitive feel can be traced in the careers of many artists. Gene Vincent originally worked within the rockabilly idiom but the vocals became smoother as the Capitol studios tried to produce a more polished sound. In the late '50s more and more rock 'n' roll stars moved away from the rockabilly influence. Eddie Cochran was too contrived vocally and musically and Ronnie Hawkins began to record at a time when fond memories of his youth in Memphis were not strong enough to produce quite the right sound. The era had gone and Rockin' Ronnie made some fine records, but rockabilly they were not.

Sun did not die along with rockabilly but they stopped leading the way. Rockabilly and the first rock 'n' roll era continued to influence everything that came after. Each new generation seems to turn back to those old records as a source of inspiration and as a point of reference. At a local level throughout the South there are still old rockabilly singers playing it like they did in '55 and the sound has never totally disappeared from view.

In 1962 the Liverpool sound was born but the Beatles started off playing Sun songs like *Blue Suede Shoes* and *Red Hot*. It is also obvious that George Harrison learned how to play the guitar from Carl Perkins' *"Dance Album"*. At roughly the same time Bob Dylan was emerging and it is no secret that Bob always wanted to be a rock 'n' roll star. His first demo was inspired by Carl Perkins' *Matchbox* and he scandalized Hibbing, Minnesota, playing *Great Balls of Fire* and *Good Golly Miss Molly* at his high school concert. Later John Fogerty and Credence Clearwater Revival borrowed greatly from Sun and just recently we have seen George Thorogood tear them apart with a mixture of Chicago blues and Sun rockabilly.

Johnny Cash

"The best country music in the world was being produced in Nashville. I knew I couldn't do that well at producing country music . . . but those guys didn't leave enough to the imagination. Can you hear I Walk the Line *with steel guitar added to it?"*

—Sam Phillips

Johnny Cash, like Jesus whom he admires, has risen twice. Once from the background of Arkansas farmboy to national stardom and again from a course heading toward self-destruction to become a national institution. His importance in the story of Sun Records is two-fold. He not only provided Sam Phillips with the incentive to record more country artists but his earlier recordings show how closely rockabilly could relate to a predominantly countrified style. Cash relied on the Sun sound although his rhythms were pure country, little influenced by R&B or the mainstream of pop and rock 'n' roll.

Born in Kingsland, Arkansas, on February 26, 1932, he was christened simply J.R. Cash. The name "Johnny" was given to him on his induction into the Air Force. His father was a sharecropper but the Depression had deprived him of a market and a drought had robbed him of the soil upon which his cotton had grown. In 1936, however, the Cashes became one of six hundred families chosen by the Federal Government to take part in the Dyess Land Colony Scheme, which was bordered by the Mississippi River. It was there that Cash grew up entirely among whites, for black families were excluded from the rehabilitation scheme. It is customary to attribute the "lived-in" quality of Cash's voice to the hard times experienced during those years, although Cash himself admits that his family never came close to starvation.

Cash made his first public appearance, aged 17, at a local talent contest, winning the first prize for singing unaccompanied and he later appeared on KLCN, Blytheville, Arkansas. His brother Roy was also on the station schedule as one of the Delta Rhythm Ramblers. Cash had his first brush with one of his country music idols at this time. In 1949 Eddie Hill and the Louvin Brothers played at the Dyess School Auditorium. Cash listened to them on WMC and made his way to the show hoping to talk with them. He was dumbstruck when Charlie Louvin came up to him and asked him where the rest room was. Cash proudly escorted him to the appropriate door and even waited outside to

Johnny Cash, 1955

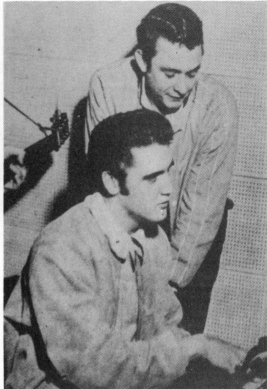

Johnny Cash and Elvis Presley

ANOTHER TWO-SIDER
BY ONE OF THE
TRULY GREAT
TALENT FINDS

●

**I WALK
THE LINE**
b/w
GET RHYTHM

SUN RECORD 241

EXCLUSIVE MANAGEMENT:
BOB NEAL
MANAGER
★ STARS INCORPORATED ★
Suite 1916, Sterick Bldg., Memphis, Tenn.

SUN RECORD
COMPANY, INC.
706 Union Ave.   Memphis, Tenn.

Johnny Cash, date unknown

*Johnny Cash and the Tennessee Two. Left to right: Luther Perkins,
Johnny Cash and Marshall Grant*

accompany him back.

Six weeks after graduation in 1950 Cash borrowed sufficient money to go to Detroit but he hated the impersonality of the large city and returned home with his first pay check. After that sobering experience he worked in a variety of jobs until the outbreak of the Korean War when he joined the Air Force for three years. While stationed in San Antonio, Texas, he met his first wife, Vivian Liberto, and when his unit moved to Germany, he took up the guitar and started writing poetry. One of his first efforts, *Hey Porter*, was published in the U.S. servicemens' magazine *Stars and Stripes* and later became his first record. In Germany he also formed a group, the Landsberg Barbarians, and appeared on local radio stations. Tapes still exist of early appearances. The Barbarians performed in the traditional hillbilly style and Cash's voice, somewhat higher than usual, was nevertheless distinctive.

After his discharge he married Vivian in San Antonio on August 7, 1954 and they set up home on Tutwiler Avenue in Memphis. Cash got a job selling vacuum cleaners to Memphis ghetto blacks. His route took him past the home of veteran jug band leader Gus Cannon, to whom he would sit and listen for hours. He also used part of his earnings to enroll in a school for radio announcers. In view of his later success, Cash can afford to recall these years without rancor. "I was the world's worst appliance salesman. Now and then the boss heard a rumor that I worked there but I didn't sell too much." The birth of a daughter meant that he had to drop out of the announcers' school but he was still singing with his guitar and went for his first audition with Sam Phillips, who turned him down because he chose to sing religious songs. Sun had known only commercial failure with religious records in the past.

Early in 1955 Cash went to see his brother Roy, then working at the Chrysler plant in Memphis. Roy Cash introduced him to co-workers Luther Perkins and Marshall Grant, who also played as a country duo on weekends. They gave Cash a gig at a church social and he became a regular member of the group. "At that time," said Grant, "we all played rhythm guitar and Johnny said 'I do most of the singing so I guess I'll carry on playing rhythm.' Luther had a little six inch speaker so he played the lead and that left me playing bass."

By the time they went for their second audition with Phillips they had forged a sound which remained basically unchanged. "The first session was really something," recalled Cash. "Luther had a little second-hand Sears amplifier and a six-inch speaker. Marshall Grant had a bass which was held together with masking tape and I had a little $4.80 guitar which I had brought back from Germany. Phillips had to be some kind of genius to get something out of that conglomeration. Luther took the metal plate from his Fender guitar and muted the strings because he played it so ragged and was trying to cover up the sound."

They played *Hey Porter* and Phillips was sufficiently impressed to promise to issue it if they could come up with another song. Legend has it that Cash wrote *Cry! Cry! Cry!* overnight. The two sides were issued on June 21, 1955, breaking into the country charts two weeks later. The record later went on to sell more than one hundred thousand copies and Phillips lent the trio money for clothes and a photographic session. They hustled gigs in Memphis and East Arkansas, although Cash resolutely refused to play honky-tonks and beer halls which were bread and butter for many struggling young country bands in those days.

It was obvious that Phillips was continuing his policy of trying to break into the lucrative country market and he probably never saw Cash as a rock artist, although he later added reverberation to *Hey Porter* to enhance the record's appeal in a rockabilly conscious market. He tagged advertisements for Cash's first record onto the bottom of his ads for Presley's last Sun records, obviously hoping to break Cash in the wake of Elvis.

As a follow-up Cash chose *Folsom Prison Blues*, which he had written after seeing Steve Cochran's performance in the movie *Inside the Walls of Folsom Prison*. It was recorded on July 29, 1955 and released on December 15. The song was recorded again in Folsom Prison in January 1968. It gave Cash one of his biggest selling albums to date and consolidated his position as a country pop superstar.

Rockabilly was breaking and Cash now had two country hits under his belt. He had toured with Presley and Perkins but was obviously not in a position to become a rockabilly legend. His voice sounded breathless and curiously out of place at anything above mid tempo but this did not stop him from writing rockabilly songs and pitching them at others. He wrote *Get Rhythm*, hoping that Elvis would record it and had two songs recorded by Carl Perkins. He also wrote *You're My Baby*, later recorded by Roy Orbison for Sun, and *Rock 'n' Roll Ruby*. Cash's acoustic guitar is decidedly ragged on both recordings and his voice is just too deep and cumbersome for "frantic chanting," as *Billboard* liked to call it.

In 1956, however, Cash did break into the pop charts with *I Walk the Line*. It was recorded on March 30, 1956, released on May 1 and reached the charts in September. Jack Clement recalls, "I wasn't too impressed with Johnny Cash at first because I like recordings with class, you know, and Cash seemed too rough but *I Walk the Line* with the humming was a class recording. I wanted to work with him after that point."

The success of *I Walk the Line* meant that the next Cash release was put back to November 1956 but Cash had to wait until October 1957, when he recorded Jack Clement's *Ballad of a Teenage Queen*, for his next hit. It was the first song he had recorded that he had not written himself. Jack Clement had also produced the record and obtained what he characterized as a "pretty sound." The song bristled with homespun philosophy, the guy gets the girl and the chorus added to the popular appeal. It did not have much to do with hillbilly music but it fitted right in with *Tammy*, *April Love* and the other biggies from that period. The flip side was much better. *Big River* had been written a few months earlier by Cash, who recalls, "I got the idea for that song when I read a story on myself in *TV Radio Mirror* magazine, written by a woman writer. The first line of her story was 'Johnny Cash has the big river blues in his voice...' I finished the song before I ever finished the article." Jack Clement produced the record and played an attractive acoustic guitar riff in the background. In fact, Clement had made Cash into a country pop artist and the man enjoyed an unbroken string of hits up to, and way beyond, the time he left Sun.

Guess Things Happen That Way was an attractive song that sounds better today than some of Cash's pop ditties from the same period. Clement was the writer and producer and the song was recorded on April 8, 1958 and released on May 20. By then most of Cash's records had piano and drums, usually played by Charlie Rich and Jimmy van Eaton, to augment the sparse sound of the

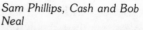
Sam Phillips, Cash and Bob Neal

Cash's first album, 1957 (Canadian version, London SU1220)

Johnny Cash on stage

Johnny Cash and Jerry Lee Lewis, Indianapolis, 1958

Tennessee Two. The record was breaking as negotiations over Cash's future were getting underway. Bob Neal, who managed most Sun acts, explains why Johnny left Sun when his three year contract was up. "In 1958, or thereabouts, Johnny had become so big that he wanted me to become his personal manager. Now Sam's arrangement with all the artists he discovered involved, I believe, a low royalty rate, about 3% on 90% of retail was the basic rate. When Johnny's contract was about to expire we talked to him. Johnny wanted to get the standard 5% royalty but Sam mentioned that he could not afford to pay it so we negotiated with several companies. Columbia's offer was basically the same as the others but it allowed an artist who was also a writer a full royalty rate whereas RCA had a clause which said that if you were a writer and artist too you got a smaller royalty rate as a writer. When the deal was announced, Sam was very upset. He said he would have done the whole deal if he thought we'd meant it." On August 1, 1958 Cash signed a long term contract with Columbia.

The last three Sun sessions produced ten songs. On May 15 four Hank Williams songs were recorded to form the basis for a proposed tribute album. In the event, only these four were included and they all suffered from the intrusion of a chorus, in particular a high pitched soprano which was meant to contrast with Cash's rough hewn baritone. It was a pity because a Hank Williams tribute album should have revealed Cash at his finest.

On July 10 Cash recorded Charlie Rich's *Ways of a Woman in Love*, a beautiful song with Rich on piano. It was issued after Cash left Sun. They also recorded *Thanks a Lot* and *Fools' Hall of Fame*. Billy Riley was playing guitar on *Fools' Hall of Fame* but the tape box was marked "Never to be released." Black singer Rudi Richardson had originally recorded the song in 1956 and although Cash's version was somewhat ragged it was finally released on *"The Rough Cut King of Country Music"* album in 1971.

The last session was held on July 18 and produced *I Just Thought You'd Like to Know* and *It's Just About Time*, which were issued in November 1958 and *I Forgot to Remember to Forget*, which was issued in June 1959. Rich was on piano again and the songs were good examples of Cash's later Sun output. The sound is mellow and inoffensive, the voice is distinctive and the songs were pretty. *I Forgot to Remember to Forget* had been written by Stan Kesler in 1955 and recorded by Presley at the time of Cash's first audition.

Initially, Cash was confined to the country market and success in the lucrative pop market only came when his sound was sweetened for popular consumption. At first sight, Cash's sound, with the throbbing electric guitar and sparse lonesome sound, seems strikingly original. We have seen, however, that one of the characteristics of early '50s hillbilly music was the strong walking bass, played on the deadened bass strings of an electric guitar. Cash stripped this sound of the fiddle and steel guitar and brought the electric guitar into sharper prominence. It is true, however, that no one had consistently recorded in this style previously.

His first hits were descriptions of Southern life in general. It was the honest poor white ethos. The main subjects were trains, prisons and lost love. Only "mother" was missing. Under Clement's guidance, however, the sound and the content changed. As Clement said, "Take Cash now. Sam Phillips was the one who saw the potential of that sound but I think I was the one who crystalized it. You know, the separation in that studio was enormous and we used overloading and distortion on Cash's sound." It was a powerful sound, created by the use of flutter echo on Cash's voice and all the instruments. The hard edge not only disguises the overt sentimentality of many of the early songs and the teenage love ballads but also the limitations of Cash's voice and Luther Perkins' instrumental technique.

On April 23, 1963 Stan Kesler on steel guitar, Bobby Wood on piano and Gene Chrisman on drums added backing tracks to several previously unissued 1956 recordings for an *"Original Sun Sound"* album, the last album to be issued on the old Sun label. The overdubbed version of *Wide Open Road* makes an interesting comparison with an undubbed alternate take later issued by Shelby Singleton. Cash was in a taunting mood:

> You said you'd had enough
> You said that you were leaving
> I said "Shove off, honey baby,
> I ain't grieving
> You can pack your bags and go out this evening
> There's a wide open road."

© Hi-Lo Music Inc.

By 1964, however, the vault had virtually run dry and all the remaining items were repackaged by Shelby Singleton between 1968 and 1971.

Cash's work for Sun includes many excellent recordings which have stood the test of time remarkably well. His sound remained unaltered at Columbia, except during one period in the early '60s when he tried to become a folk singer. Stardom gave him freedom of choice, allowing him to indulge his penchant for western ballads and to cultivate a reputation as a folklorist. He has hawked his conscience from cause to cause but has nevertheless emerged with a body of material that is indelibly etched with his own personality. Occasionally, he has managed to set his outraged conscience on a sound lyrical footing, as in the *"Bitter Tears"* album, where his interpretation of Peter LaFarge's *Ballad of Ira Hayes* is outstanding. His best work always refers back to his Sun sound, his *One Piece at a Time* hit, for example. On other occasions his infatuation with an idealized American past has intruded itself.

Johnny Cash stands with Jimmie Rodgers and Hank Williams as one of the three giants of country music. He was influenced to a degree by Ernest Tubb and Jimmie Skinner and some of his songs share the melancholy of Hank Williams but his vision and his manner of expressing it is uniquely his own. Today we can see that Cash was an important artist in the changing country scene of the '50s. He was not a hillbilly, he was not a cowboy. He was one of the first artists whom one can properly term a "country" singer.

Left to right: Unknown, Jimmy Swan, Ernie Chaffin and admirers

Texas Bill Strength

Jack Clement

David Houston

Cashing In. Sun and Country 1956–1966

For more than a year after the success of *Blue Suede Shoes*, pure country music took a back seat to rockabilly as Phillips attempted to capitalize upon the success of Carl Perkins, Warren Smith and Roy Orbison. The steady sales of Johnny Cash records throughout 1956, however, encouraged him to experiment again with country music.

The first of a new generation of Sun country artists was Ernie Chaffin, a seasoned performer working out of Long Beach, Mississippi, with steel guitarist Pee Wee Maddux, guitarist Ernie Harvey and bass player Leo Lodner. Maddux was later featured on his own show on WVMI (Biloxi, Mississippi) and later recorded for Judd Phillips' Judd label as a solo attraction. Chaffin's first Sun release was in January 1957 but its pleasant acoustic production sounded out of place in the changing times and by 1959 he had succumbed to the country pop sound.

Mack Self from backwoods Arkansas was a country singer who arrived in Memphis during 1955 and worked as a demo singer until 1957 when one of his own compositions, *Easy to Love*, was recorded. The sparse production was redolent of the hillbilly classics recorded in 1954 and 1955 and the fine backing was provided by Stan Kesler, Roland Janes and Billy Riley. It was a beautiful record released three years too late. Self recorded again in 1958 and a record appeared on the new Phillips International label. One side was a western folk ballad, *Willie Brown*, while the other side was a fine rockabilly song, *Mad at You,* with a harmony vocal supplied by Charlie Feathers.

The driving force behind the new country issues was Jack Clement who had grown up in Memphis listening to WMC. By 1956 he had gained experience as a country musician in Washington, D.C., Wheeling and Boston and had recorded for Sheraton in Boston in 1953 but he realized that his light high voice was unsuited to rockabilly or rock 'n' roll. He did not record under his own name during his first two years with Sun but with the trend toward a sweeter, pop-oriented sound that he himself had pioneered he decided that "Cash and them other guys shouldn't have all the fun."

In Clement's view, Sun was not making records quite "musical enough." He was gradually able to try a range of experiments with Cash and was responsible for getting him into the pop market. What he did like at Sun was the depth of talent and the relaxed atmosphere. He could do what he liked. Work all night on a session, write songs in Taylor's Café next door (like *Guess Things Happen That Way*) and even build a washroom in the control room. He once told Sam Phillips that he would build an office for Barbara Barnes for one hundred dollars. He got the job and canceled all sessions for a while. He also spent time helping to master recordings for his buddies on other labels and developing his own sound.

The Clement sound was country but it was not the usual Sun sound. It was light and acoustic, far from the ponderous muddy sound that Phillips had developed with Johnny Cash. It was worked out with the help of Clement's friend Jimmy C. Wilson, one of Sun's session pianists. Jack says, "Wilson was nearly as crazy as me. He lived in rooms above Taylor's Café next door. He had a pet coon which he used to bring in and chain to the piano. He was a great player if he was in the mood. His downfall at Sun was that he used to dismantle and build old guns up in his room and after he'd set fire to the place one time and then loosed off a rocket, a home made thing, they threw him out. He went to California and married Nudie the tailor's daughter."

In February 1957 Clement, Wilson and coon took off for the RCA studios in Nashville. They recorded four songs, two for Sun and two which Jack kept for RCA later on. *Ten Years* came out on Sun, a light pleasant country ballad with an epic story-song feel to it. This format was repeated in October 1958 when Jack recreated the sound at Sun on *Black Haired Man*. This was a fast, rhythmic development of the Cash beat, a gunfighter ballad of some class and a fairly successful record.

Clement also appeared on several Sun sessions as side man, notably a weird Dixieland singalong, *The Minstrel Show*, by the Clement Travelers where he played electric mandolin. Jack has always seen himself as a latter-day wandering minstrel. His unissued Sun recordings reveal more strange things, such as *Peroxide Blonde and a Hopped Up Model Ford* where he becomes a rocker, or *Tongue Tied Smith*, another gunfighter ballad about a touchy, tongue-tied cowboy.

After Clement's departure in early 1959 country issues were on a one-off basis. Among the artists who enjoyed one release on Sun or Phillips International were Onie Wheeler, "Texas" Bill Strength and David Houston. Both Wheeler and Strength disliked the casual atmosphere, which they regarded as unprofessional. David Houston's record was made at a low point in his career and was reissued by Phillips after Houston achieved success with *Almost Persuaded* on Epic. The Sun recording coupled a poor country pop song, *Sherry's Lips*, with *Miss Brown*, a fair attempt at the rock 'n' roll style. Both titles were leased from Bob Montgomery in Nashville.

The last country artist on Sun was Dane Stinit from Hartford, Kentucky. His overall sound was based on that of Johnny Cash, although his voice lacked Cash's somber brooding intensity. Stinit was first recorded on November 26, 1966 with a back-up band that included top session men Reggie Young, Bobby Wood and Tommy Cogsbill. The organist was Charles Chalmers, who later became musical director for Al Green. The session reputedly lured Sam Phillips out of semi-retirement but after a second unsuccessful record Stinit was dropped as Sun Records entered its final year.

Jerry Lee Lewis

"I knew when I heard him going up and down the keyboard and carrying on like that he was going to make it. And he did. Then he lost it and made it again."

—Malcolm Yelvington

Jerry Lee Lewis was twenty-one when he made some demonstration tapes for Sam Phillips. He was twenty-two when his second record sold six million copies but by the time he was twenty-four his career as one of the highest paid entertainers in the country had all but finished, only to revive almost a decade later in a different field.

Born in Ferriday, Louisiana, on September 29, 1935, Jerry Lee was one of the four children of Mary and Elmo Lewis. Elmo was a carpenter and played piano and guitar at church meetings and Jerry began his musical career on his father's guitar. At the age of eight, however, legend has it (a legend which, in common with many others, is propagated by Lewis himself) that he spotted a piano in his aunt's home and played his first tune. "I really gave dad and mom a start, my playing the piano without ever seeing one before. Dad was so impressed, he mortgaged the house to buy a piano for me."

When asked to name the artists who influenced him Lewis will generally reply that there were none. "I taught myself everything I knew about the piano. I wasn't influenced by anyone because I lived so far back in the country." It was natural, though, that he should grow up surrounded by the country music of Hank Williams and even Jimmie Rodgers but, in common with Presley, Bill Haley and Carl Perkins, he appears to have gone out of his way to listen to R&B bands. Lewis remembers hearing Sunnyland Slim and Tampa Red and claims that he sold newspapers and shined shoes in Haney's Big House, a dance hall in Ferriday that featured R&B bands. Lewis recalled, "Me and Jimmy Lee Swaggart, my cousin, we used to sneak into old Haney's. I loved to play the piano but it wasn't an instrument used a lot in country bands back then. I sure heard a lot of good piano playing from them R&B cats. Of the guys who came through, I guess B. B. King is more stamped more on my mind than anybody. The black guys they would come to town in them old buses, nine hundred years old, y'know, sittin' back there, feet stuck out the windows, eatin' sardines, the works. I loved it. I don't believe I was really influenced by anybody but if I could

103

play guitar like B. B. King, I'd be President of the United States. I'd be hell on wheels."

In the fall of 1948, Lloyd Paul, the Ford dealer in Ferriday, introduced a new range of models and Lewis joined the band who played in the parking lot. His set, which included *Drinkin' Wine Spo-Dee-O-Dee* (a hit at that time for Stick McGhee) lasted twenty minutes and brought him $13. In the following year, while still in school, he began work at the Blue Cat Nightclub in Natchez, Mississippi, but the distance forced him to take gigs nearer home. He still had a regular spot every Saturday on WNAT in Natchez, however, but after graduating from high school he gave up the Devil's music and entered the Bible Institute in Waxahachie, Texas. It was there that another apocryphal story about Lewis originated. At a concert given by the students, his incipient exhibitionism got the better of him and he rocked the accompaniment to *My God Is Real* and was asked to leave. As his garrulity was not to be used in the service of the Lord Lewis applied it to selling vacuum cleaners and sewing machines until late 1952 when he secured a job at the Wagon Wheel in Natchez. At that time he was playing drums, only taking over the piano stool when the leader of the combo, Paul Whitehead, doubled on accordion or trumpet.

By 1954 Lewis had built up a steady reputation and local following and had made his first record. Aunt Stella had driven him to Shreveport to audition for a Slim Whitman package tour and he cut *I Don't Hurt No More* and *If I Ever Needed You* at the KWKH studio, playing in a restrained popular country style. He also won a prize at the State Fair playing a version of Bill Nettles' *Hadacol Boogie* and in 1954 he was encouraged to go to Nashville in search of a recording contract. He says, "I remember it very well. I was turned down by every label in town. I stayed three weeks at the Bell Hotel downtown, right opposite the Continental bus station. I worked for Roy Hall in a little ol' club upstairs where Webb Pierce and Ernest Tubb and all these people used to come and get drunk and pay me to play." Unable to sustain a living, Lewis returned home and stayed around Ferriday and Natchez for at least a year until he tried his luck with Sun. "You know I started giving shows when I was just a kid. My father would load that old piano onto the back of his truck, we'd drive somewhere, unload it, I'd give a show, we'd pass the hat, he'd load it back on again and we'd go home and see what we'd got. Then in 1956 my father and I sold thirty-three dozen eggs, got in our old car and headed for Memphis to get an audition with Sun Records. We got there just in time to miss Sam Phillips who had gone to Nashville and they wouldn't let me in. I told them I was going to get an audition if I had to sit on the doorstep for three weeks."

Finally, Lewis cut a demonstration tape with Jack Clement. He saw himself as a country singer and was advised by Clement to work up some rocking songs instead of his country repertoire. By the time Clement had made the demo tape, Lewis had written *End of the Road* and reworked half a dozen country standards including *You're the Only Star in My Blue Heaven* and as much as he could remember of *Crazy Arms*. He returned to Ferriday for some weeks and heard nothing but when he got back to Memphis he found that Sam Phillips had liked his tape. Clement told him, "I was just fixing to call you. We think the record has something." Clement admits today that Lewis was "absolutely the most naturally talented artist I've ever worked with."

Jerry Lee Lewis and Sun Records came to an agreement and the old Ray Price hit, *Crazy Arms*, was chosen for the first single. It was issued on December 1, 1956, after the dubs had been well received on WHBQ and appeared at the lower end of the country charts a few weeks later. By that time Lewis was playing around Memphis or as a supporting act on a Stars Inc. show, booked by Bob Neal. Clyde Leoppard, who worked regularly out of West Memphis, says, "Jack Clement came by one night and asked if we needed a piano man. I said no since we had Smokey Joe but I went over to meet him anyway and Jack said, 'I'd like you to meet Jerry Lee Lewis.' I agreed to let him play some that night and he stopped the dance. Man, he beat that piano sore."

Lewis also worked as a session musician. In April 1957 he was on the session that produced *Matchbox* and two Billy Riley singles. He also took part in the Million Dollar Quartet session shortly after joining Sun.

The other side of Lewis's first record pointed the way toward the future. It was a storming rock number, *End of the Road*, and it was followed in April 1957 by *Whole Lotta Shakin' Goin' On*, which effectively ended his career as a small time country artist and session pianist. Suddenly in demand, his concert price jumped in one year from $50 to $10,000 and this was largely the work of Judd Phillips, who explained in detail how he came to launch a national figure.

"The first time I really noticed him was when he was a minor artist on a tour that Johnny Cash, Carl Perkins and Webb Pierce were doing. We stopped by my house for lunch in Florence, Alabama, but Jerry sat down at the piano and started to play. I heard him playing tunes like *Summit Ridge Drive* and tunes you wouldn't believe he had in his repertoire. I had in my mind that this was not just a cat well rehearsed on a few numbers. He could play. This guy had depth and it was a matter of bringing it into focus. I took him to New York and presented him to Jules Green who was managing Steve Allen and Henry Frankel who was talent co-ordinator for N.B.C. I took a real gamble in terms of Sun Records to see if a mass audience would accept this man. There was a big gamble in ensuring that every retail outlet in the United States had copies of *Whole Lotta Shakin' Goin' On* so that it was available. This represented a lot of merchandise that could have been returned. We were a small company fighting the giants. Those big labels were not really creative in their approach and did not care about developing a product after someone else had established it. We had to take a chance on taking the artist to the public. When it came down to the nitty gritty, after Carl Perkins had his accident, after we had gone someway toward getting a successful national artist, I knew the only hope to make Sun a successful and big company was that we take Jerry Lee Lewis and put everything behind him and use his talent to create all the other Sun personalities."

It was at this time that Sun hired Barbara Barnes. Lewis was starting to get a lot of fan mail and Barbara set up a fan club organization as well as writing album liner notes, organizing a regular news-sheet, chasing distributors for orders and promoting new releases. By this time, Marion Keisker had left Sun and the new secretary was Sally Wilburn. Sam also employed a stenographer, Regina Reese, and with Sam and Judd, Jack Clement and Bill Justis that was Sun's total work force as *Whole Lotta Shakin'* entered the national charts.

Jerry's version of *Whole Lotta Shakin' Goin' On* went on to sell more than 6 million copies worldwide. Its initial success in the States was largely due to Judd's gamble on guaranteed sale and Jerry's appearance on the Steve Allen show. When Presley had appeared on the same show exactly a year earlier Allen had insisted that there be no "breach of good taste" and Presley had been forced to wear a white suit with tails and carry a cane. By 1957 N.B.C.'s standards had relaxed a little and when Lewis threw furniture around the stage Allen came on from the wings and did the same.

For a follow-up, Lewis recorded a song by Otis Blackwell and Jack Hammer, *Great Balls of Fire*. It was released on November 3, 1957 and climbed into the National Top 10 on December 30. Lewis went on to perform the song in Warner Brothers' *Jamboree* movie. His stage act became the sensation of the year despite the fact that the public had grown insensitive to outrageousness from rock 'n' roll singers. Jerry could be frenzied or cool and sneering. He had received instant stardom but took it totally in his stride, probably regarding it as no less than overdue.

Great Balls of Fire was followed by *Breathless*, a gimmicky and undistinguished number when set against the man's remarkable standards but it entered the charts in both America and England. It was drifting down the English hit parade when he arrived on those shores for a promotional tour in May 1958. It did not take long for certain sections of the English press to discover that Jerry's wife, Myra, whom he had married in December 1957, was younger than their standards would allow. They patronizingly transcribed the Southern patois as he explained, "Mah wife is cute. She might look young and be young but she is growed."

On May 24 the truth came out that Myra was thirteen rather than fifteen, as had been previously thought, and that Jerry had married her before a divorce from his second wife had been finalized. Again he explained, "Myra and I are legally married. It was mah second marriage that wasn't legal. Ah was a bigamist when ah was sixteen. Ah was fourteen when ah was first married. That lasted a year, then ah met June. One day she said she was goin' to have mah baby. Ah was real worried. Her father threatened me and her brothers were huntin' me with hide whips. So ah married her just a week before mah divorce from Dorothy. It was a shotgun wedding."

The public was not satisfied and after three shows the tour was cancelled. Jerry and Myra returned to London Airport to await the airplane home and it was there that he had the last word. Looking through the morning papers he remarked, "Who is this DeGaulle? He seems to have gone over bigger'n us."

Jerry's career was effectively ruined by the adverse publicity. His return to the States was marked by an attempt by his manager, Oscar Davis, to hush up the issue. Arriving in New York, Lewis declared, "Could've made mah home there if ah'd wanted. Ah was just homesick, ah guess."

The truth came out, however, and so did a record called *The Return of Jerry*

Jerry Lee with the stars of "High School Confidential." Left to right: Diane Jergens, Russ Tamblyn, Jan Sterling, John Drew Barrymore and the immortal Mamie Van Doren.

Jerry Lee Lewis – an early Sun publicity shot

Jerry Lee Lewis with ex-rockabilly Jimmy Bowen, Nashville manager of Elektra Records

Jerry Lee Lewis and family, 50s

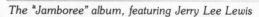

The "Jamboree" album, featuring Jerry Lee Lewis

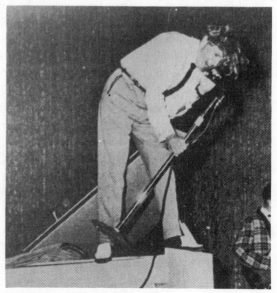

Lewis on piano (on stage), 1958

Lee, which attempted to satirize the issue by using clips from previous discs interspersed with a commentary from George Klein. For example:

Q: *"What did Queeen Elizabeth say about you?"*
A: *"Goodness gracious, Great Balls of Fire!"*

The record was not issued in England and did not sell too well in the States. In fact, Jerry returned to see his last real chart success of the '50s slide down the charts. *High School Confidential* had been written by Jerry with Ron Hargrave for a movie of the same name. It had been designed as a successor to the *Blackboard Jungle* with Jerry cast as the teenagers' delight but it turned into a vehicle for the posturing of Mamie van Doren.

Jerry's records after 1958 were characterized by a lack of chart success with the exception of his revival of *What'd I Say* which entered the Top 50 in 1961. After many rumors related to the idea that Sam Phillips was refusing to supply Jerry's records to distributors who owed him money, Jerry finally made the break from Sun on September 29, 1963 and signed with Smash, a division of Mercury Records.

His career at Smash started by copying Ray Charles' formula for success. Charles had reached the top of the charts with string laden revivals of country standards and Jerry followed with the syrupy *Pen and Paper* coupled with Charles' *Hit the Road Jack*. It did not find success and thereafter Jerry was marketed as a rock singer. This period saw the release of some good records including *She Was My Baby (He Was My Friend)*, *I'm on Fire* and *"The Return Of Rock"* album. There was also a far less successful flirtation with soul music on *"Soul My Way"* before the release of his first double-sided country single, *Another Place, Another Time/Walking the Floor Over You*, which took him to the top of the country charts. Jerry announced that he had always been country and made a slew of albums for Smash and later Mercury which grew increasingly undistinguished. There were a few attempts to break away from the formula, such as the time he recorded in London with superstars dropping in and out of the studio. There was also the *"Southern Roots"* concept album which contained some fine work. In general, though, Jerry recorded over twenty country albums in eleven years on which he sounded increasingly bored and tired. His voice was shot and his performances were obviously perfunctory. Even one of his favorite songs from way back usually failed to stir him.

Jerry was still a crazy man, though, treating the press to a string of anecdotes from back when. He had made a fortune and lost it. After twenty years in the entertainment business he was still living out of his back pocket. Still in trouble with women, "If the Lord made anything better than a woman he kept it for Himself."

In 1978 he signed with Elektra Records, who were revitalizing their country division. He signed at roughly the same time as Jack Clement, Roy Acuff and Hank Williams, Jr. His first album under the new deal arrived in the racks in March 1979 and looked and sounded far better than anything he had done for years. At the same time, the I.R.S. arrived at Jerry's Mississippi home and seized some cars and jewelry in lieu of unpaid taxes. He is definitely crazy but there ought to be a place for his larger-than-life character in today's somewhat sterile music scene.

The Lewis Style

Jerry Lee Lewis recorded prolifically for Sun. There were twenty-two singles issued on Sun and an instrumental coupling issued on Phillips International under the pseudonym of The Hawk. There were four EPs and two albums. There were also one hundred unissued masters which ran the gamut from country standards and R&B hits such as *Hound Dog*, *Let the Good Times Roll*, *Born to Lose* and *The Wild Side of Life* to hard rock and the occasional instrumental such as *Rock 'n' Roll Ruby*, *Wild One* and *Dixie*.

The variety embodied in Jerry's recordings highlights his many and varied influences. His music was a uniquely personal blend of country boogie, hillbilly, the New Orleans stomp of Fats Domino, the fast emerging rock music of Elvis Presley and the gospel music that surrounded him in his youth. One can even trace the influence of Moon Mullican, a Texas country artist who was himself influenced by the black singers working on his father's ranch. On piano and pump organ Mullican developed a style that predated Jerry's in some respects.

The Lewis style, which Phillips aptly dubbed "The Pumping Piano," was simplistic and dominated by right hand *glissandi*, especially when compared with the work of such accomplished boogie pianists as Albert Ammons or Meade Lux Lewis. In the context of his records, however, it is much more appropriate and reveals an amazing subtlety that few country pianists have brought to their work. His one solely instrumental record illustrates this. The two extended piano solos, issued under the pseudonym of The Hawk, were recorded at Jerry's last session in the old Sun studio at 706 Union Avenue, on January 26, 1960. Backing was supplied by Roland Janes on guitar, R.W. Stevenson on bass and Jimmy van Eaton on drums. *In the Mood*, a revival of the old Glenn Miller hit, is the faster of the two and Jerry begins by stabbing the bass notes although he reverts to rolling boogie styles later in the song. Unfortunately, he only attempts limited improvisation, contenting himself with embroidering the melody. *I Get the Blues When It Rains*, in contrast, is a slower paced performance, redolent of the late '40s honky-tonk style of Del Wood.

Another factor coloring Jerry's music is his ambivalent attitude toward the Almighty. He recorded a number of gospel songs during his early years with Sun and the gospel influence on his overall sound was deep. In 1958 Billy Riley turned on the tape machine as Lewis and Phillips discussed religion and the conversation went as follows:

Jerry Lee Lewis: "H-E-L-L, hell. Great God Almighty, Great Balls Of Fire ... It says make merry with the joy of God only but when it comes to worldly music rock 'n' roll—you have done talked yourself into the world and you are a sinner unless you be saved and borned again and be made like a little child and walk before God and be holy and, brother, I mean you gotta be so pure and no sin shall enter there, for it says, 'No sin shall enter there.' It doesn't say, 'Just a little bit,' it says, 'No sin, brother. Not one little bit. You gotta walk and talk with God to go to Heaven."

Sam Phillips: "Hallelujah! You're right. Now look, Jerry, religious conviction doesn't mean anything resembling extremism. You mean to tell me that you're gonna take the Bible and revolutionize the whole universe. Did Jesus Christ save all the people in the world?"

Jerry Lee Lewis: "No but he tried to."

Sam Phillips: "He sure did. Jesus Christ went around and did good. He didn't preach from one pulpit ..."

Jerry Lee Lewis: "It's what is happenin' every day. The blind are made to see. The crippled are made to walk ..."

Sam Phillips: "But, Jerry, Jesus Christ is just as real today as when he came into the world."

Jerry Lee Lewis: "You're right. You're so right you don't know what you're sayin.'"

Phillips: "Now I've studied the Bible a little bit ..."

Jerry Lee Lewis: "I have, too, I've studied it through and through. I know what I'm talkin' about."

Sam Phillips: "You mean that you can't do good to be a rock 'n' roll exponent?"

Jerry Lee Lewis: "You can do good, Mr. Phillips, don't get me wrong. You can have a kind heart and help people."

Sam Phillips: "I don't mean a kind heart. You can save souls."

Jerry Lee Lewis: "No! No! No! How can the Devil save souls? Man, I've got the Devil in me. If I didn't I'd be a Christian."

Sam Phillips: "The point I'm trying to make is, you've got no alternative ..."

Jerry Lee Lewis: "It ain't a matter of what you believe. It's what's written in the Bible. It's what's there, Mr. Phillips."

Sam Phillips: "No, no, no. If it's not what you believe then how do you interpret the Bible?"

Jerry Lee Lewis: "Man alive! There's some people, you just can't tell 'em, 'cause they just don't listen."

Both Lewis and Phillips obviously shared difficulties in reconciling a deep-seated prejudice against the Devil's music with their own largely faultless judgment of what was commercially acceptable. Jerry's periods of abject piety did not interfere with his career as a rock 'n' roll artist and he was never tempted to resume a career in the service of the Lord. Other artists with similar doubts, Little Richard, for example, eschewed the secular life for long or short periods.

Jerry Lee Lewis sneering gently, 1961

Jerry Lee Lewis and Judd Phillips, February 1961

Roland James

Jerry Lee Lewis, 1957

Jerry Lee Lewis's career with Sun Records divides itself fairly neatly into the classic sides recorded by Sam Phillips and Jack Clement in the old studio on Union Avenue and the later recordings made in the new studios in Nashville and on Madison Avenue in Memphis. It was during the latter period that various attempts were made to bring his sound into line with popular trends. Between January 1960 and February 1961 Jerry does not appear to have recorded although he may have placed a vocal track on his weakest single, *When I Get Paid/Love's Made a Fool of Me*. This break in his activity acts as a convenient watershed from which to assess his career.

The highly distinctive sound which marks his first recordings is a product of limited instrumentation, limited recording techniques and, to a lesser extent, choice of material. The prominent feature was the voice and piano of Jerry himself. He supplied the rhythmic pulse which was highlighted by the subtle touch of drummer Jimmy van Eaton. The guitar, which was almost invariably played by Roland Janes, was limited to unobtrusive rhythm support and one short solo. Janes was not an overimaginative guitarist but he was an ideal session man, able to adapt from the hard rock of Hayden Thompson and Lewis through the gentle lilting ballad style of Buddy Cunningham to the tough down home blues of Frank Frost. He played on hundreds of sessions "because I was there. Not because I possessed any particular gift that anyone else didn't have." Janes had come to Memphis from backwoods Alabama in 1956. He began work as a professional musician with Billy Riley almost immediately and it was through Riley that he came to meet Lewis, who could not afford a regular band at that time and had to work with the available session musicians.

The success of a recording depended entirely upon Lewis and on the early sides he is totally in control and rarely less than brilliant. Whether racing

Jerry Lee Lewis and Sam Phillips

through *Jailhouse Rock* to prove that he could rock as hard as Presley or drawling his way imperiously through a country ballad he was always totally in control of the session. Jack Clement and Sam Phillips added the echo which brought his voice into sharper prominence, giving it a hard crystalline edge. Sales of *Whole Lotta Shakin'* in this simple style encouraged Clement to restrain his desire to fill out the sound with more instruments. *Shakin'* is a masterpiece of power and energy, remarkable for the way Lewis controls the ebb and flow of sound, lulling the beat before storming back in the final chorus.

After *Shakin'* had been recorded they needed a flip side. Clement explained how he came to write *It'll Be Me*.

"Now defecating is an unpleasant subject and I wouldn't want my mother reading this but *Shakin'* needed a B side and I decided to write one. I liked to write at Sun 'cause most everything got cut. While I was thinking I went to the bathroom for the purpose of defecating and I got to wonder about the forms of reincarnation and the song just came to me. 'If you see a lump in the bowl, baby it'll be me and I'll be looking at you.' We changed it to 'sugar bowl' and the song came from there. It was my first free ride on the back of *Whole Lotta Shakin'*. When we were short of hits Bill Justis used to tell me, 'Why don't you go and take another of those $10,000 shits?' "

All of Jerry's hits retained the same limited instrumental format. In fact, *Great Balls of Fire* has only piano and drums. Flutter echo is used as a third instrument, giving the recording depth. It was not until 1958 that Jerry recorded with a saxophone on a version of Moon Mullican's *I'll Sail My Ship Alone*. The song was taken at a breakneck tempo which destroyed some of the poignancy of the original but it was an exceptionally good rock record. Released in November 1958 it reached number 90 in the Hot 100. The session had been held in May and was one of the few occasions when Lewis did not play piano. Charlie Rich was the piano player and Jeff Davis played the drums in place of Jimmy van Eaton. The saxophonist, Martin Willis, is scarcely audible in the background, filling out the sound. The session also produced *It Hurt Me So* and fuller versions of songs Lewis had recorded when he first came to Sun demanding an audition, *Drinkin' Wine Spo-Dee-O-Dee* and *You're the Only Star in My Blue Heaven*.

I'll Sail My Ship Alone is one of the few times when Lewis failed to rework a country standard successfully. Normally, his finest work can be found in his interpretations of hillbilly standards and folk tunes such as *Hand Me Down My Walking Cane*, *Old Black Joe* and *Silver Threads*. His versions of Hank Williams' songs are also outstanding whether he is racing his way through *Jambalaya* or recapturing Williams' melancholy in reworkings of *I Can't Help It*, *You Win Again* or *I Could Never Be Ashamed of You*. He was also in top form for a version of Billy Mize's *It All Depends (Who Will Buy the Wine)*. An old hillbilly song is one of the few things to reduce Lewis to sustained silence. "Considering what they had to work with back in those days," he said, "they made better records back then. Just like they made better cars in 1942 than they do in 1972."

Another source of material was R&B standards. Lewis recorded less during his early period than Presley but he turned in fine versions of Chuck Willis' *Hang Up My Rock 'n' Roll Shoes*, Clyde McPhatter's *Come What May*, Chuck Berry's *Johnny B. Goode* and *Little Queenie*, Louis Jordan's *Let the Good Times Roll* and Billy Ward's *Sixty Minute Man*. In fact, after his success in 1961 with *What'd I Say* he was forced to record a greater selection of R&B standards but they lack the artistic success of songs like *Little Queenie* on which Lewis perfectly interprets Chuck Berry's leering original. He does not try to imitate black vocals patterns but makes these R&B songs expressions of his own personality.

Jerry never managed to recapture the artistic success of his early recordings. He never found another drummer as sympathetic as Jimmy van Eaton and never found another producer willing to use the sparse instrumentation. Thankfully his voice did not develop Presley's plummy vibrato or lose its range but nonetheless he was never able to recapture the magic that prevailed in that tiny studio on Union Avenue.

When he emerged from a brief semi-retirement in February 1961, he opened the new Sun studio in Nashville by taking four Nashville session men, guitarists Hank Garland and Kelso Herston, bassist Bob Moore and drummer Buddy Harman and recorded four songs. *I Forgot to Remember to Forget* and *Cold, Cold Heart* which remained unissued at the time together with *What'd I Say* and *Livin', Lovin' Wreck* which were issued as a single two weeks later, giving him his only big hit since *High School Confidential*. Jerry had recorded *What'd I Say* in 1959 with the Sun house band, including Roland Janes, but it remained unissued.

In June 1961 he made *It Won't Happen With Me*, his solitary "highschool" recording. The lyrics mention Ricky Nelson, Elvis Presley and Jackie Wilson and the titles of their latest hits but it was an idiom to which he was obviously unsuited and not even a storming piano break could save the record. The session of September 9 was even less successful. He recorded *Money*, *Ramblin' Rose* and *Rockin' the Boat of Love*. Jerry's piano and Jerry Kennedy's guitar were swamped beneath the unimaginative brass and reed arrangements.

Jerry returned to Memphis in January 1962 to make his first recordings at the new Phillips studio on Madison Avenue. Reunited with Roland Janes, he reworked Junior Parker's *Feelin' Good* as *I've Been Twistin'* and as another gesture toward that forgotten craze he even re-recorded *Whole Lotta Shakin' Goin' On* as *Whole Lotta Twistin' Goin' On*. The other titles were *I Know What It Means*, which was dubbed with a chorus and issued after Jerry left Sun, and *High Powered Woman (You're the Monkey on My Back)*. This last song was based loosely on the *What'd I Say* riff and it had a fine loose and easy backing and a strong vocal from Jerry. Unfortunately, it was only one minute and forty-seven seconds long and too suggestive. It remained unissued until 1974.

In June 1962 Scotty Moore produced two sessions of R&B standards designed to recapture the success of *What'd I Say*. The titles included Fats Domino's *Hello Josephine*, Chuck Berry's *Sweet Little Sixteen*, Roy Brown's *Good Rockin' Tonight* and Gene Vincent's *Be Bop A Lula*. None of these had the magic of the old Memphis sessions but they were among the better items from the period. Too often Jerry sounds uninterested. He wants the session fee for his alimony payments, then he wants to split.

Another ghastly experiment from the same period was the teaming of Jerry with his teenaged sister Linda Gail. One session in March 1963 produced a tuneless version of the old George Jones hit *Seasons of My Heart* and two unissued songs. Jerry has never harmonized well but it was never more obvious than on these recordings. In addition, Linda Gail's voice sounds weak, thin and extremely flat.

The last Sun sessions were a pointer toward the future. They were recorded in Memphis three days before his contract expired and included modern country sounds which did not seem to have dated when issued by Shelby Singleton, the new owner of the Sun repertoire, over five years later. The titles included *One Minute Past Eternity, Invitation to Your Party, I Can't Seem to Say Goodbye* and *Love on Broadway*. There was a chorus led by Noel Gilbert and a simple countrified backing from Roland Janes, Scotty Moore and others. The boom in country sales had not started and with the exception of *Carry Me Back to Old Virginia* all the titles were suppressed until Shelby Singleton took over. The overall sound was remarkably similar to Jerry's Smash/Mercury country recordings and all the suppressed titles from Jerry's last Memphis session went on to become hits.

There has been one more development concerning Lewis's recordings. After the death of Elvis Presley, Singelton's Sun label issued a single of *Save the Last Dance for Me* and an album, *"Duets."* Both sailed into the country and pop charts on the strength of the rumor that the other voice belonged to Elvis Presley. As Presley was in the Army in Germany when *Save the Last Dance for Me* was recorded it is extremely unlikely that he is the mystery voice. It belongs, in fact, to Jimmy Ellis or one of the burgeoning number of Elvis imitators.

Jerry Lee's classic records were performed in a style that can be called "country-rock." It lacks the acoustic and primitive feel of much rockabilly and the over-production of much commercial rock 'n' roll. Jerry is certainly strongest when he is reworking country material. His enthusiasm jumps out of the grooves. Some critics have remarked that Jerry is handicapped because he does not write his own material. It is certainly true that he has written very little, although he maintains that he could if he wanted to. Jerry thinks that Hank Williams killed himself through his writing. "All of your great writers . . . it takes something out of you. You get in different moods . . . You get all boozed up, I mean it's not worth it." He compensates by treating other writers' songs as if they were his own. Jerry has never been cowed by a good song, always believing that he can make a greater version and this self-confidence has usually been well justified. He has been an instantly recognizable performer at every stage of his career but remains at his greatest on his early Sun recordings.

Dickey Lee and the Collegiates

Edwin Bruce, 1957

Jerry Lee Lewis and Ray Smith

Barbara Pittman

Ray Smith on stage

Ray Smith

The End of an Era

At the time Jerry Lee Lewis was achieving his greatest success, primitive rockabilly was giving way to the fuller sound of rock 'n' roll, characterized by the pre-Army recordings of Elvis Presley. We have seen that Sam and Judd Phillips intended to use Jerry's fame to promote the rest of the Sun catalog and from 1957 until the commercial death of rock 'n' roll in 1960, the Phillips brothers produced a strain of hard rock singers. Some of these new Sun artists, most notably Ray Smith, modeled their approach on Jerry Lee Lewis.

Session drummer Jimmy van Eaton later took an overview of the whole period. "First off, there was Elvis, just guitars and bass. Then *Blue Suede Shoes* hit with drums and after that, everything had to have drums. Then, Jerry Lee hit with *Shakin'*, which had a piano. After that, everything had to have a piano. Later, everything had to be like Charlie Rich. That's the way it was. Things started to fall apart after Jack Clement and Bill Justis left. We were in a groove but it just disappeared."

One of the first in the hard rocking style was Edwin Bruce who made two unsuccessful discs for Sun in 1957 and 1958. He was only sixteen years old but had previously recorded with Bill Flagg on the latter's rockabilly recordings. Bruce recorded for Sun in a rock-a-ballad style and *Rock Boppin' Baby* might have achieved national impact if it had enjoyed the advantage of being promoted by one of the major companies. His second record, *Sweet Woman/Part of My Life*, was recorded in January 1958 and released in April. Bill Justis produced the session and Dickey Lee and Jimmy Smith were among the backing musicians but it also failed to attract any attention. Bruce returned to the family business in Memphis until 1965 when he recorded for RCA Victor in Nashville. In 1968 he was signed by Fred Foster at Monument and his *"Shades of Ed Bruce"* album, released in September 1969, brought him some belated recognition which he has developed into a strong career in country music.

Tommy Blake was in a similar mold. His first disc was a revival of T. V. Slim's *Flat Foot Sam* but the failure of his second release meant that he too was dropped from the roster. Blake had begun his career in country music on KRUS (Ruston, Louisiana) but was only recorded as a rock artist by Sun. Among the sides he left behind were the frantic *Shake Around* and *I Dig You, Baby*.

Junior Parker wrote *Mystery Train* and Sun released it as a follow-up to

117

Feelin' Good in late 1953. It reappeared with the addition of "Phillips" to the composer credits in the Fall of 1955 as Presley's last single for Sun. Another version was recorded in August 1959 by Vernon Taylor. The new version reflected the change in public taste. The primitive sparse sound of Presley's rockabilly version had now given way to a fuller, sax led production and the subtle understated beat was now reinforced by the drumming of Jimmy van Eaton. The flip side was also an updated rockabilly song, Roy Orbison's *Sweet and Easy to Love*, with the piano of Charlie Rich in evidence. Taylor himself was a twenty-one-year-old singer from Maryland who, unlike most other Sun artists, had previously recorded for another label, Dot in Gallatin, Tennessee.

Of far less consequence were the gestures toward high school music and the first artist to be recorded in this unique and forgettable style was Rudy Grayzell, formerly a straight country singer who had known success in 1953 with *Looking at the Moon and Wishing on a Star,* for Abbott Records. His only disc for Sun, *Judy,* was produced by Roy Orbison. It had conversational lyrics which mentioned Presley in an attempt to get the pubescent audience to identify with the song but still had shades of Gene Vincent and classic rockabilly.

Jimmy Isle's *Together/What a Life* was in the mode of the typical highschool songs, developed by Jerry Keller and the others in the Brill Building. Isle's inane lyrics, impoverished melody and tuneless vocals render his records arguably the worst issued on Sun. He was apparently undeterred by his conspicuous lack of talent and went on to record for S.P., Talent and even Roulette Records.

George Klein, a Memphis deejay, and confidant of Elvis Presley produced a more interesting disc, designed to appeal to University of Tennessee jocks. *U.T. Party* was essentially a dance workout number, preserving a priceless slice of period deejay patter interspersed with Charlie Rich's piano:

> Before you make the scene, we'll have a little warm-up routine
> The girl with the little curl, easy now, honey
> Now Daddy-O, let's see if you can make the loop
> And for you in blue, it's an easy two.

This period also saw some releases from Barbara Pittman who had begun her career as a featured vocalist with Clyde Leoppard's Snearly Ranch Boys. She possessed a fine husky voice, was capable of storming rock numbers and excelled on slow ballads. Stan Kesler wrote some songs to highlight her vocal range and although she recorded the trite *Eleventh Commandment* she also turned in a fine jazz-tinged version of Charlie Rich's *Handsome Man* at the same session. She left Memphis in 1960, went to Chicago but returned in the late '60s after her career had just about finished.

Presley's influence was still very strong in this era and most labels had a poor man's Presley. Sun tried out quite a few including Hayden Thompson and Dicky Lee, whose debut, *Good Lovin'*, bore a remarkable resemblance to Presley's *Too Much*. Lee was a local Memphis teenager, discovered by Dewey Phillips and recorded by him on his first record, *Dream Boy*. As a favor to Dewey, Jack Clement signed Dickey to Sun and it was only after he had done so he found that he had made quite a good deal. "Dickey was only a kid but he had all 'round talent. Eventually, he came good, writing the country classic *She Thinks I Still Care* and then going Top Ten with *Patches*." This was all still in the future, however, and after two singles and some session work Lee moved on to Beaumont, Texas, with Clement and song writer Allen Reynolds. They broke into the pop market on TCF-Hallway and Smash, later returning to Memphis and working at the Sounds of Memphis studio in the late '60s. Dickey returned to country music under contract to RCA, having gained an introduction from Sun's Billy Sherrill and Jack Clement who were well established in Nashville by then. He currently records for mercury.

Five singers in particular tended to base their styles on Jerry Lee Lewis. Of these, Charlie Rich and Carl Mann became best selling artists on the Phillips International label and both developed distinctive styles that will be discussed later. The others were Ray Smith, Cliff Thomas and Carl McVoy.

Ray Smith never achieved the individual identity that Rich and Mann have shown throughout their careers. A Kentuckian, he came to Sun because his manager was a friend of Sam Phillips. He first recorded on May 9, 1958 while Lewis was in the midst of his problems in England. He made four titles that day including his first single, *So Young/Right Behind You Baby*, and Charlie Rich's *Break Up*. Smith was primarily a pianist but he played rhythm guitar on this session while Rich played piano and directed proceedings. The same group re-assembled in October when Smith cut *Why Why Why* and *You Made a Hit* for his second single. These two sessions account for Smith's finest work although their success is largely due to the strength of Rich's material and musical direction.

Smith went on to enjoy a hit in 1959 with *Rockin' Bandit* but it was a poor gimmicky number that owed its inspiration to the Olympics' *Western Movies* without being half as good. Late in 1959 and through 1960 Smith recorded under the direction of Bill Justis in Nashville, using some of the top session men, in an attempt to get Judd Phillips' Judd label off the ground. It was here that he achieved his only national hit, *Rockin' Little Angel*, which was based on a nursery rhyme. From Judd, Ray Smith has moved on to innumerable labels and still seeks the elusive hits. He was based in Hamilton, Ontario, and was in demand for rock revival shows before his death in November 1979.

Cliff Thomas also displayed a pronounced Lewis influence. He was a college kid from Mississippi who sang in a harsh rock style while brother Ed supplied the piano accompaniment and Barbara Thomas filled in with back-up vocals. The trio worked out of Jackson, Mississippi, as Cliff Thomas, Ed and Barbara. They issued four singles on Phillips International under that name or as Bobbie and the Boys. Cliff and Ed later resurfaced on Jackson's Ace label and on several other local labels but they never did as well as their first single for Phillips, *Treat Me Right*. Ed Thomas was a fine pianist and he and Cliff have remained in music as well as helping to run the family shirt business. They have written soul hits for Barbara Lynn and Peggy Scott and Jo Jo Benson.

Lastly, the Lewis influence can be heard in the recordings of Carl McVoy who came to Memphis from Mississippi with a rearrangement of the evergreen, *You Are My Sunshine*. At that time, Bill Cantrell, Quinton Claunch and Ray

Cliff Thomas with Ed and Barbara

Carl McVoy

Harris had persuaded local record store owner Joe Cuoghi to put up the money for an independent label. McVoy was taken to Nashville to record and was signed as the first artist. Bill Cantrell says, "Quinton Claunch and I wrote *Tootsie* in that fast style Jerry Lee had for the flip side of the record and we put it out as the first record on the Hi label." When it began selling well Cuoghi received offers from other companies offering to buy the masters but he refused to sell and eventually lost money because he could not collect from the distributors. He solved this problem by signing with London Records but it was too late to do anything with McVoy's single. Cuoghi tried to recoup some of his losses by selling the masters to Sam Phillips for $1500 and Phillips re-released the record on Phillips International in June 1958. McVoy recorded another eleven songs for Phillips but a follow-up was not issued and he returned to Hi to work as a pianist with the Bill Black Combo. Most of his recordings at Sun had been demos of country songs, very much in the style of his cousin Jerry Lee Lewis. Though unreleased, they show the way in which Jerry himself would turn almost a decade later.

Sun at the Crossroads

The Memphis recording industry expanded after Sun had given it an injection of success. A plethora of small labels began operating although most went bankrupt within a few years. Among the casualties were Summer Records owned by Jack Clement and Play Me owned by Bill Justis. Both Hi and Stax Records eventually eclipsed the success of Sun and Phillips International in the '60s. Problems at Sun revolving around the business methods and conflicting lifestyles of the two brothers prevented capitalization on the new musical trends and Sun ended as it had begun—a small label recording local musicians and supplying a local market.

Toward the end of 1958, however, Sun was still a booming concern. Recordings by Johnny Cash, Jerry Lee Lewis and Bill Justis were securing national airplay and a few artists of great potential had been acquired. There were problems but these centered around management changes. At the time of Judd Phillips' departure there developed what Bill Fitzgerald called an "ego clash" between Phillips and his producers. "I worked for Sam between 1959 and 1968," said Fitzgerald, "and I was the only guy he didn't fire." Jack Clement was in the middle of these disputes which often set in when success starts fading. "Slim Wallace and Scotty Moore cut *Tragedy* for Fernwood at Hi studios but they had no echo so I ran it through the tape machine that we had down at 706 Union. Of course, the thing became a big hit and Sam was real mad about it. This was an early clash but eventually Sam and I found we could not get on any more. It came to a head in March 1959 when Bill Justis asked Sam to leave the studio because he was working and needed to concentrate. Bill was fired for insubordination and I was fired for laughing at them."

Jimmy van Eaton recalled that things started going downhill after Jack and Bill were fired. "At first Sam brought in Ernie Barton who was pretty bad and then there was Charles Underwood who was not much better." In 1959 Bill Fitzgerald became general manager of the Sam C. Phillips International Corporation because "Phillips wanted to look after his radio interests in Memphis (WAGI and WHEE) and Florida and move into the property business." Fitzgerald's promotional manager was Cecil Scaife who stayed with Sun almost to the end before moving to Nashville.

Sam and Judd Phillips fell out after Judd faced payola allegations. "The Judd label originated," said Judd, "at the end of 1958 because Sam and I had a real separation. Most of the artists felt they had a raw deal but there were markets like Chicago and New York where it was foolish even to sample our product in. You couldn't get any juke box or airplays. I felt that we were right to concentrate on Jerry Lee, to get him really hot in order to get the promoters interested in the others as well. At that time the payola investigations started. A lot of people wrongly felt that I had paid deejays for plays. A group of people put up a million dollars for the Judd label and gave me a free hand. I went right out there and got smash hits." Unfortunately, the hits became few and far between. Judd was a far better promotion man than a label boss and he moved on to manage Jerry Lee Lewis. Judd admits that he liked to spend and this had been the cause of another split soon after Judd first worked as Sun's promotion manager in 1952. Now, Sam has said, "I would bring Judd in and explain our financial position, show him where we didn't have the money and he'd still go back out on the road and overspend."

Sam Phillips was undoubtedly one of the greatest record producers. He could galvanize an artist into giving their finest performances but the raw driving sounds that he had so perfectly captured had been supplanted by smoother, over-produced pop rock. Phillips went into semi-retirement from the record business, partly because he was unable to "feel" the new music and Sun seemed to lack direction. The growing album market was ignored to a large extent. Bob Neal noticed an increasing reluctance to commit capital. "Sam told me that he wanted to get enough money to take care of the future. Actually, if he had preferred to go the other way he could have had a major label in these days. Sam was always conservative really. He used the main distributors and his credit was good so there would have been no financial holdups but he just didn't operate as a major. He didn't press discs in half-millions, he pressed day-by-day and consequently other labels got to covering him because they had the disc available. Imperial did this on *Raunchy*; it was so easy on an instrumental." Sam had made it though. "One day in the winter of '58–'59," recalled Bill Justis, "Sam came to see Jack and myself and he said, 'Well, boys, I'm a millionaire.'"

In the new era the majors reasserted their dominance. Sun still had the Johnny Cash back catalog but Jerry Lee Lewis' sales potential was at its lowest ebb. Sun and Phillips International were able to make a mark in the '60s with Charlie Rich and Carl Mann but were no longer market leaders.

Sun in the Evening

"Memphis is an historical center for music. The first and greatest Soul City and it was the Phillips International Corporation that laid the foundations."

—Knox Phillips

The new Phillips International label had been launched in the Fall of 1957 and had inaugurated a phase of expansion. New studios opened in Memphis and, later, Nashville. Sun and Phillips International did not become major companies in the '60s but the revenue gained from hiring the studios to the new labels enabled the Phillips Corporation to retain some hold on the recording activity of Memphis and the mid-South.

Jack Clement and Bill Justis were followed by Ernie Barton who had made a couple of passable records in the country rock style. Barton signed the excellent Mississippi rocker Mack Allen Smith to Sun but was fired before anything was issued. He was followed by Charles Underwood who began a disastrous schmaltzy trend. Underwood was followed by Scotty Moore who came back to Sun in a new capacity. "I had been working with Fernwood and some other guys at Echo studios," he recalls, "and then I met Sam Phillips and Bill Fitzgerald again. I played on a few sessions and then they were looking for some new permanent staff and soon I was production head for both the Madison Avenue and Nashville studios. That lasted from 1961 through 1965 at which time I went into independent production. I worked for a time with Billy Sherrill who is a big wheel in Nashville right now but in the early '60s he had just gotten out of playing with R&B and rock bands and was into production with Sun."

By 1961, when Scotty rejoined Phillips, the old studio on Union Avenue where he had recorded the vital new music with Presley six years earlier had been vacated and two new ones replaced it. The new Memphis studio was not far away at 639 Madison Avenue and it was opened midway through 1960. The Nashville studio was opened in February 1961 on 17th Avenue in the heart of what would become "Music Row". Phillips was one of the first independent producers to open up in Nashville but he sold his facility before the Nashville scene bloomed in the late '60s.

Phillips must have expected the success of 1956–1958 to breed further success. Phillips International was created to cope with tax complexities and the diversification of musical tastes at the close of the rock 'n' roll era. In the new climate a second label with a new image was needed and this became particularly important after 1957 when radio began Top 40 programming and record stores began stocking a wider range of records. Another important factor was explained by Bill Fitzgerald. "Phillips International had been formed because the deejays had to apportion air time and if we released six discs on Sun they could not play them for fear of some payola problem or other. If we spread them over two labels we could get more air play. Also we could split our markets and use different distributors if we had any problems as we sometimes did."

The first batch of Phillips International releases appeared on September 23, 1957 and among them was *Raunchy*, a rock 'n' roll instrumental written by saxophonist and in-house producer Bill Justis and guitarist Sidney Manker. It provided an immediate Top 10 hit for the new label, entering the charts in November 1957 and briefly reaching number one in December.

Justis had not joined Sun as a featured performer but as a session musician and musical arranger just before the formation of the new label. The basis of his "Orchestra" was Roland Janes, Billy Riley and James van Eaton, but to these veterans of the rockabilly era were added more guitarists, brass and vocal groups. The pianist was usually Jimmy Wilson or Charlie Rich. It is no exaggeration to say that this group played on most Sun and Phillips International releases between the end of 1957 and the end of 1960.

The melodies Justis employed for his own recordings were usually watered down blues, carried by the high smooth tone of his saxophone. The overall sound was part of a new trend in rock 'n' roll when instrumentals by Duane Eddy, the Champs (including Dean Beard who had previously auditioned for Sun), Johnny and the Hurricanes and others were enjoying considerable, if brief, commercial success. Justis paid for the *Raunchy* session himself, "the musicians, the studio, everything. It was my idea. . . . I had a sax player to play lead but he got sick so I played it myself. I was out of shape on the sax and got an off-tone and I think that was what helped to sell it. My job at the studio didn't alter after that hit. I had to turn down a lot of lucrative tours in order to fulfill my commitments to the studio. I did do some TV shows, though. Bandstand in Philadelphia and things like that."

Justis's start in the business had been a calculated move. "I was living in Memphis and was working at various jobs around town. I wanted to be in music but never had been professionally, not really.

"One night I was reading a newspaper article about a guy in New York named Buck Ram who had to do with the success of the vocal group scene. I read about how much money he had made out of rock 'n' roll so I said 'that's for me.' I immediately set out for a record store and bought $80 worth of all time rock 'n' roll hits. The ones that set the styles. I studied the stuff and found it was so simple yet basic and savage and that it was difficult to perform.

"This was 1956. Soon after that I was hired by Barbara Pittman to arrange a session at Sun. Sam Phillips complimented me on the work I had done for her and asked me to come to see him sometime. I had arranged a session with Wink Martindale at WHBQ for the OJ label so I took the Martindale tape to Sam and he asked me to work with him."

Justis's career as an artist which had begun so remarkably with *Raunchy* spanned six singles and an album. The follow-up sounded predictably similar and on subsequent flops Justis tried a fuller orchestration, approximating Billy Vaughn on some cuts. His last record for Phillips International was *Flea Circus*, a song that had been pitched at him by a young guitarist, Steve Cropper, who went on to make some of the classic Memphis recordings with Otis Redding and the Stax-Volters.

Justis left Phillips in March 1959. "I was fired for insubordination. Sam Phillips and some of his cronies came into the studio one night when I was trying to record Charlie Rich. We recorded often at night, incidentally, because as Sun's fame grew you couldn't get anything done during the day for cats sitting on the doorstep trying to audition. Even when I left early in the morning there'd be some guy sitting on the front steps with his guitar. Anyway, on this occasion Sam came in and they were making merry. . . . I stood for it for as long as I could then I told them to get out. . . . Sam fired me and he fired Jack Clement at the same time for laughing at what I'd said. It was actually a good break for Jack and me because we both started making money after that, which is kinda important if you live in this country."

Raunchy had been one of the first instrumental hits but Sun soon started following crazes. The '60s proved to be a struggle against the slide into obscurity and the releases were of an uneven standard. A lot of good music was recorded, though, particularly by Charlie Rich and Carl Mann, two artists of considerable talent with new and quite individual styles.

In September 1958 Charlie Rich made his debut on Phillips International as a featured artist with the first of ten singles which were to make him the label's biggest selling artist. Rich had also joined Sun as a session musician and can be heard on many sides, including some by Jerry Lee Lewis and Johnny Cash. He also played for Judd Phillips' Judd label and it was over two years before his talent was given free rein.

Rich was born in Colt, a small town in northern Arkansas. He left there to join the Air Force, forming a group known as the Velvetones in which he doubled on piano and tenor saxophone while his future wife, Margaret Ann, shared the vocals. He was a Stan Kenton fan and modeled the group's style on Kenton's music. After he finished his stint in the Air Force he returned to farming with his new wife. "It wasn't really what I wanted to do but I felt I needed to build up a little security. Of course, I always figured maybe I could play a little on the side just for my own pleasure.

"So we tried the farming thing for a year or two. The first year was fine, the second year was so-so. We started out the third year and it rained and rained. We couldn't get the crops in."

Rich had been set up in farming by his uncle who owned a large plantation near West Memphis. He offered to bail Rich out but Rich was unwilling; he was not a farmer.

"I didn't know what I was going to do but I had made some inroads into the music scene in Memphis by playing with some of the groups and jobbing here and there as a piano player. I had a little Webcor tape recorder and a rented piano at the house and I made some tapes, some terrible little tapes of some stuff I had written along with my wife. We got enough money some way to get in the union and I started working kinda regular in Memphis, like piano bar type stuff, after-hours joints." Fred Cook, now station manager at WREC, remembers visiting clubs and seeing Rich whom he describes as the "best white jazz piano player I ever saw."

Charlie was discovered at the Sharecropper Club in West Memphis by Bill Justis who recalls, "He was just too jazzy for Sun, all thirteenths. I gave him a bunch of Jerry Lee Lewis records and told him to come back when he could get that bad. His voice was fine but his songs and arrangements were too complicated." He was brought in as a session pianist but he tried to adapt to the rock 'n' roll style. He recorded some demos such as *Rock 'n' Roll Party* and *Breakup* which was recorded by Ray Smith on Judd and Jerry Lee Lewis on Sun.

The first session which featured Charlie as a solo attraction was produced by Bill Justis on August 17, 1958. The band, as usual, comprised Roland Janes, Billy Riley and Jimmy van Eaton. They made *Whirlwind* and *Philadelphia Baby* which were issued on the Phillips International label later that year. The style was rock 'n' roll, modeled on Jerry Lee Lewis.

There was another session resulting in an instrumental single that was issued under the pseudonym Bobby Sheridan on Sun and then, on October 14, 1959, Charlie and the usual band recorded *Lonely Weekends*. It started a career that was to make him the most important artist after 1958. He had developed a peculiar off beat, that he still uses today on up tempo recordings. It has its origins in songs like the Coasters' *Searchin'* and was paralleled in the music of Dallas Frazier and in the hit recordings of the Hollywood Argyles. Charlie has always expressed his feelings in his own way. His deep Presley-ish voice and jazz-tinged piano stood out from the rest of the instrumentation. He also excelled on slow ballads such as *There Won't Be Anymore*, which he has recorded for three companies.

As a songwriter Rich had developed an ability to produce atmospheric, wine-soaked ballads which only occasionally display the self-pitying remorse found in so much country music. He suffers a lot through his songs but rarely does he moralize. Experiment was always a vital part of his music and this is amply illustrated in the fifty unissued Sun recordings which range from rock 'n' roll trivia like *Popcorn Polly* through such varied and distinctive songs as *Juicehead Blues*, *No Headstone on My Grave* and *Mountain Dew*. It shows Charlie's unique blend of country, rock, jazz and blues that have suffused all of his finest recordings.

Despite his prodigious talents Rich was unable to sustain his national success and in 1961 he followed Bill Justis to RCA, recording for their Groove subsidiary, and subsequently Smash, Hi, Epic and United Artists. Phillips had enough songs in the can to issue singles up to 1965 when Charlie had another

Buddy Blake Cunningham, 1969

Charlie Rich, 1959

Ace Cannon

Bill Justis

The Phillips Int. Studio, 639 Madison Ave., Memphis

Carl Mann

big hit with *Mohair Sam* on Smash. Again, he was unable to sustain the success and he moved on to Hi. His most successful affiliation was with Epic which came about through Billy Sherrill who had worked with Charlie at Sun. Charlie moved to Nashville and after a few unsuccessful years he belatedly achieved superstardom in the country pop market with *The Most Beautiful Girl in the World*. Rich deserves his success but it is unfortunate that such a talented writer, pianist and singer had to deny the people his real talents in order to sell them records. He appeared on television in England in 1976, surrounded by a thirty piece orchestra and chorus. He looked bored and sounded bored and spent most of the broadcast away from the piano. He only caught fire during two songs, *Big Boss Man* and *Breakup*, which harked back to his earlier days as the master of white R&B.

The only other successful artist during Sun's declining years was Carl Mann who has enjoyed a long and checkered career in the music industry. Carl, with his group, the Kool Kats, came from near Jackson, Tennessee, and in 1958, after leaving school they recorded for the small Memphis label, Jaxon which was owned by Jim Stewart. Their first record, *Gonna Rock and Roll All Night*, was published by Phillips' Knox Music and in 1959 the record was brought to Phillips' attention and Mann was offered a contract with Phillips International. His band was also put under contract and guitarist Eddie Bush later had one single issued on Phillips International, as he had on Jaxon. The bass player was Robert Oatswell and the drummer was W. S. Holland who had left the Carl Perkins Band to stay in Memphis and Jackson where he undertook session work for some time before joining Johnny Cash.

Carl Mann was only seventeen when he became a part of the Memphis recording scene but he had already evolved the basis of a very effective late rock 'n' roll style with Eddie Bush that worked extremely well on old standards such as *Mona Lisa*, *Pretend* or *South of the Border*. Bill Justis recalled how Carl came to Sun. "One day, Carl Perkins' drummer, W. S. Holland, came in and said he had a group from Jackson, Tennessee, led by Eddie Bush. Jack Clement set up a session for them. Carl Mann was the pianist. He sang a demo of *Mona Lisa* and while he was playing Conway Twitty came in and said that he liked the tune. Soon afterward, his M-G-M record of it came out, styled after Carl's demo. Our promo man, Cecil Scaife, insisted that we put it out on Carl and it became a hit."

Mann was not able to recapture the impact of his first million selling single but he did become Phillips International's best selling artist after Charlie Rich and his recordings continued to be released after he left the company in 1962 following a dispute over the ownership of his songs. He later recorded briefly for Monument Records before getting out the music industry, working in garages and timber mills in Memphis and Jackson. He resurfaced in 1973 with ABC-Dot in Nashville and enjoyed some minor success. Just recently, he has found himself in demand in Europe where he has given some of the best rock 'n' roll performances in the various revival shows.

Carl enjoyed seven single releases on Phillips International together with an album. He usually retained his own style of rolling piano and carefully controlled vocals, complemented by Eddie Bush's dampened guitar. When Elvis recorded *I'm Coming Home,* he followed Carl's vocal style very closely while Floyd Cramer imitated the piano.

Usually, Mann's sessions were produced in Memphis although two took place in Nashville, produced by Scotty Moore. Among the session musicians were Charlie Rich and Al Jackson, who later played on many of the Hi recordings in late '60s and early '70s.

Phillips had little national success in the '60s, apart from Rich and Mann. His previous policy of building up local acts was not successful and, as a result, his producers resorted to plagiarizing other hit formulas. This was the era of insipid soft rock when it seemed that all male singers were called "Bobby" but there were also some pioneering experiments in what would later become country rock and white R&B. Some of the lesser known issues on Sun were good, contributing in a positive way to the maelstrom of ideas then in evidence.

Most of the issues, however, were far from good and very few were strikingly original. Many of the session musicians later went on to become important but they played poor pop music for Sam Phillips.

Among the artists who recorded for Sun was Brad Suggs, a local singer who had worked for years with Slim Rhodes' country band. He had previously recorded as a rockabilly artist for Meteor and had played on countless sessions. He reemerged in 1959 as a band leader in the Bill Justis mold and as a producer. The Brad Suggs Orchestra included Ace Cannon on saxophone, Larry Mohoberac on piano and D. J. Fontana on drums. Together, they provided some competent if unexciting musicianship.

Buddy Cunningham, whom Jimmy van Eaton characterized as having "no talent to speak of," had been the first local artist to appear on Phillips International. One of the few outsiders from the period was Tracy Pendarvis from Florida who recorded three singles of some potential. If freed of unnecessary embellishments they would have harked back to the rockabilly era. More typical, however, were five releases by Tony Rossini and three by Harold Dorman issued between 1960 and 1963.

Tony Rossini fitted right in with Paul Anka, Pat Boone and the crud at the top of the charts in those days. An impressive array of accompanists could not produce the innocuous sound required. Rossini was only fourteen and probably did not know that his producer, Scotty Moore, had revolutionized rock guitar six years previously. Scotty found "it was really quite hard going for me to manufacture pop sounds even though I had done okay at Fernwood. I was used to the more straightforward capturing of a sound, like with Elvis or Frank Frost. We cut a really good blues album on him in '62 that was really so different from Tony Rossini." So it was that Rossini's micro-talent was teamed with Scotty Moore, Larry Mohoberac and Al Jackson. They labored to produce some songs to get the wee ones hot and runny, including *Meet Me (After School)* and *Vacation Time.* Another session, which produced *New Girl in Town,* had an even more impressive line-up of sidemen including Booker T., Steve Cropper, Roland Janes and Scotty Moore.

The pop ballads of Harold Dorman were blacker in approach and marginally more successful than Rossini's sessions. Dorman had just enjoyed an amazing hit on Rita, *Mountain of Love*, one of the best pop songs from 1960. His follow-ups on Sun were less successful and he left the label after three sessions in 1961 and 1962.

The Phillips studio also tried cover versions of other trends and crazes. In 1958 Bill Pinkney, former singer with the Drifters, combined with Bill Justis and Roland Janes to produce *After the Hop*, an answer disc to Danny and the Juniors' *At the Hop*. In 1959 an intriguing cover version appeared of Ernie Fields' current hit, *In the Mood*. The artist was "The Hawk."

"At that time," recalled Bill Fitzgerald, "Jerry Lee Lewis was having some problems so we decided to try him on Phillips International with some instrumentals. I called him The Hawk in order to get some interest going on him again. We also recorded *Dixie* and I guess we should have issued it because we sure needed to restore public approval of him in some way."

This was also a time of reissues. Not only were compilations appearing of Sun's greatest hits but when Roy Orbison had a national hit in July 1960 with *Only the Lonely* on Monument, Sun reissued *Sweet and Easy to Love* as a single followed by an album. Orbison listened with horror, remembering that "the songs were overdubbed with saxophones, trombones and terrible things, trying to update them—but it didn't work."

Four years later an even more interesting reissue appeared in the form of Smokey Joe's 1955 recording of the *Signifying Monkey*. It had been given a primitive reggae feel by the addition of extra drumming and it was issued in the month when the bluebeat sensation, *My Boy Lollipop*, by Millie reached the number two slot in the national charts.

It was not a great period for popular music and Sun did nothing to lead the way as they had done in the mid '50s. Memphis led the way out of the doldrums with some fine mid '60s soul but Sun was not there and it was left to some new faces to set the pace, although many of them had paid the rent playing in Phillips' studios over the years.

The Memphis Sound

By 1964 the sound of Sun and Phillips International was increasingly tied to the Memphis sound as a whole. The Nashville experiment had been dropped, the studio had not produced any hits for Phillips since *What'd I Say* back in 1961. The new Nashville sound had been developed in the late '50s and early '60s by top A&R men like Chet Atkins of RCA, Owen Bradley of Decca and Don Law of Columbia. Country music had gone pop, it was dubbed "uptown country" or "countrypolitan." Some of the best session musicians also appeared for Sun, men like Floyd Cramer, Hank Garland, Bob Moore, Lightnin' Chance and Buddy Harman but they were unable to help Sam Phillips find hits for his artists.

Trade paper advertisements still proclaimed "The Latest Hit from Sun" but by the mid '60s new releases were only distributed locally. Bill Fitzgerald said, "Our national sales dived during the '60s but they remained steady in Memphis and the mid-South area. That was until 1968, early that year, when both labels ceased activity. The last few years had seen Knox Phillips and his friends trying out new styles but it was in 1968 that Sun actually folded. Sam and I and Buddy Cunningham went to work on a new project at Holiday Inn at that time but that folded too. We could no longer find any artists who were as good as the ones we had previously."

Fitzgerald finally moved to Nashville to run the R&B label Seventy-7 and Knox Phillips, Sam's eldest son, continued to run the Madison Avenue studio profitably. Shelby Singleton had recorded *Hey Paula* at Phillips studio and it was still in great demand by local companies and others wanting to get the Memphis sound. Sun product was still leased to foreign licensees, which provided a steady income but the competition provided by Hi, Stax and Sounds of Memphis had forced Phillips out of the manufacturing business. The rivals had grown up with soul, funky pop and country music and, to a large extent, they cornered the market.

At the start of the '60s, the R&B scene was dominated by Ray Charles, Sam Cooke, Jackie Wilson and others who could reach a white audience through their capacity to work with smooth arrangements. In 1961, however, an instrumental combo, the Mar-Keys, had a national hit with *Last Night*, on Satellite Records, and a new sound came into being. Satellite was a Memphis label owned by Jim Stewart and his sister, Estelle Axton. Satellite became Stax, the name being a play on Stewart and Axton and the Mar-Keys, whose follow-up, *Diana*, was also a hit were only the first in a line of tougher, funkier R&B musicians who played the new soul music. The Mar-Keys, a racially mixed group, included Albert Jackson and Don Nix among others who were to become important in southern music over the next decade.

Stax changed the R&B and soul scene and dominated it throughout much of the '60s in direct competition with the Tamla complex and other northern labels whose sound derived partially from the "Memphis Soul Stew." An interesting comparison between Memphis and Detroit soul sounds may actually be heard on Sun. In November 1966 vocalist James Thomas and his group The Climates assembled at Madison Avenue to cut *No You for Me*, which had a riffing brass section and the close ties with '50s R&B normally found in southern soul. The other side, *Breaking Up Again*, was a direct copy of the Tamla group sound with its bouncing beat and breathless vocals.

The sound of the Climates was somewhat similar to that produced by the Goldwax label in Memphis between 1964 and 1968. This is hardly surprising since Goldwax used the Sun studio and the same session men. These included Tommy Cogsbill, Bobby Wood, Reggie Young, Mike Leech, Bobby Emmons and Gene Chrisman in the rhythm section and Charles Chalmers, Floyd Newman and Andrew Love on brass. Most of these musicians recorded for Sun and Cogsbill later went on to become a producer at Stax.

Rufus Thomas also returned to the recording scene on Stax with some novelty dance numbers but the Stax sound was more properly identified with Booker T. Jones and his group, the MG's. They had their own hits and played on many sessions. The Volt label was formed in 1962 and later the Hip subsidiary was added to the fold and Billy Riley returned to cut some white funk for them.

As the '60s moved into the '70s Stax faced increasing competition from Hi, a label that started with rock 'n' roll and struggled through the early '60s with the help of hits from the Bill Black Combo, Gene Simmons and Ace Cannon. All three were former Sun artists and much of the production work at Hi was done by Quinton Claunch, Bill Cantrell and Ray Harris who had all worked for Sun. In 1964 Claunch quit to form Goldwax with local drug store owner Rudolph "Doc" Russell and at that time black jazz/blues musician Willie Mitchell came into the scene as a session man, having worked with Home of the Blues label. During the late '60s he took over from Ray Harris who moved back to Tupelo, Mississippi. This was the time when Mitchell started concentrating on soul music which was rewarded with the fantastic success of Al Green.

Hi illustrates the changing musical face of Memphis. The label started with rockabilly and country from Carl McVoy, Jay B. Loyd and Tommy Tucker before moving on to the Bill Black Combo, mainstay of the label for some years. Their incredible success started in 1960 with *White Silver Sands* and the group included a vast number of top Memphis sidemen including Gene Simmons whose cover version of Johnny Fuller's horror rock song *Haunted House* reached number eleven on the *Billboard* charts in August 1964.

Both Stax and Hi far outsold Sun during the mid and late '60s but they have in turn run into hard times just recently. After Stax finished their association with

Bill Black & Bill Cantrell

Booker T and the M.G.s

Left to right: Rudolph "Doc" Russell, Stan Kesler
and Quinton Claunch

Gene Simmons

Atlantic they sold out to Gulf+Western. After buying themselves out of that disastrous deal with the help of a loan from Polydor they went through some more changes of ownership before ending up in the hands of Fantasy, the small Berkeley jazz label. By this time all of their major artists had gone and the converted cinema on McLemore Avenue that served as a studio and store had been auctioned off together with other assets. Hi also changed distribution from London, with whom they had been affiliated for almost twenty years, to Cream, a new label formed by Al Bennett who had founded and sold Liberty Records. The cool Memphis soul of Al Green and Ann Peebles now sounds out of place in the disco-oriented black market of today and the label is currently short of hits.

Memphis in the '60s was a city of musical experiment. This was also true in the country music scene. Eddie Bond proclaimed the "All New Memphis Sound" on his own labels like Tab and Stompertime but one of the first on the market with small time country labels was M. E. Ellis with Erwin and Zone. A little later Glo-Lite, owned by Bill Glore, came into the picture. Glore had bought out Ellis and along with men like Lewis Willis continues to champion the Memphis country scene. Labels like E-Volve, Blake, Cotton Town Jubilee, Western Lounge and a score of others flitted across the local country market.

Sometimes they built their own small studio but mostly used Phillips. Even Fernwood, despite one major and several minor hits, did not have impressive facilities.

The Rita label had a massive hit with Harold Dorman's *Mountain of Love* but owners Ira Vaughn, Billy Riley (who sold his share just before Dorman hit) and Roland Janes did not have a good studio nor the capital to improve it. Vaughn ran other short lived labels like Nita and Roland Janes had some luck with his Renay label, leasing the million selling *I'm Moving On* by Matt Lucas to Smash. He has lately set up the Sonic studio for custom work. Riley too has been involved in a multitude of minor recording activities, working with Mojo, Home of the Blues, Myrl and other labels. "I just keep on trying. The scene in the '60s was wide open to anyone who could hit with a new sound. I spent some time out West, wrote a lot of songs, lost or sold a lot of songs, made a lot of recordings but I kept returning to Memphis and all the time the business was altering. There was great turmoil in the city, everybody coming and getting involved, hoping to hit with something. Stax and Hi actually made it and I keep thinking maybe I will too. I made the national charts in '72 on Entrance and I figure that eventually it will happen for me." After a spell with the Nashville Sun label, reactivated by Shelby Singleton in 1969 when, as always, he made some marvellous recordings, Riley is now living in Jonesboro, Arkansas, living proof of the fact that talent is not always rewarded commercially. His latest recordings were made in the Phillips studio on Madison with the old gang including Jimmy Van Eaton. Recordings like *Good Old Rock 'n' Roll/Blue Monday* on Southern Rooster are a powerful indication of just how rockabilly can be developed instead of imitated.

Stan Kesler is another with a great involvement in the recording activity of the city. He began as a sideman with Clyde Leoppard and then did session work and toured with Presley in 1954 while emerging as a songwriter. Then, in 1958, as Clyde Leoppard recalls, "I planned to put in a studio with Stan Kesler so we rented a room on North Main to do custom work. Scotty Moore was then working just nearby with Fernwood and he loaned us $1500 to buy some Ampex equipment off the guy who owned Moon Records. That was our beginning in recording. Jack Clement then came in with us for a short while with his Summer label and we moved out to a new studio at Madison and Manassas. This was the Echo studio and a lot of masters were cut there for a lot of labels, although the Phillips studios were close by and they were doing a lot of business also. As a matter of fact, the reason Stan put in the Echo studio was that he had hit material on his labels but was having to record at Sun."

Kesler was then in partnership with businessmen Drew Canale, Paul Bomarito and Gene Lucchesi which produced Crystal Records in 1957 and the Pen, Dingo and XL labels in 1959. Kesler's best prospect was a young Mexican, Domingo Samudio, who recorded as Sam the Sham and the Pharoahs and after a few misses a tune called *Wooly Bully* started to sell and proved too hot to handle. It was sold to M-G-M and became the fourth biggest selling record of 1965. Kesler went on to lease masters to Phillips International and other labels.

There were still many young musicians coming to Memphis in search of success with the Memphis Sound, now a mixture of the rockabilly legacy and soul music. One of the door-knockers was Mac Davis who had written Sam the Sham's first record and did session work for Phillips and on the Judd recording by Tommy Roe. He later went on to write *In the Ghetto*, picked up by Elvis, and have his own hits and television series.

Many other top country music writers began their careers playing in the clubs in Memphis, later migrating to Nashville. Charlie Rich was one. He was followed by John Hartford who wrote *Gentle on My Mind* and went on to make some idiosyncratic bluegrass records for Warner Brothers and Flying Fish. Country writers Bill Rice and Jerry Foster got started at Fernwood and Memphian Rita Coolidge also performed regularly in the city. Similarly "Rockabilly" Swan developed his love for rock 'n' roll in Memphis and came out with international progressive rockabilly hits in the '70s. Even Jesse Winchester grew up playing R&B and gospel in Memphis before moving to Canada. He played with the Amazing Rhythm Aces who recorded their hit, *Third Rate Romance*, at Phillips studio.

By 1968 Sam Phillips had become involved in the vast Holiday Inn hotel and motel chain and agreed to launch the Memphis based corporation into the record business. The new label pursued a policy similar to Sun, using local or hitherto unknown talent and Holiday Inn releases featured sides by Charlie Feathers and Charlie Freeman, concentrating on country sounds.

The last years of Sun and Phillips International saw very few country releases with the exception of Dane Stinit. There had been a single-minded preoccupation with pop-soul and R&B. This trend had begun around 1962 with the recording of Frank Ballard from Jackson, Tennessee, bluesman Frank Frost and soul-pop artist Jeb Stuart.

There were only five releases on Phillips International between 1964 and 1966 when it folded. Sun lasted two years longer but only had twenty singles to show for its last four years. Seven of these were accounted for by the still active club band of Billy Adams and Bill Yates. They had been together for many years and Adams had appeared on a dozen or more labels in a variety of musical styles. The Sun recordings were usually recreations of R&B standards. This was hardly original but the standard of the performances was excellent. On *Betty and Dupree* and *Trouble in Mind* there is a toughness not usually found even in southern pop records and the style is akin to that of swamp pop group Cookie and the Cupcakes. Bill Yates, who also recorded as Gorgeous Bill, was pianist with the Adams group. The group also had several up and coming young musicians including Wayne Perkins and Donald "Duck" Dunn.

Knox Phillips was increasingly involved in the later issues as was another of Sam's sons, Jerry Phillips. The latter organized a white R&B band called the Jesters in 1966 and they recorded several sessions from which *Cadillac Man* was issued. This turned out to be a one-off issue, as was *I'm Gonna Move in the Room with the Lord* by Brother James Anderson, whose record issued as Sun 406 was supposed to inaugurate a "Gospel Series." Although fourteen titles were recorded only one was issued, and this in 1967, four years after the recordings had been made.

Sun only issued one more single, a contemporary soul disc by the Load of Mischief, although several others were scheduled to appear and some deejay pressings may have been made. The Phillips International Studio remained in operation, however, and Knox became a director of Mempro and Memphis Music Incorporated, organizations which exist to promote recording activity in the city. In the '70s there have been the "Memphis Music in May" Awards. Among those fêted have been Judd Phillips, B. B. King, Jerry Lee Lewis, Ray Harris and Willie Mitchell. Sam Phillips was the first to receive an honor and he received another one in 1979.

In the '70s, the third Phillips brother, Tom, has been most actively involved in producing records. He runs the Select-O-Hit record store and one stop from Chelsea Avenue, next to the old E-Volve, Erwin and Glo-Lite studios where his sons Skip and Jerry now do custom recording work. Tom bought all the old Sun returns and overstock for 3¢ a disc which ensured that his warehouse was a popular place. Elvis records have not been found there for ten years or more but it was still possible to pick some of the great classics of Sun Records until comparatively recently. Tom has also started many small labels catering to the local country, R&B, soul and gospel markets in conjunction with Judd Wood and Quinton Claunch at Goldwax. Phillips operated Black Gold, S-O-H and Philwood.

Judd Phillips gave up recording altogether. He sold out his interest in the Judd label to N.R.C. in Atlanta and concentrated on managing Jerry Lee Lewis, guiding his protégé to great heights in the country music field. He later became Southern regional manager for Phongram/Mercury. Sam Phillips had joined Ray Harris in opening a new studio in Tupelo, Mississippi, in 1972 but he had retired from record production after the Holiday Inn label folded in 1968. Jack Clement had this to say to him, "Sam's early success with Carl, Cash, Elvis was entirely Sam's. I was into making things musical, Sam was not. He understood

Frank Frost

Bill Yates and band

Jeb Stuart

Billy Adams, Bill Yates with Tommy Ruble, MC of the Admiral Benbow in Mempnis

Tom Phillips

Sam, Knox and Jerry Phillips

one thing that I didn't back then, he understood feel in music."

Sam Phillips made a lot of money in the record business and even more from his other interests but most devotees of Memphis music would agree that he deserved it all. Doug Poindexter, whose band was used to create the early Elvis sound, sums it up, "He's got a lot of credit coming to him. Sam has built music up in Memphis from nothing. As far as I'm concerned, he's the creator." Phillips' own line on this has never varied. "Until rock 'n' roll came long, the worst discrimination in America was in music. You had pop music for a certain type of people; you had country music which was supposedly for another class and you had what was called 'race' music, black music. I just hope I played some part in breaking that segregation down in some way."

A New Dawning

"I remember old Elvis when he Forgot to Remember to Forget,
And when young Johnny Cash hadn't seen this side of Big River yet,
And when Sun was more than the daylight shinin' on Memphis,
Tennessee
N' old Luther and Lewis and Perkins was pickin' and playin' them
songs for me.

—Chip Taylor
The Real Thing
© Blackwood Music Inc. & Back Road Music Inc.

For more than a year Sun Records remained dormant. Interest in the label was largely confined to specialist record collectors, particularly in Europe. Credence Clearwater Revival, however, demonstrated that the unvarnished Sun sound could be translated into marketable pop product and for a short time John Fogerty's group became the most successful band since the Beatles. In the U.S.A. there was also a country music revival and renewed interest in Elvis Presley.

Elvis was persuaded to do a television special for NBC in which he performed all his old hits and reminisced about the old days. Clad somewhat ridiculously in black leather, he was accompanied for part of the show by Scotty Moore and D. J. Fontana. Best of all, he still sounded great. Sam Phillips, of course, no longer possessed any Elvis tapes except the Million Dollar Quartet and a few odds and ends but Presley's reemergence was accompanied by a recognition of his importance in the gestation of rock 'n' roll and this inevitably reflected upon the role of Sam Phillips. The new rock fanzines and magazines carried long retrospectives on both Phillips and Presley.

We have seen that country music was reasserting its importance and fringe artists were regularly in the pop charts. Spearheading the revival was Johnny Cash and trailing a little way behind were former Sun artists Jerry Lee Lewis, Conway Twitty, Dickie Lee, Charlie Rich, David Houston, Edwin Bruce and Carl Perkins. It was clear, therefore, that Sun's extensive back catalog could be successfully repackaged as top selling album product. In fact, Judd Phillips and Jerry Lee Lewis had hoped to obtain all their old masters with the intention of marketing them via their own label but this move was forestalled by the entrance of Shelby Singleton, Jr.

Shelby had been introduced to country by his first wife, Margie Singleton, who was a regular performer in the early '50s on the Louisiana Hayride. He hung around the Hayride until 1957 when he began work for Mercury, introducing fine Southern performers into the roster. Among these were J. P. Richardson (the Big Bopper), Johnny Preston and Bruce Channel whose *Hey Baby* became one of the biggest hits of 1961. Singleton became one of the most gifted and successful producers at Mercury and was responsible for the sustained success of Brook Benton. He had no formal musical training but he had an undeniable talent for bringing out commercial arrangements and also acted as an energy catalyst, encouraging both session musicians and featured artists after many wasted takes. Setting up his own independent production company on Belmont Boulevard in Nashville he quickly realized the potential of the Sun catalog and clinched a deal with Sam Phillips on July 1, 1969, in which Phillips became a minority shareholder in the newly formed Sun International Corporation.

The deal was signed at a very propitious moment for on June 9 Johnny Cash broadcast the first program in his highly successful television series. The show had been scheduled as a vacation replacement for Hollywood Palace but it gained such high ratings that Cash was invited back for another season.

Sleepy La Beef

Million Dollar Quartet album sleeve, awaiting release

Shelby S. Singleton

Singleton, of course, had been in at the start of the country-pop boom with Jeannie C. Riley and he began repackaging the old Sun product for the rock market.

All the old Sun singles by Johnny Cash, Jerry Lee Lewis, Roy Orbison, Carl Perkins and Jack Clement were reissued on the new Sun International label and new recordings were issued both on Sun and Midnight Sun, designed to cater to the black market. Shelby soon bowed out of soul after a few hits, "We got the sales but the artists were too much trouble." From that point he concentrated on country music. Shelby has actively carried on the Sun spirit, continuing to record modern interpretations of that old Sun sound with Billy Lee Riley, Sleepy LaBeef, Jimmy Ellis, Bobby Lee Trammell and others.

Singleton leased the repackaged Sun albums to companies around the world. These albums were fine for rack sales and mail orders in the country market but we were aware that in Europe there was a market for a more substantial reissue program, giving collectors a chance to hear unissued recordings as well as the accepted rarities. We convinced Phonogram in London to issue *"Sun Rockabillys"* which collected together many of Sun's most obscure and best rockabilly titles. Its sales far exceeded expectations and other issues followed. Since 1975 the reissues have been carried on by Charly Records, the current licensee. It is now possible for us to hear not only the hits but most of the marvelous, and some of the not so marvelous, blues, country and rockabilly records produced at Sun.

Rock music is essentially a transitory medium; today's smasheroonie is tomorrow's golden oldie. The music of the '50s often sounds stilted but the music that Sam Phillips recorded by Elvis Presley, Jerry Lee Lewis, Carl Perkins and Johnny Cash is in no way overshadowed by their later output; rather, the reverse is true. The twenty or so titles recorded by Presley in the little studio at 706 Union represent a promise that was never fulfilled while those of Lewis, Cash, Rich, Perkins and a host of minor artists remain their very best work. As Jack Clement said, "Back then, you know, we had the feeling that we were really creating something; that, in a sense, we were making history."

What They Did and Where They Are Now

The following entries are not intended as complete biographies; rather, they provide supplementary biographical information on artists and personalities mentioned in the text.

JOHNNY ACE—Born John Marshall Alexander, June 9, 1929, Memphis. Educated LaRose Grammar School and Booker T. Washington University. Served in Navy during World War II. Member of Beale Streeters, blues artists who began by backing B. B. King. Signed with Duke in 1952 and achieved huge success before and after his death in Houston on December 25, 1954.

WOODROW ADAMS—Born Tchula, Mississippi, 1917. A tractor driver and sometime guitarist for Howlin' Wolf, Willie Nix and Robert Nighthawk. He modeled his vocal, harmonica and guitar style on Wolf. Adams ran a band called the Boogie Blues Blasters. Recorded for Chess, Sun, Meteor and Home Of The Blues.

ALTON & JIMMY—Alton Lott and Jimmy Harrell, both guitarists. Recorded a session for Sun in a late rock style on June 5, 1959. Backing by Billy Riley and Jimmy van Eaton. Alton Lott has since recorded as a solo artist.

RAY B. ANTHONY—Born Rayburn Anthony in Jackson, Tennessee. Colleague of Carl Mann and recorded for Sun with backings provided by Mann's band in October 1957. Singer and composer, runs Arlue Recording. In 1978 came through with a hit on Mercury, *Shadow of Love*.

FRANK BALLARD & THE PHILLIP REYNOLDS ORCHESTRA—From Jackson, Tennessee. Recorded in a R&B vein for Phillips Int. on March 18, 1962. Band members included Frank Reed, Clarence Render, James Matthews, Chester Maxwell, Kurl McKinney and Ike Price.

BARBARA BARNES—Now Barbara Sims, living in Louisiana and teaching English at Louisiana State University. Left Sun in the Fall of 1960 having worked for three years on administration of Sam's affairs and artist promotion.

SMOKEY JOE BAUGH—Born Joseph E. Baugh, July 25, 1932, Helena, Arkansas. Began playing piano professionally in 1947 around Memphis and West Memphis. Member of Clyde Leoppard band with Buddy Holobaugh who recalls 'Smokey traveled with Sun tours and later with Bill Black's Combo. Ace Cannon took over the combo when Bill died and Smokey stayed with him and was also featured on his recordings. Since 1970 we have had our own band playing out of Waco, Texas, known as the Midnight Cowboys.' Shortly after his Sun record, Smokey recorded for Clyde Leoppard's Fonofox label in a novelty rock style on songs like *Perfect Girl*. Joe also played session piano, notably for Jimmy Pritchett on Crystal Records.

DEAN BEARD—Born Texas. Recorded two rockabilly sessions in Dallas in 1957 that were leased to Atlantic. Previously recorded one unissued session for Sun, including *Rakin' & Scrapin'* and *Rock Around the Town*. Later the piano player for The Champs, who recorded for Challenge.

BLACKWOOD BROTHERS—Country/gospel group formed in Kosciusko, Mississippi, 1934 by Ray, Doyle, James and R.W. Blackwood. Their recordings influenced Elvis Presley who nearly became a member of their associated group, The Songfellows, in 1954. James and R.W. with Bill Lyles and Jack Marshall recorded four unrelased titles for Sun in 1962.

TOMMY BLAKE—Born in Shreveport, Louisiana. Blake played country radio (KTBS and KRUS) in the late '40s and early '50s after a stint in the Marines. He later joined the Big 'D' Jamoree in Dallas. Between 1956 and 1966 he recorded for Buddy (Marshall, Texas), RCA, Sun, Recco and Chancellor.

BOBBY 'BLUE' BLAND—Born January 27, 1930, Rosemark, Tennessee. Moved to Memphis 1948. Played with Billy 'Red' Love and other influential Delta musicians. First recording was *Dry Up Baby* (Modern 848). Entered Armed Services 1952, joined Johnny Ace Revue after discharge, having signed with Duke Records. First smash hit, *It's My Life Baby*, 1955 followed by years of consistent success in R&B market.

EDDIE BOND—Born July 1, 1933, Memphis. Worked with Campbell & Son as a salesman until 1956 when he signed with Mercury Records. Previously worked clubs and package tours out of Memphis with his band, The Stompers. Since 1958 has been heavily involved with Memphis country music scene with his own labels and radio and TV shoes on WHBQ and KWEM. Composed the original unused score for 1973 movie *Walking Tall* about legendary lawman Buford Pusser. Stood for sheriff, 1974.

CHARLEY BOOKER—Born Moorehead, Mississippi, 1925. Recorded for Blues & Rhythm and RPM. A contemporary of Boyd Gilmore and Willie Love. Recorded one unissued sesssion for Sun, later issued on Charly (England).

ED(WIN) BRUCE—Born Memphis, 1941. Recorded for Sun as a teenager. Later got through college, worked in the family business and then turned to country music in Nashville with RCA, Transonic, Monument, Epic and UA.

JIM BULLEIT—Born Indiana, 1909. Worked as a radio announcer in Los Angeles for CBS before moving to WSM (Nashville), 1943. Started Bullet Records in 1946, one of the South's earliest successful record labels. After exchanging recordings with Sam Phillips in 1950 and 1951 Bulleit bought into Sun in 1952. He later sold his share and eventually got out of the record business in 1954. Bullet was the first label to record B. B. King and Ray Price. The masters now belong to Dot (MCA/ABC Records). Bulleit still lives in Nashville and has been successful in the confectionery (candy) business.

ALBERT 'SONNY' BURGESS—born Newport, Arkansas, 1931. In Army 1951-1953, returned to farming near Newport after discharge. Started performing in country music in 1955, turning professional in 1956 with his band, the Pacers, which comprised Jack Nance (guitarist, trumpeter and lately roadie with the Jackson Five), Ray Kern Kennedy (piano), Johnny Ray Hubbard (bass) and Russell Smith (drums, later drumming for Jerry Lee Lewis). In 1959 Burgess toured with Conway Twitty, leaving the group with drummer Bobby Crafford who recorded an unissued session with Sun. In 1964 Burgess recorded the first of many releases for Razorback (Little Rock, Arkansas), having previously recorded for Arbur and TSBS as well as Ara and Rolando (owned by Sun session guitarist Roland Janes). Burgess also worked as a salesman for a St. Louis company and currently runs a shoe store in Little Rock.

CHESTER BURNETT (HOWLIN' WOLF)—Born West Point, Mississippi, June 10, 1910 and raised in the Delta. Taught how to play guitar by bluesman Charlie Patton. Wolf emerged as a bluesman after the War while working as a DJ with KWEM (West Memphis, Arkansas). Began recording in 1951 for Phillips and moved to Chicago after a tussle between Chess and RPM for his services. Stayed with Chess until his death in January 1976, although he recorded one album for the Rolling Stones label.

JOHNNY BURNETTE—Born March 25, 1934, Memphis. Top school football player and boxer. Later roamed the South and West, holding a variety of jobs before persuading his brother Dorsey and guitarist Paul Burlison to join him in a rockabilly trio. Auditioned for Sun and was rejected. Later recorded for Von before going to New York and winning Arthur Godfrey's *Talent Hour* show three times in a row. Recorded rockabilly for Coral in 1957-58. Split up with the other members of the trio and moved to California. Later joined with Dorsey to peddle songs before joining Liberty where he enjoyed several popular hits before his death on August 14, 1964.

DORSEY BURNETTE—Born December 28, 1932, Memphis. Career with Johnny until 1960 when he had his first successes on Era with *Tall Oak Tree* and others. He recorded for innumerable country labels in a pop-country style of no great distinction before his death at Canoga Park, California on August 19, 1979.

LITTLE MILTON (CAMPBELL)—Born September 17, 1934, Inverness, Mississippi. Sang in church choir and took up guitar at age 10. By 1950 he was playing in a trio around Memphis where he came to the attention of Sam Phillips and Ike Turner. Recorded for Sun with his 'Playmates of Rhythm', later recording for Meteor in Memphis before moving to St. Louis to record for Bobbin in 1958. Signed with Checker in Chicago in 1961 and Stax in 1971. Still retains his blues roots and has enjoyed several large soul hits. Now with Glades Records.

BILL CANTRELL—Born Hackleburg, Alabama. Met Sam Phillips during his radio days in Birmingham and Florence. Played with the Dixie Blue Seal Flour Boys in Nashville prior to sessions with Meteor, Sun and OJ. Co-founded Hi Records with Joe Cuoghi and Ray Harris. Still a shareholder. No longer an active performer.

JOHNNY CARROLL—Born 1938, Memphis. Recorded for Decca in Dallas and Nashville in 1956. On June 23, 1957 recorded at Cliff Herring's studio in Ft. Worth, leasing the tape to Sam Phillips. George Jones was on guitar at this session. Carroll later recorded for Warner Bros. and Rollin' Rock.

JEAN CHAPEL—Born Jean Amber in Neon, Kentucky. Played in a group with her sisters on WHIS in W. Virginia, later moving as solo to Renfro Valley Barn Dance in Mt. Vernon, Kentucky. Moved to Memphis and played with Clyde Leoppard before recording *I Won't Be Rocking Tonight* for Sun. Later recorded for RCA before becoming a song writer in Nashville. Has written songs for Eddy Arnold, Dean Martin and Roy Rogers.

JACK CLEMENT—Born Jack Henderson Clement, 1931, Memphis. Country musician in Washington, Boston and Baltimore until 1953 when he returned to Memphis. Member of the Buzz and Jack bluegrass duo in early '50s and Slim Wallace's Dixie Ramblers 1955. Recorded for Sheraton, Sun and RCA and has been in production with Fernwood, Sun, Summer, Epic, RCA and others. Owns Jack Music, a movie production company and JMI Records. Latest recording affiliation under his own name is Elektra for whom he recorded an album, *"All I Want To Do In Life"* (1978).

JAMES COTTON—Born Tunica, Mississippi, July 1, 1935. Ran away from home and played harmonica with every major artist in the Delta area in the early 1950s. Later left for Chicago, joining Muddy Waters and then embarked on a solo career in a progressive blues vein with Verve-Forecast and Buddah. Was under contract to Sun for one year from August 12, 1953.

BUDDY CUNNINGHAM—Born Jackson, Mississippi. Recorded for Sun as B.B. Cunningham and Buddy Blake. Formed Cover Records in 1957 and has been involved in several Memphis labels including Sam Phillips' Holiday Inn label in 1968.

JIMMY DEBERRY—Born November 17, 1911, Crumrod, Arkansas. Contracted to Sun for one year from February 25, 1953, having been introduced to Phillips by Walter Horton. Recorded with Horton and by himself. Other details unknown.

BUD DECKELMAN—Born Harrisburg, Alabama, April 2, 1937. Served in U.S. Air Force during War then moved to Chicago and Memphis. Formed a hillbilly band in 1950. Recorded the local hit *Daydreamin'* for Meteor in 1954, song later picked up nationally by Jimmy Newman. Signed with M-G-M in 1955. Formed Shelman Publishing with Bill Cantrell in 1960s. Currently emcee of Mid South Jamboree.

JACK EARLS—Born August 23, 1932, Woodbury, Tennessee. Trained as a baker and worked in Memphis. Formed a band with Bill Black's brother, Johnny Black, in 1954. Recorded for Sun in 1956 with Bill Black and Luther Perkins and also with own band, the Jimbos. Earls kept some of his early recordings which were later issued on Olympic Records, for whom he recorded a comeback session in 1975, having previously recorded for Fortune and Ry-Ho. Now lives in Detroit.

BILLY "THE KID" EMERSON—Born William R. Emerson, December 21, 1929, Tarpon Springs, Florida. Father was a piano player and Billy got a job playing with the Billy Battle Band in 1946. In Army 1952-1954, came to Memphis after his discharge and was brought to Sam Phillips by Ike Turner. Signed one year contract January 11, 1954, recorded same day. Later recorded with Elven Parr's band on April 24, 1954 and with his own band on later sessions. Contract renewed for a two year period. Went to Chicago on leaving Sun in 1956, recording for Chess, his own Tarpon label, Vee Jay, M-Pac and other small Chicago labels.

CHARLIE FEATHERS—Born Charles Arthur Feathers, June 12, 1932, Myrtle near Holly Springs, Mississippi. Listed in Memphis City directory 1955 as full time musician. Recorded for Sun and Flip in a hillbilly style but is most famous for his rockabilly recordings with Meteor, King, Kay, Memphis and Redneck. Has also recorded for Ace, Hi, Walmay, Philwood, Shelby Co., Barrelhouse, EMI-Harvest, Rollin' Rock and Vetco. Has used pseudonyms such as Charlie Morgan and Jess Hooper. In 1973 he began to play regularly with his family band at Harpers Lounge in Memphis where he was filmed by the BBC (England) as part of a documentary on the creators of popular music.

NARVEL FELTS—Born November 11, Keiser, Arkansas. Learned music in high school and recalled 'I listened to most all country artists on the radio. Hank Snow I liked and Johnny Ray in pop.' Moved to Malden, Missouri, where he knew Bill Rice, Jerry Foster and John Hartford. Recorded for Sun 1957 but sessions unissued. Continued in country and popular music with Pink, Mercury, Hi, M-G-M, Renay, RCA, ARA but his biggest hit was *Honey Love* (Pink 702) which was recorded in Memphis and leased from Hi. Since 1974 he has been a successful country artist with ABC/Dot (now MCA) after a few minor hits with Cinnamon. Has reworked R&B standards for the country market including *Drift Away* and *Reconsider Me*.

THE FIVE TINOS—A northern based doo-wop group who were the only black vocal group (apart from the Prisonaires) to have a record issued on Sun in the '50s. Group comprised Melvin Walker, Marvin Walker, Melvin Jones, Haywood Hebron and Luchrie Jordan. Sun #222 recorded May 25, 1955 with instrumental support from Calvin and Phineas Newborn, Moses Reed, Jewell Briscoe, Robert Garner and Robert Banks.

FRANK FLOYD—Born October 11, 1908, Tacapola, Mississippi. Played medicine shows throughout South in talking blues style mixed with hillbilly and pop. Settled in Memphis as a part time pig farmer in 1950 and became a radio favorite with the Eddie Hill Band. Lived in Memphis intermittently until 1972 when he moved to Cincinnati. Now plays the college circuit with blues and folk musicians since his rediscovery by Steve LaVere.

CHARLIE FREEMAN—Born Waynesboro, Arkansas. Country DJ on WABO. In 1964 formed E-Volve with Charles King. He recorded on E-Volve and leased songs to Holiday Inn and Sun International, notably *From Saigon To Little Rock*.

FRANK FROST—Born April 15, 1936, Auvergne, Arkansas. Guitar, harmonica and vocalist. First played with guitarist Jack Johnson and drummer Sam Carr in St. Louis in 1957. Carr is the son of delta musician Robert Nighthawk, from whom Frost's band and style is descended. Recorded by Scotty Moore for Phillips Int. in 1962 and Jewel in 1965, having also played dates with Sun artists Carl Perkins and Carl Mann in the early '60s. Now works a day job in Lula, Mississippi and plays bars on the weekends. One compilation album issued by Jewel 1973.

ROSCO GORDON—Born West Memphis, Arkansas. After leaving Sun he left for New York, becoming a successful R&B artist. Recorded for Old Town as part of Rosco and Barbara and appeared in a movie, *Rock Baby Rock It*, in 1958. Recorded for a plethora of labels including RPM, Chess, VJ, Calla, Rae-Cox, Bab Rock, Jomada and ABC.

HARDROCK GUNTER—Born Sidney Louie Gunter Jr. in Birmingham, Alabama, February 27, 1925. First worked as a salesman then started working in radio around Birmingham in 1940's. Recorded *Birmingham Bounce* for Bama in 1948. Has worked on WWVA (Wheeling, W. Virginia) since 1954 and has also recorded for Bullet, Decca, M-G-M, Sun, King, Cross-Country, Cullman, Morgan, Starday, Gee-Gee and Heather. Currently lives in Denver, Colorado.

RED HADLEY—Born Covington, Tennessee. One of the first country bands to record for Sam Phillips (on November 13, 1952). Recorded *Tennessee Drag*, *If This Is Love, Boogie Ramble* and *I'd Be A Millionaire,* titles were leased to Trumpet. He recorded for Meteor in a honky-tonk vein. The band included 'Junior' Hadley (guitar), Red Hadley (piano), Dave Simmons (steel guitar), Paul Brazile (guitar) and Houston Stokes (drums). Junior, later known as Jay, also recorded for Shelby Co. Records in Memphis, and Glo-Lite Records.

EDDIE HILL—Born Knoxville, Tennessee, 1922. Began playing country music and working as an announcer with WNOX in Knoxville prior to moving to Memphis and Nashville and, finally, Decatur, Alabama. Made his first and best recordings for Apollo and Mercury in the early '50s.

RAYMOND HILL—Born Clarksdale, Mississippi. A contemporary of Ike Turner and co-founder of the Top Hatters. Played around Clarksdale with Billy Gayles before joining Ike Turner's Kings of Rhythm. Recorded for Sun in 1952 and 1954. Purveyor of honking sax solos on *Rocket 88* and other records. Also recorded for Aladdin, Cobra and Federal. Now deceased. His father, Henry Hill, recorded for Sun with Dr. Ross.

GLENN HONEYCUTT—Born Belzoni, Mississippi, May 2, 1933. Moved to Memphis 1940 and attended Humes High School. Entered Army 1952 after holding several jobs in Memphis and playing part time. Left Army 1955, formed Glenn Honeycutt and Rhythmaires, which included Jack Clement who introduced Honeycutt to Sun. Later recorded for Topp-ett, Black Gold and Fernwood. Has worked for U.S. Postal Service since 1958. Now lives in Walls, Mississippi. Cousin of Elvis Presley.

EARL HOOKER—Born Clarksdale, Mississippi, 1930. Raised in Chicago, taught guitar by Robert Nighthawk. Spent most of his life touring from St. Louis to Florida and back again. First recorded in Miami for Rockin' in 1952 and came to Sun in 1953. Afflicted with TB from 1956 he stayed home more in the years before his death but recorded frequently. Died Chicago, April 21, 1970.

WALTER HORTON—Born April 6, 1918, Horn Lake, Mississippi. Raised in Memphis (father worked for the city corporation). Traveled throughout the South with Floyd Jones, Big Joe Williams and others in the '30s. Moved to Chicago after working in Memphis as a chef and cab driver. Returned to Memphis to record for Phillips in 1951 and returned periodically thereafter. Made his home in Chicago playing with Muddy Waters and as a solo act. Still records for specialist labels.

DON HOSEA—Pianist and vocalist with Sun and Rita. Enjoyed a hit with *John Henry* (Rita 1010), recorded at Echo studios, Memphis where Hosea worked as a producer and session musician. In 1970 Hosea reemerged as the producer on Guy Drake's redneck smash of that year, *Welfare Cadillac* (Royal American 1), recorded in Florida.

D.A. HUNT—Born Daniel A. Hunt, Mumford, Alabama, 1920. Came to Sun 1953 and recorded two songs with a distinct Lightnin' Hopkins influence. Possibly died circa 1964.

ROLAND JANES—Born Alabama, 1934. Moved to Memphis in 1956 and became a full time musician with Sun. Originally influenced by Grady Martin and Hank Garland but able to handle rock, blues and country music with equal ease. Session musician for Rita, Nita, Pen, Dingo, Summer, Erwin, Zone, Fernwood and his own Ara and Rolando Records. Owns Sonic Sound Studio in Memphis. Worked as band member for Billy Riley, starting in C&R Club in Helena, Arkansas, where the band got its first gigs.

HAROLD JENKINS (CONWAY TWITTY)—Born Friars Point, Mississippi, September 1, 1933. Jenkins played with the Phillips County Ramblers in Helena, Arkansas, with steel guitarist John Hughey. Recorded for Sun in 1956 but recordings unissued until 1970 (Birchmount Records, Canada). Recorded as Harold Jenkins and His Rockhousers. Recorded for Mercury 1956 and later MGM (1958). Recorded briefly for ABC in 1963 and then joined Decca (later

MCA) where he has become a phenomenally successful country artist based in Nashville since 1965.

THE JESTERS—Rock band formed 1966 by Teddy Paige and Jerry Phillips (son of Sam Phillips). Recorded prolifically for Sun in R&B and rock 'n' roll revival style but only one disc issued. Other members were James Dickinson (who went on to make a solo album for Atlantic produced by Knox Phillips), Billy Wulfers and Eddie Robertson. Paige later worked with Shelby Singleton in Nashville.

BILL JOHNSON—Born Augusta, Georgia. Real name Johnny Lee Hamilton. Recorded for Sun in January 1960 in an Augusta studio. Musicians included Hubert Perry, St. Clair Pinckney, John Winfield, Albrister Clark and Sammie Jackson. Also recorded for Federal, S.S.S. and for Duke with Junior Parker.

JONES BROTHERS—Recorded for Sun January 28, 1954 in a gospel style. Group comprised Charles Jones, Jake McIntosh, William Gresham, John Brye, Charles Bishop, James Rayford, Eddie Hollins and Walter Oliver.

BILL JUSTIS—Born Birmingham, Alabama, October 14, 1927. Moved to Memphis at age 5 and became interested in music through his mother who was a concert pianist. Played saxophone in high school and later influenced by Duke Ellington. Formed a dance band at age 15 and after going to college played with professional dance bands during the vacations. Did post grad work in music theory and started working in record business because he needed extra money after getting married in 1954. After leaving Sun he formed the short-lived label, Play Me, and then joined RCA-Groove as an artist and producer, later moving to Smash where he also recorded prolifically. Later with Monument and Sound Stage 7 in Nashville for whom he produced big hits by the Dixiebells. Has done arrangements for Kenny Rogers and many others.

B. B. KING—Born Riley King, Indianola, Mississippi, September 16, 1925. Moved to Memphis after the War to be with his cousin, Bukka White. Eventually got a job as a DJ on WDIA and formed a band which also played over KWEM with Sonnyboy Williamson. Later played as a trio with Johnny Ace and Earl Forrest. Became one of Memphis' and Sam Phillips' first major acts. *Three O'Clock Blues* was a huge success, prompting his move from Memphis. Started touring and recorded hundreds of songs for RPM–Modern. Was one of the first black singers to become a businessman, beginning with the formation of his own labels in Memphis in early '50s.

SLEEPY LA BEEF—Born Thomas Paulsley LaBeff, Smackover, Arkansas, 1935. One of the best rockabilly artists still performing. Recorded prolifically since the '60s for Starday, Mercury (*All Alone* was a hit), Dixie, Gulf, Picture, Crescent, Wayside, Columbia and Plantation. Moved to Houston in 1953 and has played shows and television all around Texas, Louisiana and Tennessee. Now records for Shelby Singleton's Sun International label.

DICKEY LEE—Born Richard Lipscomb, Memphis, September 21, 1943.

Went to college Memphis State and recorded for Sun in 1957 in a hard rock style. Moved to Beaumont where he worked with Jack Clement and Hallway Records. Enjoyed the sickie hit, *Laurie*, and a monster with *Patches*. Later moved to Nashville after writing the C&W classic, *She Thinks I Still Care*. Has recently renewed his career with RCA and, more recently, Mercury.

CLYDE LEOPPARD—Born Arkansas. Moved to Memphis 1949 from Marianna, Arkansas, with his western swing band. Originally a guitarist who took up bass in 1952 and later switched to drums. Ran a semi-professional band in Memphis and West Memphis for 15 years while working for Standard Life Inc. Currently owns a studio in Memphis, heading the VU label and undertaking custom work for other labels such as Divine, the gospel label.

JOE HILL LOUIS—Born Lester Hill, September 23, 1921, Whitehaven, Tennessee. Became a cook and chauffeur to the Canale family in the late '40s. Obtained the name "Joe Hill Louis" from the Canale boys after a victory in a boxing match. Played around Memphis, working for WDIA as the Pepticon Boy. Continued to do odd jobs for the Canales and began recording for Columbia in 1949. Also recorded for The Phillips, Modern, Sun, Checker, Rockin', Ace, Big Town, House of Sound and Vendor. Died August 5, 1957, from tetanus.

COY "HOT SHOT" LOVE—Very little known. Signed a one year contract with Sun from January 8, 1954. Then living at Gayoso Street, Memphis and working as a commercial sign maker.

BILLY "RED" LOVE—Born Milton Love. Singer and pianist who made many unissued recordings for Sun and *Drop Top* that was leased to Chess. Signed with Phillips on July 31, 1951 and recorded with Willie Nix, Rosco Gordon and others. Moved to Detroit 1954 with Sonnyboy Williamson (Rice Miller). Some of his unissued Sun recordings now available on Charly (UK).

JAMES MATTIS—Co-founder of Music Sales Distributors and worked for WDIA in early '50s. Co-founded Duke in 1951 and sold it to Don Robey's Peacock label in Houston on August 2, 1952. Has since owned the Starmaker label.

WINFIELD "SCOTTY" MOORE—Born Gadsden, Tennessee, December 27, 1931. Graduated from high school in 1948, worked as a mechanic and a hatter. Took up the guitar and played conventional country music on WBRO (Washington, DC). Came to Memphis 1951, playing guitar on Eddie Hill's *Hot Guitar* (Mercury) where he imitates other guitarists including the pioneer rockabilly style of Merle Travis. Played on two Sun recordings before Presley's first disc. Soon became Presley's first manager. Returned to Memphis after Presley entered the Army. Worked for Fernwood and then Sun. Later moved to Nashville, setting up Music City Recorders, working as a freelance producer and playing in a group with D.J. Fontana, What's Left.

BOB NEAL—Born Robert Neal Hopgood, Belgian Congo. Resident of U.S.A.

since 1930. Started work for WMPS in Memphis in 1942, working with country music, drama and childrens programs. Opened a record store at 505 Main Street, Memphis in 1952 and started his Memphis Promotions Agency, signing Sonny James. He was Presley's manager in 1955, working out of 160 Union Avenue. In 1956 he formed Stars Inc. with Sam Phillips, later becoming Johnny Cash's full time manager in 1958. In 1960 he moved to Shreveport and then to Nashville where he worked for the Wil-Helm Agency and then his own Neal Agency, later absorbed into the William Morris Agency. Not involved in the record industry as such, although Roy Orbison did see one promotional EP issued on the Star Incorporated label. Quit Morris Agency in 1979.

WILLIE NIX—Born Memphis, August 6, 1922. First entertainment experience as a dancer with minstrel shows. Worked as a drummer with Sonnyboy Williamson and Willie Love during the late '40s. Led his own band and called himself the "Memphis Blues Boy." Worked on KWEM and recorded for Sam Phillips (who leased titles to RPM, Chess) and issued a single on Sun. Later worked for Chance and Sabre. Reputedly returned to Memphis after a stint in Chicago.

PINETOP PERKINS—Born July 7, 1913 in Belzoni, Mississippi. Joe Willie 'Pinetop' Perkins was raised with Boyd Gilmore and joined the KFFA King Biscuit Boys in Helena, Arkansas. A fine session pianist he recorded unissued sides for Sun under his own name and with Earl Hooker. Has since moved to Chicago and still does session work.

THOMAS WAYNE (PERKINS)—Born Batesville, Mississippi, July 22, 1940. Brother of Luther Perkins, guitarist with Johnny Cash 1955-67. First recorded for Mercury in 1956 and then for Fernwood, Capehart, Santo and Chalet as well as Phillips International in 1962. Worked as a session guitarist in Nashville (sometimes with Scotty Moore's Music City Recorders) until his death in an auto accident in 1971.

JUNIOR PARKER—Born Herman Parker, West Memphis, March 3, 1927. First recorded for Modern after playing with Sonnyboy Williamson and Howlin' Wolf in 1948 and 1949. Moved to Sun in 1953 and joined Duke in 1954. Also recorded for Mercury, Capitol, Blue Rock, Minit and UA. Parker lived comfortably in Houston despite sporadic chart success. His death, during an eye operation, in November 1971 was a surprise.

DICK PENNER—Born Chicago, Illinois, 1936. Moved to Dallas 1937 and learned country guitar at age 16. Moved to Denton, Texas, 1955 to attend North Texas State University. Met Wade Moore and Roy Orbison at this time and composed the million selling *Ooby Dooby* with Wade Moore (born Amarillo, Texas, 1933). Recorded for Sun with Wade Moore and as a solo act. Moore went on to join Orbison in Nashville but Penner got out of music and became a professor of English at Tennessee University, Knoxville. Still composes songs, most recent success was *Otis, Janis, Jimi and Me*, recorded by Mac & Katie Kissoon (Youngblood, UK).

EARL PETERSON—Born February 24, 1927, Paxton, Illinois. Peterson gave up law studies in favor of country music. In his late teens, he played on WOAP (Owosso, Michigan) and then WOEN (Mt. Pleasant, Michigan) with Earl's Melody Trails Show. Doubled as farming editor and announcer. Recorded for his own Nugget label *(Take Me Back to Michigan / Michigan Waltz)* before moving to Memphis in 1954 and recording for Sun. Recorded for Columbia 1955. In 1960 he established his own station, WPLB in Greenville, Michigan. Became ill with cancer 1965 and died in 1971.

DEWEY PHILLIPS—Premier Memphis deejay in the 1950's who was instrumental in the success of Elvis Presley. Dewey himself recorded for Fernwood Records. The tunes included *If It Had To Be You* which Jack Clement said 'Dewey used to whistle all the time'. He had formed The Phillips in 1950. He died in 1969 before his contribution to the Memphis music scene had been properly acknowledged. He was only interviewed properly once (by Stanley Booth for *Esquire* magazine.

JOHNNY POWERS—Born John Pavlik, E. Detroit, Michigan, 1938. Learned guitar from his father and from country music on the radio. First played semi professionally in 1954 with Jimmy Williams and the Drifters who had a show on WDOG (Marine City). In 1957 Powers paid $100 at the Fortune Studio to record *Honey Let's Go To A Rock & Roll Show* and *Your Love* which were released by Fortune on the Hi-Q label. In 1958 recorded *Rock Rock* for Fox Records in Detroit with a band that included Stanley Getz (from Jack Scott's band). Powers was managed by Tommy Moers who got him a session with Sun. Four songs were recorded and two released at the beginning of 1959. Later recorded for Tee-Pee Records (New York) and Tamla (unissued). Formed Power House Productions in 1969, leasing product to Holiday Inn, Bell Records and his own labels.

MAGEL PRIESMAN—One record issued on Sun in 1958. According to Bill Justis she "was from up north." Phillips may have issued her record because she had a blind child to support.

THE PRISONAIRES—Inmates of Tennessee State Penitentiary, Nashville. Black vocal group recorded by Phillips at the Penitentiary and subsequently on three occasions in Memphis.

Johnny Bragg (lead tenor). Born 1921. Entered Penitentiary May 8, 1943 and formed the Prisonaires the following year. Allowed out on parole in 1956, he allegedly violated terms of parole and was inducted back into the Penitentiary. Has been back to jail since and was released again, following the death of his wife, in 1979. Has recorded for Excello, Decca and Elbejay.

Other members: William Stewart (guitar, musical director and baritone). Entered Penitentiary 1940. Born and raised in Macon County, Tennessee. Ed Thurman (tenor). Born Nashville. Entered Penitentiary August 16, 1940; Marcell Saunders (bass). Born Chatanooga, Tennessee. Entered Penitentiary 1951; John Drue (tenor). Born Lebanon, Tennessee. Joined Prisonaires on entering Penitentiary in January 1951.

RANDY AND THE RADIANTS—Recorded several sessions for Sun, principally on October 19, 1964 and September 16, 1965. Two singles were issued in a pop vein. Personnel: Randy Haspel, Bill Slais, Howard Calhoun, Mike Gardner and Ed Marshall.

TEDDY REIDEL—Born June 7, 1937, Quitman, Arkansas. Vocalist and pianist in a style similar to that of Jerry Lee Lewis and, especially, Carl Mann. Recorded for Vaden (some titles leased to Atco including the hit *Judy*). Recorded one session with Sun (*Me and My Blues* and *Step*) which was unissued. Written several hit country tunes and writes specifically for Sonny James. Recorded under the name Reddell. Resides Hever Springs, Arkansas.

"SLIM" RHODES—Born Ethmer Cletus Rhodes, Pocohontas, Arkansas, 1913. Led a country band and joined WMC (Memphis) in 1944. Later had a syndicated television show (which included the only TV appearance of Malcolm Yelvington). Rhodes died in 1966 but his band has been continued by various members of his family. The band recorded for Sun, Gilt Edge, Cotton Town Jubilee and Rhodes own Silver Star and Rhodes labels. The various band members were Spec, Dusty, Bea Rhodes, John Hughey, Neil George, Bertha Sipes, Dottie Moore (who recorded for King Records 1963-1965) and Brad Suggs. Spec has appeared frequently on TV, including *Hee-Haw*, and Rhodes' niece, Sandy, worked as a session vocalist on most of Al Green's Hi recordings and had an album released on the Berkeley based Fantasy label.

Johnny Powers

Jim Williams

Narvel Felts

Mack Allen Smith, 1956

PAUL RICHY—Born Paul Richey, Arkansas. Moved to Memphis 1954. Made one record for Sun on March 11, 1960, *The Legend Of The Big Steeple*. Phillips met Richy at a DJ convention in Nashville and brought him up to Memphis, teaming him with Charlie Rich, Brad Suggs, Bob Stevenson, Roland Janes and Jimmy van Eaton. The record was issued by Sun after Jack Clement took the demo of *Steeple* to Porter Wagoner in Nashville who had a hit with the song. Richy currently works in Nashville as a session musician and song writer.

BILLY (LEE) RILEY—Born October 5, 1933, Pocohontas, Arkansas. Came to Memphis 1955 and got a job with the Industrial Coverall Company while working as a part time country singer. Under contract to Sun 1956-1959. Left Sun in early 1958 but resigned later that year until 1960. Worked extensively as a session musician. Part owner of the Rita, Nita and Mojo labels. Recorded under the pseudonyms Skip Wiley, Lightnin' Leon, Jivin' Five, Megatons, Rockin' Stockins, Sandy & The Sandstones, Darren Lee. Labels include Sun, Rita, Nita, Brunswick, Home Of The Blues, Mojo, Dodge, Checker, Pen, Mercury-Smash, Fire, Fury, Myrl, Hip, Sun Int., Entrance, Crescendo, and Southern Rooster. Plays drums, bass, guitar, harmonica and has worked as a commercial songwriter, record producer, session man and cabaret act. Currently lives in Jonesboro, Arkansas, working as a painter and recording for Knox Phillips.

RIPLEY COTTON CHOPPERS—Country gospel group from Ripley, Tennessee. Included Ernest Underwood, Jettie Cox, R.M. Lawrence and Raymond Kerby. Recorded one session for Sun on July 11, 1953, including *Blues Waltz*, *Roses And Sunshine*, *Silver Bells* and *Pretty Baby*. Disappeared into the mists of time.

DR. ISIAH ROSS—Born October 21, 1925, Tunica, Mississippi. Started playing harmonica when he was nine. Entered the Army December 1943, went overseas to the Philippines and Southwest Pacific. Left the Army 1948, recalled 1950, discharged and married 1951. Ross had played over KFFA (Helena, Arkansas) and WROX (Clarksdale, Mississippi) before the War and had toured around the South with a variety of guitarists. After his discharge he decided to make his living from the music business. First recorded for Phillips in 1951 (Phillips leased some titles to Chess) and again 1953-5 when Ross had some singles issued on Sun. Signed a one year contract October 5, 1953. Worked with a group and also as a one man band, playing guitar left handed. Left for Flint, Michigan, 1954. Has since recorded for specialist labels including Testament, Big Bear and Oldies Blues.

MACK SELF—Born Helena, Arkansas, 1930. Came to Memphis 1955 to audition as a country artist. One disc was issued on Sun and later a rockabilly disc (a duet with Charlie Feathers) was issued on Phillips International coupled with a gunfighter ballad. After his Sun contract expired in 1959 Self moved on to work with M.E. Ellis and his best seller was *Four Walls Of Memories* (Zone 1085) issued in Memphis in 1965. Currently lives in West Helena and produces songs and demo tapes for Twin Records and Central Songs in Nashville.

HOWARD SERATT—Born Manila, Arkansas, March 9, 1922. Crippled by polio at age 18 months. Seratt played harmonica with Ted Henderson's hillbilly band in Blytheville, Arkansas (featured over KLCN). Worked in Michigan 1947-8 in defense plants and later on the Farmersville, California potato farms. Religious conversion in 1948 when he became a gospel musician and returned to Arkansas. Managed by KLCN deejay Larry Parker. In April 1954 he recorded for Sun, having previously made a record at Sun for the gospel label—St. Francis. Seratt moved back to California in 1955 and now runs a jewelry store in Hemet. His nephew, Kenny Seratt works in country music.

BILLY SHERRILL—Born Winston, Alabama. Played sax and piano in a white R&B band throughout the late '50s and came to Nashville 1958. Met Sam Phillips 1960 and worked four years as Sun's producer in Nashville. Now head of CBS/Epic's Nashville operation, having moved to Epic in 1964.

GENE SIMMONS—Born, Tupelo, Mississippi, 1933. Recorded for Sun on moving to Memphis in late '50s. Has recorded since for Hi, Epic, Hurshey and his own studio in Tupelo. He recalls, "I began in music at age 15, playing dances in Tupelo and then in Memphis with Clyde Leoppard. I played shows throughout the Tri State area until 1959 when I went on tour in Canada. I got back in 1960 and worked at the Cotton Club in 1961 then I joined the Bill Black Combo and worked for Hi Records. I wrote several songs at the time, including *Muddy Ole River* for Dane Stinit for Sun. My latest release as of July 1973 is *Good Ole Country Music* (Hurshey 01A). Greatest success came in 1964 with a pop hit, *Haunted House,* (Hi 2076)." An earlier Hi session including *Going Back to Memphis* had been leased to the Checker label in 1960 without success.

SHIRLEY SISK—Born Ernestine Brooks, Memphis. First recorded for Sam Phillips as a pianist/vocalist with Judy Dismukes on guitar. The session was on February 8, 1952 when *Let Me Count The Curls* and *Mean Old Memphis* were recorded. Dubs were sent to Chess (who assigned matrix numbers but the record was never issued). Contract was also signed with Acuff Rose in Nashville. By the late '50s Sisk was back in Memphis, working out of the Echo studios as a pianist and organist. She was featured on a Phillips International disc by the Memphis Bells and in her own right on Sun 365, recorded at the Echo studio on Manassas Avenue in 1961. Recently she owned Permanent Records in Memphis, which did not live up to its name.

MACK ALLEN SMITH—Born, Carrolton, Mississippi, 1938. Learnt some guitar from Mississippi John Hurt. Recorded for Sun with his band, The Flames in 1959. The tape including *Sandy Lee* and *Mean Woman Blues* left Sun with producer Ernie Barton before it could be released. Smith later made excellent recordings for Vee Eight, Statue, Delta Sound and other local Mississippi labels. He has kept the Delta sound alive to the present and has fine country rock albums issued on Ace and Delta Sound (US) and on Redneck, Checkmate and Charly (UK).

RAY SMITH—Born October 30, 1934, in Melber, Kentucky. Recorded for

Sun and Judd Records in Memphis during the late '50s and early '60s. Recorded under his own name and several aliases for a profusion of other labels including Warner Brothers., Infinity, NRC, Tollie, Diamond, Goldies, Smash, Celebrity Circle and Goldband. More recently, he has worked in country music and has recorded for Cinnamon, Corona, Boot, Zirkon, Wi and, most recently, for Rockhouse in Amsterdam. Beginning in country music, he has worked as a session pianist in several genres. His largest hits came for Judd where he recorded *Rockin' Little Angel* (Judd 1016) in 1960. Albums on Judd and Crown followed but he could not sustain his success. Lived in Hamilton, Ontario, Canada until his death, November 29, 1979, of a suicide-shooting.

WARREN SMITH—Born February 7, 1933, Louise, Mississippi. Lived mostly in Texas, apart from spells in Memphis 1955-1959 and Hollywood, 1959-1962. Recorded for Sun, Liberty, Mercury, Skill and Jubal. Recently a personnel manager in Longview, Texas, although he toured England in a rockabilly revival show and recorded for EMI-Harvest and Lake Country. Died January 30, 1980 of a heart attack.

"TEXAS" BILL STRENGTH—Born Houston, Texas. Recorded for Sun in July 1960 by which time he was resident in St. Paul, Minnesota. Had previously recorded for Dot, Coral, Capitol and, more recently, for Starday and Brite Star Records. Strength was a top country artist and deejay in the early '50s and began his career in Houston in the late '40s on KTHT, KLEE, KNUZ and KATL. During 1948-1950 worked with Congress of Industrial Organizations, traveling the U.S.A. to sing at conventions and union meetings. Moved to WEAS, Atlanta, and then KWEM, West Memphis. Left Memphis in 1956 as top deejay. Cut seven titles for Sun backed by Scotty Moore, Brad Suggs, Larry Mohoberac, Bob Stevenson and D. J. Fontana. Died in an automobile accident, September 1973.

BILLY SWAN—Born Cape Girardeau, Missouri, 1932. Heavily influenced by Jerry Lee Lewis. Swan came to Memphis in 1962 and peddled songs on Bill Black's labels. His song, *Lover Please*, first recorded by Dennis Taylor on Bill Black's Louis label was a hit for Clyde McPhatter in 1962. In the '60s, Swan worked as a writer, musician and even security guard to Elvis. Produced Tony Joe White's *Polk Salad Annie*. In '70s, toured with Kris Kristofferson and had hits with *I Can Help* and others, pioneering a new wave of rockabilly.

BILL TAYLOR—Born Tuscaloosa, Alabama, 1932. Left high school 1949 and traveled to Memphis to work in music. Vocalist, songwriter and trumpeter, he was influenced by Bunny Berigan, Bobby Hackett and Dizzy Gillespie and by the country music that surrounded him. Joined Clyde Leoppard in 1950 and had one recording issued on Flip in 1955. Left Memphis in '55 to play with Bob Wills. Also recorded rock 'n' roll in the late '50s under the name William Tell Taylor for Flame Records. Returned to Memphis 1961 and joined Jerry Lee Lewis as musical arranger and trumpeter. Also a songwriter for Lewis and others.

VERNON TAYLOR—Born November 9, 1937, Sandy Spring, Maryland. Played in high school band and over WARL (Arlington, Virginia) in 1955. Mac Wiseman signed him to Dot in 1957 and he later appeared on the Dick Clark show. Also recorded for Ridgecrest.

BOBBY LEE TRAMMELL—Born Jonesboro, Arkansas. A much recorded Southern rocker who has turned back to country music. Wrote *Shirley Lee*, recorded by Ricky Nelson and has recorded on Fabor, Radio, Atlanta, Decca, ABC, Atlantic, Sims and his own Soun-Cot label. Recorded for the revived Sun label in 1978 with, *It's Not My Fault*.

IKE TURNER—Born Clarksdale, Mississippi, November 5, 1931. Taught piano by Pinetop Perkins and formed the Kings of Rhythm while still in high school. Held down a deejaying job on WROX (Clarksdale) and later became a talent scout in Tri State area for both Sam Phillips and RPM/Modern. Recorded many interesting and vital blues artists, including Howlin' Wolf and B. B. King, before moving to St. Louis in 1956 and teaming up with Annie Mae Bullock, or Tina Turner. The rest, as they say, is history.

CONWAY TWITTY—See Harold Jenkins.

JIMMY VAN EATON—Born Memphis, December 23, 1937. Session drummer for Sun and other labels 1956-1961. Recorded under his own name for Nita. Worked for Mid South Vendors servicing jukeboxes in '60s. Formed his own Ivy label in 1974 and played on Billy Riley's sessions in 1978. Occasionally races cars at Millington, Tennessee speedway.

MARCUS VAN STORY—Born Memphis. Plays bass and guitar, participated in many early Sun rockabilly sessions and played on the road with Warren Smith and the Sun package tours. Before becoming a professional musician he worked as a welder with Guy Burnette Company and Houck Pianos. Sometime owner of a club adjacent to Memphis fairgrounds, film actor and other occupations. Latest recordings for Tom Phillips' Select-O-Hit following an album for Barrelhouse in Detroit.

ONIE WHEELER—Born November 10, 1921, Sikeston, Missouri. Played radio shows throughout Missouri and Arkansas during 1940s, forming the Ozark Cowboys in 1950 and moving to Nashville where he gained a recording contract with Okeh and Columbia. Joined Roy Acuff as harmonica player in 1965 and led his own bands on tours of Vietnam. Recorded for multitude of minor labels, his biggest hits coming with Columbia in 1957 and Royal American in 1972.

DAVID WILKINS—Born Memphis. Recorded for Phillips International 1962, one of a number of young Memphis singers and songwriters who were forging a new country sound. Wilkins is now a hugely successful country singer with MCA having worked with several small labels before joining Shelby Singleton's Plantation label in 1969, leaving to work for MCA in 1973.

JIM WILLIAMS—Born Memphis. Educated near Elvis Presley and was musically inspired by Presley's success. He says, "Like Elvis I lived in a government housing project in Memphis and then when Johnny Cash began to have local hit records I decided it was time to go down and see Sam Phillips and find fame and fortune. At that time, I had a sixteen piece dance band called the Dixielanders which played top dance venues and show gigs in the Mid South. I took the nucleus of my band in 1956 and formed a rock group. My Sun release was done in consultation with Jack Clement and Sam Phillips and when it was issued I went on tour with other Sun artists throughout mid America. I became friends with Roy Orbison, Scotty Moore and Bill Justis, who have helped me in my later work." Williams became an Air Force pilot and now works for TWA. Has also recorded for Dot and Ace and has his own studio in Kansas City.

MAGGIE SUE WIMBERLY—Born Muscle Shoals, Alabama, 1941. Discovered for Sam Phillips by Bill Cantrell while singing in a gospel group, the Harmonettes. She recalls, "I had never given much thought to country music before I went into the Sun studios to cut *How Long*. I had been raised on gospel and country was a whole new world for me. I liked country then for the same reason I like it now: I feel comfortable singing it and it's so down to earth." Now recording under the name Sue Richards and enjoying minor country hits for Epic, ABC-Dot and, most recently, MMI labels.

And, last but by no means least . . .

THE SUN STUDIO, 706 UNION AVENUE, MEMPHIS—Originally a radiator repair shop, the old studio was given up by Sun in 1960. It had always been rented and during the '60s it had several new tenants including a barber and auto repair companies. Today, it is owned by a Memphis company who have restored it and use it on a sightseeing tour connected with the Presley legend. As Jack Clement said, "It's not really the way it was."

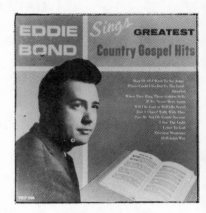

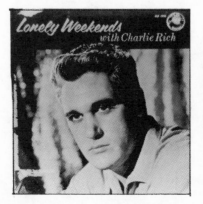

Appendix One: Label Listings

There follows a numerical listing of all records released on Sam Phillips' Sun, Flip and Phillips International labels. Many of the records listed were subject to more than one pressing. In general, we have followed details given on the initial pressing. On the early issues we have followed details given on the 78 rpm issue if it differed from the 45 rpm issue.

'The Phillips' Label

This label, sub-titled 'The Hottest Thing in the Country' was issued in August 1950 and has no issue number.

Joe Hill Louis	Matrix (on label)	(on wax)
Gotta Let You Go	9001	100-2
Boogie In The Park	9002	101-2

Sun Label

174 *Jackie Boy and Little Walter*
Blues in My Condition U-49
Sellin' My Whiskey 50

175 *Johnny London*
Drivin' Slow 51
Flat Tire 52

176 *Walter Bradford and the Big City Four*
Dreary Nights 53
Nuthin' But the Blues 54

177 *Handy Jackson*
Got My Application Baby 55
Trouble (Will Bring You Down) 56

178 *Joe Hill Louis*
We All Gotta Go Sometime 57
She May Be Yours (But She Come to See Me Sometimes) 58

179 *Willie Nix—The Memphis Blues Boy*
Seems Like a Million Years 59
Baker Shop Boogie 60

180 *Jimmy and Walter*
Easy 61
Before Long 62

181 *Rufus 'Hound Dog' Thomas Jr.*
Bearcat (The Answer to Hound Dog) 63
Walkin' in the Rain 64
Note: "The Answer to Hound Dog" omitted from re-pressings

182 *Dusty Brooks and His Tones*
Heaven or Fire (Vocal, Juanita Brown) 65
Tears and Wine (Vocal, Juanita Brown and Joe Alexander) 67

183 *D. A. Hunt*
Lonesome Ol' Jail 69
Greyhound Blues 70

184 *Big Memphis MaRainey—Onzie Horne Combo*
Call Me Anything, But Call Me 71
No Means No 72

185 *Jimmy DeBerry*
Take a Little Chance 73
Time Has Made a Change 74

186 *Prisonaires*
Baby Please 75
Just Walkin' in the Rain 76

187 *Little Junior's Blue Flames*
Feelin' Good 77
Fussin' and Fightin' Blues 78

188 *Rufus Thomas Jr.*
Tiger Man (King Of The Jungle) 79
Save That Money 80

189 *Prisonaires Confined to the Tennessee State Prison, Nashville, Tenn.*
My God Is Real 81
Softly and Tenderly 82

190 *Ripley Cotton Choppers*
Silver Bells 83
Blues Waltz 84
Note: "Hillbilly" stamped in red on label.

191 *Prisonaires Confined to the Tennessee State Prison, Nashville*
A Prisoner's Prayer 85
I Know 86

192 *Little Junior's Blue Flames*
Love My Baby 88
Mystery Train 89

193 *Doctor Ross*
Come Back Baby 90
Chicago Breakdown 91

194 *Little Milton*
Beggin' My Baby 92
Somebody Told Me 93

195 *Billy "The Kid" Emerson*
No Teasing Around F-10
If Lovin' Is Believing 11

196 *Hot Shot Love*
Wolf Call Boogie 12
Harmonica Jam 13

162 - SUN RECORDS

503 *Charlie Feathers*
I've Been Deceived   20
Peepin' Eyes   21

504 *The Miller Sisters*
Someday You Will Pay   22
You Didn't Think I Would   23

Phillips International Label

3516 *Buddy Blake*
You Pass Me By   P-301
Please Convince Me   302

3517 *Hayden Thompson*
Love My Baby   305
One Broken Heart   306

3518 *Barbara Pittman*
Two Young Fools in Love   303
I'm Getting Detter All the Time   304

3519 *Bill Justis and His Orchestra*
Raunchy   309
Midnight Man   310

3520 *Johnny Carroll*
That's the Way I Love   307
I'll Wait   308

3521 *Cliff Thomas Ed and Barbara*
Treat Me Right   311
I'm on the Way Home   312

3522 *Bill Justis and His Orchestra*
College Man   313
The Stranger (Vocal by the Spinners)   314

3523 *Wayne Powers*
My Love Song   315
Point of View   316

3524 *Bill Pinky and the Turks*
After the Hop   317
Sally's Gota Sister   318

3525 *Bill Justis and His Orchestra*
Wild Rice   319
Scrougie   320

3526 *Carl McVoy*
You Are My Sunshine   H-2002
Tootsie   203

3527 *Barbara Pittman with the Bill Justis Orchestra*
Cold Cold Heart   P-321
Everlasting Love   322
Note: First pressing omits "With the Bill
   Justis Orchestra"
     First pressing misprints "Everlasting
Heart" (P-322)

3528 *Ernie Barton*
Stairway to Nowhere   323
Raining the Blues   324

3529 *Bill Justis Orchestra*
Cattywumpus   325
Summer Holiday   326

3530 *Lee Mitchell—The Curley Money Combo*
The Frog   327
A Little Bird Told Me   328

3531 *Cliff Thomas Ed and Barbara*
Sorry I Lied   329
Leave It to Me   330

3532 *Charlie Rich*
Whirlwind   331
Philadelphia Baby   332

3533 *Mickey Milan with the Bill Justis Orchestra*
Somehow Without You (with the Montclairs)   333
The Picture (with Chorus)   334

3534 *Ken Cook*
Crazy Baby   335
I Was a Fool   336

3535 *Bill Justis and His Orchestra*
Bop Train   337
String of Pearls—Cha Hot Cha   338

3536 *Clement Travelers*
The Minstrel Show   338
Three Little Guitars   339

3537 *Jimmy Demopoulos*
Hopeless Love   339
If I Had My Way   340

3538 *Cliff Thomas*
All Your Love   341
Tide Wind   342

3539 *Carl Mann*
Mona Lisa   343
Foolish One   344

3540 *Edwin Howard*
Forty 'Leven Times   345
More Pretty Girls Than One   346

3541 *Ernie Barton*
Open the Door Richard   347
Shut Your Mouth   348

3542 *Charlie Rich*
Rebound   349
Big Man   350

3543 *Bobbie and the Boys*
To Tell the Truth   351
Silly Blues   352

3544 *Bill Justis and His Orchestra*
Flea Circus   353
Cloud Nine   354

3545 *Brad Suggs*
706 Union   355
Low Outside   356

3546 *Carl Mann*
Rockin' Love   357
Pretend   358

3547 *Memphis Bells*
The Midnite Whistle   361
Snow Job   362

3548 *Mack Self*
Mad at You   359
Willie Brown   360

3549 *Brad Suggs Orchestra and Chorus*
I Walk the Line   363
Ooh Wee   364

3550 *Carl Mann*
Some Enchanted Evening   365
I Can't Forget (and the Gene Lowery Chorus)   366

3551 *Sonny Burgess*
Sadie's Back in Town   367
A Kiss Goodnite   368

Note: Flip 503 and Flip 504 were also released on Sun 503 and Sun 504 respectively, and certain Sun releases appeared with Flip labels. Sun 227, 228, 231 and 237 are examples, being issued between October 1955 and March 1956. The Flip 500 series ended before this time.

The Flip label ceased operations in 1956 because of the prior existence of a registered label of the same name. This was the Flip label owned by Ed Wells, based in Los Angeles which in 1956 had a major hit with *A Casual Look* (Flip 315) by The Six Teens.

3552 *Charlie Rich*
Lonely Weekends (The Gene Lowery Chorus) 369
Everything I Do Is Wrong 370

3553 *Barbara Pittman with Gene Lowery Singers*
The Eleventh Commandment 371
Handsome Man 372

3554 *Brad Suggs*
Cloudy 373
Partly Cloudy 374

3555 *Carl Mann*
South of the Border (with
the Gene Lowery Singers) 375
I'm Coming Home 376

3556 *Don Hinton*
Jo Ann (with the Gene Lowery Singers) 377
Honey Bee 378

3557 *Jeb Stuart with Gene Lowery Singers*
Sunny Side of the Street 379
Take a Chance 380

3558 *Eddie Bush*
Baby I Don't Care 381
Vanished 382

3559 *The Hawk*
In the Mood 383
I Get the Blues When It Rains 384

3560 *Charlie Rich with Gene Lowery Singers*
Schooldays 385
Gonna Be Waiting 386

3561 *Danny Stewart*
Somewhere Along the Line 388
I'll Change My Ways 389

3562 *Charlie Rich*
On My Knees 390
Stay 391

3563 *Brad Suggs*
My Gypsy 392
Sam's Tune 393

3564 *Carl Mann*
Wayward Wind 394
Born to Be Bad 395

3565 *Jimmy Louis*
Gone and Left Me Blues E-101
Your Fool 100

3566 *Charlie Rich*
Who Will the Next Fool Be P-396
Caught in the Middle 397

3567 *Jeb Stuart*
Dream 398
Coming Down with the Blues 399

3568 *Nelson Ray*
You're Everything 400
You've Come Home 401

3569 *Carl Mann*
If I Could Change You 402
I Ain't Got No Home 403

3570 *Jean Dee*
My Greatest Hurt 404
Nothing Down (99 Years to Pay) 405

3571 *Brad Suggs*
Elephant Walk 406
Catching Up 407

3572 *Charlie Rich*
Just a Little Bit Sweet 408
It's Too Late 409

3573 *Mikki Wilcox*
I Know What It Means 410
Willing and Waiting 411

3574 *Freddie North*
Don't Make Me Cry 412
Someday She'll Come Along 413

3575 *Jeb Stuart*
Betcha Gonna Like It 414
Little Miss Love 415

3576 *Charlie Rich*
Easy Money 416
Midnight Blues 417

3577 *Thomas Wayne*
I've Got It Made 418
The Quiet Look 419

3578 *Frank Frost*
Crawlback 421
Jelly Roll King 423

3579 *Carl Mann*
When I Grow Too Old to Dream 424
Mountain Dew 425

3580 *Jeb Stuart and the Chippers*
I Ain't Never 427
In Love Again 428

3581 *David Wilkins*
Thanks a Lot 479
There's Something About You 480

3582 *Charlie Rich*
Sittin' and Thinkin' 429
Finally Found Out 430

3583 *David Houston*
Sherry's Lips 431
Miss Brown 432

3584 *Charlie Rich*
There's Another Place I Can't Go 433
I Need Your Love 434

3585 *Jeanne Newman*
Thanks a Lot 435
The Boy I Met Today 436

3586 *The Quintones*
Times Sho' Gettin' Ruff 437
Softie 438

Sun Label: Extended Play Records

EPA 107 *Jerry Lee Lewis:* "The Great Ball of Fire"
Mean Woman Blues; I'm Feelin' Sorry; Whole Lot
of Shakin' Going On; Turn Around.

EPA 108 *Jerry Lee Lewis*
Don't Be Cruel; Goodnight Irene; Put Me Down; It
All Depends (on Who Will Buy the Wine).

EPA 109 *Jerry Lee Lewis*
Ubangi Stomp; Crazy Arms; Jambalaya; Fools
Like Me.

EPA 110 *Jerry Lee Lewis*
High School Confidential; When the Saints Go
Marching In; Matchbox; It'll Be Me.

EPA 111 *Johnny Cash:* "Sings Hank Williams"
I Can't Help It; You Win Again; Hey Good
Looking; I Could Never Be Ashamed of You.

EPA 112 *Johnny Cash*
Rock Island Line; I Heard That Lonesome Whistle;
Country Boy; If the Good Lord's Willing.

EPA 113 *Johnny Cash*
I Walk the Line; Wreck of the Old '97; Folsom
Prison Blues; Doin' My Time.

EPA 114 *Johnny Cash:* "His Top Hits"
Guess Things Happened That Way; Ways of a Women in Love; Next in Line; Train of Love.

EPA 115 *Carl Perkins*
Blue Suede Shoes; Movie Magg; Sure to Fall; Gone, Gone, Gone.

EPA 116 *Johnny Cash*
You're the Nearest Thing to Heaven; I Can't Help It; Home of the Blues; Big River.

EPA 117 *Johnny Cash*
Cry! Cry! Cry!; Remember Me; So Doggone Lonesome; I Was There When It Happened.

Sun Label: Long Playing Records
(Early issues used LP prefix, later replaced by SLP on repressings).

LP 1220 *"Johnny Cash with His Hot and Blue Guitar!"*
Johnny Cash
Rock Island Line; I Heard That Lonesome Whistle; Country Boy; If The Good Lord's Willing; Cry! Cry! Cry!; Remember Me/So Doggone Lonesome; I Was There When It Happened; I Walk the Line; Wreck of the Old '97; Folsom Prison Blues; Doin' My Time.

LP 1225 *"Dance Album of Carl Perkins"*
(reissued as *"Teenbeat—The Best of Carl Perkins"*)
Carl Perkins
Blue Suede Shoes; Movie Magg; Sure to Fall; Gone, Gone, Gone; Honey Don't; Only You/Tennessee; Wrong Yo Yo; Everybody's Trying to Be My Baby; Matchbox; Your True Love; Boppin' The Blues. (Jacket of *Dance Album* lists All Mama's Children, which is not on the album)

LP 1230 *"Jerry Lee Lewis"*
Jerry Lee Lewis
Don't Be Cruel; Goodnight Irene; Put Me Down; It All Depends; Ubangi Stomp; Crazy Arms/Jambalaya; Fools Like Me; High School Confidential; When the Saints Go Marching In; Matchbox; It'll Be Me.

LP 1235 *"Johnny Cash Sings the Songs That Made Him Famous"*
Johnny Cash
Ballad of a Teenage Queen; There You Go; I Walk the Line; Don't Make Me Go; Guess Things Happen That Way; Train of Love; The Ways of a Woman in Love; Next in Line; You're the Nearest Thing to Heaven; I Can't Help It; Home of the Blues; Big River.

SLP 1240 *"Johnny Cash—Greatest"*
Johnny Cash
Goodby Little Darlin'; I Just Thought You'd Like to Know; You Tell Me; Just About Time; I Forgot to Remember to Forget; Katy, Too/Thanks a Lot; Luther's Boogie; You Win Again; Hey Good Lookin'; I Could Never Be Ashamed of You; Get Rhythm.

SLP 1245 *"Johnny Cash Sings Hank Williams and Other Favorite Tunes"*
Johnny Cash
I Can't Help It; Yoi Win Again; Hey Good Lookin'; I Could Never Be Ashamed of You; Next in Line; Straight A's in Love/Folsom Prison Blues; Give My Love to Rose; I Walk the Line; I Love You Because; Come in Stranger; Mean Eyed Cat.

SLP 1250 *"Million Sellers"* (repressed as "Sun's Gold Hits")
Various Artists
Jerry Lee Lewis—Whole Lotta Shakin' Going On;

Johnny Cash—I Walk the Line; Carl Perkins—Blue Suede Shoes; Jerry Lee Lewis—You Win Again; Carl Mann—Mona Lisa; Charlie Rich—Lonely Weekends; Bill Justis—Raunchy; Johnny Cash—Guess Things Happen That Way; Jerry Lee Lewis—Breathless; Charlie Rich—Stay; Carl Mann—I'm Coming Home; Carl Perkins—Boppin' the Blues.

LP 1255 *"Now Here's Johnny Cash"*
Johnny Cash
Sugartime; Down the Street to 301; Life Goes On; Port of Lonely Hearts; Cry! Cry! Cry!; My Treasure/Oh Lonesome Me; So Doggone Lonesome; You're the Nearest Thing to Heaven; Story of a Broken Heart; Hey Porter!; Home of the Blues.

LP 1260 *"Roy Orbison at the Rock House"*
Roy Orbison
This Kind of Love; Devil Doll; You're My Baby; Trying to Get to You; It's Too Late; Rockhouse/You're Gonna Cry; I Never Knew; Sweet and Easy to Love; Mean Little Mama; Ooby Dooby; Problem Child.

LP 1265 *"Jerry Lee's Greatest!—Jerry Lee Lewis"*
Jerry Lee Lewis
Money; As Long As I Live; Frankie and Johnny; Home; Hello, Hello, Baby; Country Music Is Here to Stay/Let's Talk About Us; What'd I Say; Breakup; Great Balls of Fire; Cold Cold Heart; Hello Josephine.

LP 1270 *"All Aboard the Blue Train"*
Johnny Cash
Blue Train; There You Go; Train of Love; Goodbye Little Darling; I Heard That Lonesome Whistle; Come in Stranger/Rock Island Line; Give My Love to Rose; Hey Porter; Folsom Prison Blues; The Wreck of Old '97; So Doggone Lonesome.

SLP 1275 *"Original Sun Sound of Johnny Cash"*
Johnny Cash
Always Alone; Country Boy; Goodnight Irene; Wide Open Road; Thanks a Lot; Big River/Belshazah; Born to Lose; New Mexico; I Forgot to Remember to Forget; Two Timing Woman; Story of a Broken Heart.

Phillips International Label: Long Playing Records

PLP 1950 *"Cloud Nine"*
Bill Justis and His Orchestra
Raunchy; Cloud 9; Rollin'; The Stranger; College Man; Flea Circus/Flip Flop and Bop; Cattywumpus; The Snuggle; Scroungie; Wild Rice; Moose Jaw.

PLP 1955 *"The Martini Set"*
Graham Forbes and the Trio
All of You; Nobody Else But Me; Lady Is a Tramp; Wait 'til You See Her; Love; From This Moment On/Love for Sale; Will You Still Be Mine; My Romance; Jericho; Autumn In New York; Adios.

PLP 1960 *"Like—Mann"*
Carl Mann
South of the Border; Wayward Wind; Walkin' and Thinkin'; Mona Lisa; I Can't Forget You; If I Ever Needed You/I Ain't Got No Home; I'm Bluer Than Anyone Can Be; Island of Love; Pretend; Baby I Don't Care; I'm Coming Home.

PLP 1965 *"Chuck Foster at Hotel Peabody Overlookin-Old Man River"*
Chuck Foster
Oh You Beautiful Doll; Woodchoppers Ball; Cimarron; La Borrachita; Oh; Slow Poke Medley/Patricia; South; Corn Ball Medley; Begin the Beguine; Josephine; Moritat (Mack the Knife).

PLP 1970 *"Lonely Weekends"* with
Charlie Rich
Lonely Weekends; School Days; Whirlwind; Stay; C. C. Rider; Come Back/Gonna Be Waitin'; Apple Blossom Time; Breakup; That's How Much I Love You; Rebound; Juanita.

PILP 1975 *"Hey Boss Man!"*
Frank Frost with the Night Hawks
Everything's Alright; Lucky to Be Living; Jelly Roll King; Baby You're So Kind; Gonna Make You Mine; Now Twist/Big Boss Man; Jack's Jump; So Tired Living By Myself; Now What You Gonna Do; Pocket Full of Shells; Just Come On Home.

PILP 1980 *"Eddie Bond Sings Greatest Country Gospel Hits"*
Eddie Bond with the Eddie Bond Band
Most of All I Want to See Jesus; Where Could I Go But to the Lord; Satisfied; When They Ring Those Golden Bells; If We Never Meet Again; Will I Be Lost Or Will I Be Saved/Just A Closer Walk with Thee; Pass Me Not Oh Gentle Saviour; I Saw the Light; Letter to God; Precious Memories; Hallelujah Way.

PILP 1985 *"Rhythm Blues Party"*
Frank Ballard with Phillip Reynolds Band
Is There Anybody Here; Do Wa Diddi; Just Leave It With Me Baby; After Hours; Drown in My Own Tears; Something in My Mind/Do You Really Love Me; I Just Can't Help It; If That's the Way It Is; Rollin' In; Trouble Down the Road; You Gotta Learn to Rock and Roll.

Appendix Two: Current Sun Albums

Part 1: The following are albums of Sun recordings issued by Charly Records, the British licensee. They are available through mail order from: Sun Rise Records, 25 Lenham Road, Platts Heath, Lenham, Kent, England. Anthologies are followed by an alphabetical listing by artist.

Sun—The Roots of Rock Vol 1 'Catalyst'
CR 30101
Howlin' Wolf - High Way Man, **Sleepy John Estes** - Registration Day, **Roscoe Gordon** - T-Model Boogie, **Junior Parker** - Mystery Train, **Jimmy Deberry** - Take a Little Chance, **Smokey Joe Baugh** - The Signifying Monkey, **Jerry Lee Lewis** - Hello Hello Baby, **Billy Adams** - Reconsider Baby, **Johnny Cash** - Give My Love to Rose, **Carl Perkins** - I'm Sorry I'm Not Sorry, **Billy Lee Riley** - Rock with Me Baby, **Jack Earls** - Crawdad Hole, **Roy Orbison** - You're My Baby, **Ray Smith and Charlie Rich** - Sail Away, **Charlie Rich** - Closed For Repair, **Harold Dorman** - Wait Till Saturday Night.

Sun—The Roots of Rock Vol 2 'Sam's Blues'
CR 30102
Howlin' Wolf - Howlin' for My Baby, California Blues, California Boogie, C. V. Wine Blues, My Troubles and Me, Look-A-Here Baby, Decoration Day, Well That's All Right, **Little Milton** - I Love My Baby, Rode That Train All Night Long, Lonesome for My Baby, If Crying Would Help Me, Somebody Told Me, Runnin' Wild Blues, Beggin' My Baby, **Houston Boines** - Carry My Business On.

Sun—The Roots of Rock Vol 3 'Delta Rhythm Kings'
CR 30103
Ike Turner - Get It Over Baby, How Long Will It Last, I'm Gonna Forget About You, You Can't Be the One For Me, Why Should I Keep Trying, **Bonnie Turner** - Old Brother Jack, Love Is a Gamble, Way Down in the Congo. **Johnny O'Neal** - Ugly Woman, Dead Letter Blues. **Raymond Hill** - Somebody's Been Carryin' My Rollin' On. **Billy Emerson** - Hey Little Girl, When My Baby Quit Me, Cherrie Pie, No Greater Love, Red Hot.

Sun—The Roots of Rock Vol 4 'Cotton City Country'
CR 30104
Charlie Feathers - Defrost Your Heart. **Doug Poindexter** - My Kind of Carryin' On. **Red Hadley** - I'd Be a Millionaire. **Maggie Sue Wimberly** - How Long. **Luke McDaniel** - Uh Babe. **The Miller Sisters** - Chains of Love. **Billy Lee Riley** - Trouble Bound. **Carl Perkins** - Sweethearts Or Strangers. **Jerry Lee Lewis** - It All Depends. **Ernie Chaffin** - Feelin' Low. **Mack Self** - Easy to Love. **Warren Smith** - Blue Days and Sleepless Nights. **Johnny Cash** - Come In Stranger. **Jack Clement** - The Black Haired Man. **Jeanne Newman** - Thanks a Lot. **Dane Stinit** - Sweet Country Girl.

Sun—The Roots of Rock Vol 5 'Rebel Rockabilly'
CR 30105
Carl Perkins - Everybody's Trying to Be My Baby. **Ray Harris** - Lonely Wolf. **Gene Simmons** - Crazy Woman. **Narvel Felts** - My Babe. **Patsy Holcomb** - I Wanta Rock.

Warren Smith - Dear John. **Dean Beard** - Rakin' and Scrapin'. **Tommy Blake** - Flatfoot Sam. **Jerry Lee Lewis** - Hillbilly Music. **Billy Lee Riley** - Pearly Lee. **Cliff Gleaves** - Love Is My Business. **Ken Cook** - I Fell in Love. **Johnny Carroll** - Rock It. **Billy Lee Riley** - Betty and Dupree. **Carl Mann** - Ubangi Stomp. **Sonny Burgess** - Sadie's Back in Town.

Sun—The Roots of Rock Vol 6 'Sunset Soul'
CR 30106
Frank Frost - You're So Kind, Pocket Full of Shells, Lucky to Be Living, So Tired Living by Myself. **Big Lucky Carter** - Gonna Break That Lock. **Arbee Stidham** - Please Let It Be Me, My Head Belongs to You, You Can't Live in This World By Yourself. **Frank Ballard** - Trouble Down the Road, You Gotta Learn to Rock 'n' Roll. **Tony Austin** - Blue Suede Shoes. **Billy Adams** - Rock Me Baby. **Jeb Stuart** - Just Walkin' in the Rain, I Bet You're Gonna Like It. **The Climates** - No You for Me. **Brother James Anderson** - I'm Tired My Soul Needs Resting.

Sun—The Roots of Rock Vol 7 'Sun Blues'
CR 30114
Handy Jackson - Got My Application Baby, Trouble (Will Bring You Down). **Willie Nix** - Seems Like a Million Years, Baker Shop Boogie. **Little Junior's Blue Flames** - Feelin' Good, Fussin' and Fightin' Blues. **Rufus Thomas** - Tiger Man, Save That Money. **Hot Shot Love** - Wolf Call Boogie, Harmonica Jam. **James Cotton** - Cotton Crop Blues, Hold Me in Your Arms. **Doctor Ross** - Boogie Disease, Juke Box Boogie. **Eddie Snow** - Ain't That Right, Bring Your Love Back Home to Me.

Sun—The Roots of Rock Vol 8 'Sun Rocks'
CR 30115
Sonny Burgess - My Baby, I Love You So, Mr. Blues, So Glad You're Mine, One Night, Little Town Baby, So Soon, Tomorrow Night. **Billy Riley** - One More Time, Let's Talk About Us, Searchin', She's My Baby. **Warren Smith** - Do I Love You, Who Took My Baby, I Like Your Kinda Love, Who.

Sun—The Roots of Rock Vol 9 'Rebel Rockabilly Vol 2'
CR 30116
Billy Lee Riley - Swannee River Rock. **Sonny Burgess** - All My Sins Are Taken Away. **Joe Baugh** - She's a Woman, Hula Bop. **Ken Cook** - Don't Be Runnin' Wild, (Problem Child), I Was a Fool. **Dick Penner** - Move Baby Move. **Eddie Bond** - This Old Heart of Mine. **Dean Beard** - Long Time Gone. **Carl Perkins** - Your True Love. **Jerry Lee Lewis** - It Won't Happen with Me. **Luke McDaniel** - High High High. **Mack Vickery** - Fool Proof. **Tommy Blake** - You Better Believe It. **Rudy Grayzell** - Judy. **Cliff Thomas** - Leave It to Me.

Sun—The Roots of Rock Vol 10 'Cotton City Country Vol 2'
CR 30117
Clyde Leoppard Band - Split Personality. **Charlie Feathers** - Peepin' Eyes. **Malcolm Yelvington** - Drinkin' Wine Spo-Dee-O-Dee. **Howard Seratt** - Troublesome Waters. **Slim Rhodes Band** - I've Never Been So Blue. **Miller Sisters** - Got You on My Mind, Someday You Will Pay. **J. R. and J. W. Brown** - Drunk! **Johnny Cash** - Two Timin' Woman. **Ernie Chaffin** - Heart of Me, Laughin' and Jokin'. **Onie Wheeler** - Tell 'Em Off. **Ken Cook** - Jenny. **Warren Smith** - Goodbye Mr. Love. **Billy Riley** - Sweet William. **Jerry Lee Lewis** - Settin' the Woods on Fire.

Sun—The Roots of Rock Vol 11 'Memphis Blues Sounds'
CR 30126
Raymond Hill - My Baby Left Me, You've Changed, I'm Back Pretty Baby. **Earl Hooker** - The Hucklebuck. **Eddie Snow** - I'm a Good Man, I Got to Put You Down. **Shy Guy Douglas** - Shy Guy's Back in Town, Detroit Arrow Blues. **Guitar Red** - Go Ahead On, Baby Please Don't Go. **Walter Bradford** - Reward For My Baby. **James Cotton** - Straighten Up Baby. **Five Tino's** - Don't Do That. **Ed Kirby** - Troubled. **The Prisonaires** - Just Walkin' in the Rain. **The Southern Jubilees** - There's a Man in Jerusalem.

Sun—The Roots of Rock Vol 12 'Union Avenue Breakdown'
CR 30127
Jimmy DeBerry - Party Line Blues. **Joe Hill Louis** - Treat Me Mean and Evil. **Willie Nix** - Prison Bound Blues, Take a Little Walk with Me. **Walter Horton** - Walter's Boogie. **Albert Joiner Williams** - Talkin' Off the Wall, Sweet Home Chicago, Rhumba Chillen. **Woodrow Adams** - The Train Is Coming. **William Stewart** - Rattlesnakin' Mama, They Call Me Talkin' Boy. **Dr. Ross with Henry Hill** - That Ain't Right. **Dr. Ross** - Texas Hop. **Pinetop Perkins** - Pinetop's Boogie Woogie. **Chris Booker** - Walked All Night. **Boyd Gilmore & Earl Hooker** - Believe I'll Settle Down.

Sun—The Roots of Rock Vol 13 'Rockabilly Sundown'
CR 30128
Ray Smith - You Made A Hit, So Young. **Gene Simmons** - I Done Told You. **Dickey Lee** - Good Lovin'. **Conway Twitty** - Give Me Some Love. **Mack Self** - Vibrate. **Dick Penner** - Cindy Lou. **Jack Earls** - Hey Slim. **Mack Self** - Willie Brown. **Ernie Chaffin** - Linda, I'm Lonesome. **Slim Rhodes** - Take and Give. **Eddie Bond** - Double Duty Lovin'. **Sleepy La Beef** - Too Much Monkey Business, Honey Hush. **Jimmy Ellis** - Blue Moon of Kentucky.

The Blues Came Down From Memphis
CR 30125
Doctor Ross - The Boogie Disease, Juke Box Boogie, Come Back Baby, Chicago Breakdown. **James Cotton** - Cotton Crop Blues. **Willie Nix, 'The Memphis Blues Boy'** - Baker Shop Boogie, Seems Like a Million Years. **Rufus 'Hound Dog' Thomas Jr.** - Bear Cat, Tiger Man (King of the Jungle). **Jimmy DeBerry** - Take a Little Chance, Time Has Made a Change. **Sammy Lewis & Willie Johnson Combo** - I Feel So Worried, So Long Baby Goodbye.

Sun Sounds Special 'Raunchy Rockabilly'
CR 30147
Junior Thompson - How Come You Do Me. **Rhythm Rockers** - Jukebox Help Me Find My Baby. **Sonny Burgess** - Truckin' Down the Avenue, Daddy Blues. **Smokey Joe Baugh** - Listen to Me Baby. **Vernon Taylor** - Your Lovin' Man. **Hayden Thompson** - Blues Blues Blues, Fairlane Rock. **Ray Smith** - Willing And Ready, Shake Around. **Edwin Bruce** - Baby That's Good. **Jimmy Wages** - Miss Pearl. **Dick Penner** - Fine Little Baby. **Danny Stewart** - I'll Change My Ways. **Don Hosea** - Never Did I, John Henry.

Sun Sounds Special 'Shoobie Oobie'
CR 30148
Billy Emerson - Shim Sham Shimmy, Little Fine Healthy Thing, Something for Nothing, When It Rains It Pours, Move Baby Move. **Rosco Gordon** - The Chicken, Cheese and Crackers, Shoobie Oobie. **Five Tinos** - Gonna Have to Let You Be. **Prisonaires** - That Chick's Too Young to Fry, Surleen, Frank Clement, Rocking Horse. **Four Dukes** - Baby Doll. **Hunki Dori** - Why Don't You Use Your Head, I Want My Baby Back.

Sun Sounds Special 'Memphis Beat'
CR 30149
Cliff Thomas - Sorry I Lied, Treat Me Right, I'm on My Way Home. **Ernie Barton** - Stairway to Nowhere, Raining the Blues. **Billy Adams** - Trouble in My Mind, Betty and Dupree, Got My Mojo Working. **Charlie Rich** - There Won't Be Anymore. **Bill Johnson** - Bobaloo. **Don Hinton** - Honey Bee. **Vel-Tones** - Fire. **Barbara Pitman** - I'm Getting Better All the Time. **Jeb Stuart** - I Ain't Never. **Harold Dorman** - Uncle Jonah's Place. **Ray Smith** - Rockin' Bandit.

Sun Sounds Special 'Tennessee Country'
CR 30150
Earl Peterson - Boogie Blues, In the Dark. **Doug Poindexter** - Now She Cares No More for Me. **Howard Serrat** - I Must Be Saved. **Malcolm Yelvington** - It's My Baby, I've Got the Blues (Way Down Blues), Goodbye Marie, Rockin' with My Baby. **Ernie Chaffin** - I'm Lonesome, Please Don't Ever Leave Me. **Onie Wheeler** - Jump Right Out of This Jukebox. **Teddie Reidel** - Me and My Blues. **Carl McVoy** - Born to Lose. **Texas Bill Strength** - I Guess I'd Better Go, Call of the Wild. **Dane Stinit** - Ghost of Marylou.

The Best of Sun Rockabilly Vol 1
CR 30123
Carl Perkins - Put Your Cat Clothes. **Harmonica Frank** - Rockin' Chair Daddy. **Jack Earls** - Slow Down. **Roy Orbison** - Domino. **Ray Harris** - Come On Little Mama. **Miller Sisters** - Ten Cats Down. **Warren Smith** - Ubangi Stomp, Red Cadillac and a Dlack Moustache, Uranium Rock. **Sonny Burgess** - We Wanna Boogie. **Billy Riley** - Rock with Me Baby. **Jerry Lee Lewis** - Milkshake Mademoiselle. **Slim Rhodes** - Romp and Stomp. **Gene Simmons** - Drinking Wine. **Malcolm Yelvington** - Rockin' with My Baby. **Hayden Thompson** - Love My Baby.

The Best of Sun Rockabilly Vol 2
CR 30135
Sonny Burgess - Going Home, Fannie Brown. **Ray Harris** - Where'd You Stay Last Nite. **Jack Earls** - Sign on the Dotted Line, Let's Bop. **Mack Self and Charlie Feathers** - Mad at You. **Malcolm Yelvington** - It's Me Baby, Yakety Yak. **Carl Perkins** - Pink Pedal Pushers, You Can Do No Wrong. **Edwin Bruce** - Sweet Woman. **Ray Smith** - Right Behind You Baby. **Johnny Carroll** - That's the Way I Love. **Carl McVoy** - Tootsie. **Eddie Bond** - Rockin' Daddy. **The Jesters** - Cadillac Man

Don't You Step on My Blue Suede Shoes—Various Artists
CR 30119
Jerry Lee Lewis - Whole Lotta Shakin' Goin' On, Great Balls of Fire, High School Confidential. **Carl Perkins** - Matchbox, Blue Suede Shoes, Honey Don't. **Johnny Cash** - I Walk the Line, Folsom Prison Blues. **Charlie Rich** - Whirlwind, Rebound. **Roy Orbison** - Go Go Go. **Sonny Burgess** - We Wanna Boogie. **Billy Lee Riley** - Red Hot. **Carl Mann** - Mona Lisa. **Bill Pinkney** - After the Hop. **Warren Smith** - Miss Froggie

Junior Parker and Billy 'Red' Love The Legendary Sun Performers
CR 30135
Feelin' Good, Mystery Train, Love My Baby, Fussin' and Fightin' Blues, Sittin' at the Window, Sittin' at the Bar, Sittin'

Drinkin' and Thinkin', Feel So Bad, Gee I Wish, Hart's Bread Boogie, The News Is All Around Town, Blues Leave Me Alone, If You Want to Make Me Happy, There's No Use, Early in the Morning, A Dream.

Sonny Burgess—The Legendary Sun Performers
CR 30136
Red Headed Woman, Restless, Going Home, Ain't Got a Thing, Find My Baby for Me, Tomorrow Night, You're Not the One for Me, Thunderbird, We Wanna Boogie, Feel So Good, Y.O.U., My Bucket's Got a Hole in It, All My Sins Taken Away, Sally Brown, I Love You So, Sadie's Back in Town.

Johnny Cash 'Old Golden Throat'
CR 30005
Big River, Luther's Boogie, You Are My Baby, Folsom Prison Blues, Hey Porter, Next in Line, Oh, Lonesome Me, Belshazah, Get Rhythm, Rock Island Line, Country Boy, Train of Love, I Walk the Line, Katy Too, Ballad of a Teenage Queen, Meaneyed Cat.

The Original Johnny Cash
CR 30113
Don't Make Me Go, Next in Line, Home of the Blues, Give My Love to Rose, Guess Things Happen That Way, Come In Stranger, The Ways of a Woman, You're the Nearest Thing to Heaven, I Just Thought You'd Like to Know, It's Just About Time, You Tell Me, Goodbye Little Darling, The Story of a Broken Heart, Down the Street to 301, Blue Train, Born to Lose.

Sun Sounds Special 'Johnny Cash'
CR 30153
Cry Cry Cry, I'm So Doggone Lonesome, There You Go, I Heard That Lonesome Whistle Blow, Doin' My Time, If the Good Lord's Willing, Wide Open Road, Two Timin' Woman, Cold Cold Heart, Hey Good Lookin', I Could Never Be Ashamed of You, Always Alone, Thanks a Lot, I Forgot to Remember to Forget, New Mexico, I Couldn't Keep from Crying.

Charlie Feathers Rockabilly's Main Man
CR 30162
Peepin' Eyes, I've Been Deceived, Wedding Gown of White, Defrost Your Heart, Mad at You, I Forgot to Remember, Uh-Huh Honey, Mound of Clay and others.

Rosco Gordon The Legendary Sun Performers
CR 30133
Let's Get High, Real Pretty Mama, T-Model Boogie, Dr. Blues, Just Love Me Baby, Love with Me Baby, Bop with Me Baby, Decorate the Counter, Love for You Baby, That's What You Do to Me, Tired of Living, If You Don't Love Me Baby, Dream On Baby, Do the Bop, Sally Jo.

Howlin' Wolf The Legendary Sun Performers
CR 30134
My Baby Walked Off, Smile at Me, Bluebird, Everybody's in the Mood, Chocolate Drop, Come Back Home, Dorothy Mae, Highway Man, Oh Red, My Last Affair, Howlin' for My Baby, Sweet Woman, C. V. Wine Blues, Look-A-Here Baby, Decoration Day, Well That's All Right.

Jerry Lee Lewis and His Pumping Piano
CR 30002
Friday Nights, Wild One, Whole Lot of Twisting, Dixie, Rock and Roll Ruby, Carry On, Sail Away, Pumping Piano, Hound Dog, Hong-Kong Blues, Rocking the Boat of Love, Near You, Cool, Cool Ways, Ooby, Dooby, Someday, Shanty Town.

Rare Jerry Lee Lewis Volume 1
CR 30006
Sixty Minute Man, Release Me, Sick and Tired, Let the Good Times Roll, Slipping Around, Little Green Valley, So Long I Am Gone, Crazy Heart, Set My Mind at Ease, I Know What It Means, High Powered Woman, Billy Boy, Wild Side of Life, When My Blue Moon Turns to Gold Again, Instrumental, My Quadroon.

Rare Jerry Lee Lewis Volume 2
CR 30007
Mexicali Rose, Lucky Old Sun, Ole Pal of Yesterday, All Night Long, Come What May, I Don't Love Nobody, Tomorrow Night, Shame on You, Carolina Sunshine Girl, Instrumental, I Forgot to Remember to Forget, No More Than I Get, Nothing Shaking, Just Who Is to Blame, Born to Lose, Long Gone Lonesome Blues.

Jerry Lee Lewis 'Nuggets'
CR 30121
Sweet Little Sixteen, Hello Josephine, I've Been Twistin', It Won't Happen with Me, Ramblin' Rose, When I Get Paid, Love Made a Fool of Me, I Get the Blues When It Rains, In the Mood, Ubangi Stomp, It'll Be Me, Put Me Down, I'm Feelin' Sorry, The Ballad of Billy Joe, Baby Baby Bye Bye.

Jerry Lee Lewis 'Nuggets' Vol 2
CR 30129
Crazy Arms, Hillbilly Music, Turn Around, Night Train To Memphis, My Blue Heaven, It Hurt Me So, I Can't Help It, When the Saints Go Marching In, Whole Lot o' Shakin' Goin' On, I'll Sail My Ship Alone, Friday Nights, Just Who Is to Blame, I Can't Trust Me in Your Arms Anymore, Hello Hello Baby, High Powered Woman, Crawdad Hole.

Jerry Lee Lewis 'The Essential Jerry Lee Lewis'
CRM 2001
Whole Lotta Shakin', Don't Be Cruel, Down the Line, Let the Good Times Roll, Jambalaya, High School Confidential, Jailhouse Rock, Lewis Boogie, Hound Dog, What'd I Say, Lovin' Up a Storm, Wild One, Great Balls of Fire, Singing the Blues, Little Queenie, Mean Woman Blues, Sixty Mintue Man, Lovesick Blues, Breathless, It'll Be Me.

The Original Jerry Lee Lewis
CR 30111
Crazy Arms, End of the Road, It'll Be Me, Whole Lotta Shakin' Going On, You Win Again, Great Balls of Fire, Down the Line, Breathless, High School Confidential, Fools Like Me, Breakup, I'll Make It All Up to You, Lovin' Up a Storm, Big Blon' Baby, Livin' Lovin' Wreck, What'd I Say

Carl Mann—'Gonna Rock 'n' Roll Tonight'
CRL 5008
Till I Waltz Again with You, Gonna Rock 'N' Roll Tonight, Why Do I Keep Telling Lies to Me, Look at That Moon, Paradise, I'm Left, You're Right, She's Gone, No One to Talk To, Red Sails in the Sunset, I'm Coming Home, South of the Border, Mountain Dew, Rockin' Love, If I Could Change You, Pretend, You Win Again, Mona Lisa.

Carl Mann The Legendary Sun Performers
CR 30130
Mona Lisa, Rockin' Love, Pretend, Kansas City, I'm Coming Home, Walkin' and Thinkin', If I Ever Needed Love, Don't Let the Stars Get in Your Eyes, Ain't Got No Home, Look at That Moon, Baby I Don't Care, I'm Bluer Than Anyone Can Be, Mexicali Rose, Ubangi Stomp, Walkin' the Dog, Mountain Dew.

Carl Perkins 'Rocking Guitarman'
CR 30003
Blue Suede Shoes, Roll Over Beethoven, Sweathearts, A Stranger, Perkins's Wiggle, Honky Tonk Gal, You Can Do No Wrong, What Do You Want, When You're Crying, Bopping the Blues, Caldonia, Lonely Street, I Care, Y.O.U., Glad All Over, Honey Don't, Dixie Fried, Her Love Rubbed Off.

The Original Carl Perkins
CR 30110
Movie Magg, Turn Around, Let the Jukebox Keep On Playing, Gone Gone Gone, Blue Suede Shoes, Honey Don't, Boppin' the Blues, All Mama's Children, I'm Sorry I'm Not Sorry, Dixie Fried, Matchbox, Your True Love, Forever Yours, That's Right, Glad All Over, Lend Me Your Comb.

Sun Sounds Special 'Carl Perkins'
CR 30152
Boppin' the Blues, Right String Baby, Only You, I'm Sorry I'm Not Sorry, I'm Sure to Fall, You Can't Make Love to Somebody, Everybody's Tryin' to Be My Baby, Forever Yours, Do No Wrong, Pink Pedal Pushers, Put Your Cat Clothes On, Perkins Wiggle, Roll Over Beethoven, Y.O.U.

Roy Orbison 'The Big O'
CR 30008
Rock House, It's Too Late, You're Gonna Cry, Ooby Dooby, You're My Baby, Mean Little Mamma, Fool's Hall of Fame, The Cause of It All, A True Love, Goodbye, Love Struck, The Clown, One More Time, Problem Child, Chicken Hearted, I Like Love, Domino.

Charlie Rich 'Lonely Weekends'
CR 30004
Lonely Weekends, The Ballad of Billy Joe, Big Man, Rock and Roll Party, Unchained Melody, Right Behind You Baby, Break Up, C.C. Rider, Rebound, It's Too Late, You Are Gonna Be Waiting, Who Will the Next Fool Be, Midnight Blues, Stay, I Need Your Love, Sittin' and Thinkin'.

The Original Charlie Rich
CR 30112
Whirlwind, Philadelphia Baby, Rebound, Big Man, Lonely Weekends, Everything I Do Is Wrong, Sad News, Red Man, Who Will the Next Fool Be, Caught in the Middle, Easy

Money, Midnite Blues, Sittin' and Thinkin', I Finally Found Out, There's Another Place I Can't Go, I Need Your Love.

Billy Lee Riley The Legendary Sun Performers
CR 30131
Red Hot, Rock With Me Baby, Flyin' Saucers Rock 'N' Roll, No Name Girl, I Want You Baby, Wouldn't You Know, Got the Water Boilin', Down by the Riverside, Rock with Me Baby, That's Right, Baby Please Don't Go, Open the Door Richard, Sun Goin' Down On Frisco, Workin' on the River, Lookin' for My Baby, Pilot Town Louisiana.

Sun Sounds Special 'Billy Lee Riley'
CR 30151
Pearly Lee, Swannee River Rock, She's My Baby, Just One More Time, Let's Talk About Us, Searchin', Betty and Dupree, Sweet William, Trouble Bound, Wouldn't You Know, Itchy, Nitty Gritty Mississippi, Tallahassee, San Francisco Lady, Kay, Old Home Place.

Warren Smith The Legendary Sun Performers
CR 30132
Red Cadillac and a Black Mustache, Rock 'N' Roll Ruby, Ubangi Stomp, Miss Froggie, Got Love if You Want It, So Long I'm Gone, Uranium Rock, Dear John, The Golden Rocket, I Like Your Kinda Love, Sweet Sweet Girl, Tonight Will be the Last Night, Who, I'd Rather Be Safe Than Sorry, Black Jack David, Goodbye Mr. Love.

Part 2: U.S.A.: At the time of going to print, the following are available in the U.S.A.

S	100	Johnny Cash and the Tennessee Two—Original Golden Hits Vol. 1
S	101	Johnny Cash and the Tennessee Two—Original Golden Hits Vol. 2
S	102	Jerry Lee Lewis—Original Golden Hits Vol. 1
S	103	Jerry Lee Lewis—Original Golden Hits Vol. 2
S	104	Johnny Cash and the Tennessee Two—Story Songs of Trains and Rivers
S	105	Johnny Cash and the Tennessee Two—Get Rhythm
S	106	Johnny Cash and the Tennessee Two—Showtime
S	110	Charlie Rich—Lonely Weekends
S	111	Carl Perkins—Original Golden Hits
S	112	Carl Perkins—Blue Suede Shoes
S	113	Roy Orbison—The Original Sound
S	119	Johnny Cash and Jerry Lee Lewis—Sunday Down South
S	123	Charlie Rich—A Time for Tears
S	124	Jerry Lee Lewis—Monsters
S	125	Johnny Cash and Jerry Lee Lewis Sing Hank Williams
S	127	Johnny Cash—Original Golden Hits Vol. 3
S	128	Jerry Lee Lewis—Original Golden Hits Vol. 3
S	132	Charlie Rich—The Early Years
S	133	Charlie Rich—The Memphis Sound
S	134	Charlie Rich—Sun's Golden Treasures
S	135	Sun's Best of Charlie Rich
PO	245	Charlie Rich—Arkansas Traveler
PO	246	Johnny Cash—Country Gold
PO	247	Jerry Lee Lewis—From the Vaults of Sun
PO	248	Jerry Lee Lewis, Charlie Rich, Johnny Cash —Greatest Hits Vol. 1
PO	249	Jerry Lee Lewis, Charlie Rich, Johnny Cash —Greatest Hits Vol. 1
PO	249	Jerry Lee Lewis, Charlie Rich, Johnny Cash —Greatest Hits Vol. 2

"Golden Rock and Roll"—
Jerry Lee Lewis
SUN 1000
Whole Lotta Twistin' • Rock And Roll Ruby • Sick And Tired • When I Get Paid • The Return Of Jerry Lee • Milk Shake Madamoiselle • Pumping Piano Rock • Let The Good Times Roll • Livin' Lovin' Wreck • Feel So Good • High Powered Woman • Hello Hello Baby • My Bonnie • Ubangi Stomp • Hong Kong Blues • I've Been Twistin' • Ooby Dooby • My Quadroon • Rockin' The Boat Of Love • Lewis Boogie

"Superbilly"
Johnny Cash
Sun 1002
I Walk The Line • Folsom Prison Blues • Guess Things Happen That Way • Ballad Of A Teenage Queen • Big River • There You Go • Give My Love To Rose • Hey Porter • Get Rhythm • Cry, Cry, Cry • Luther Played The Boogie • Katy Too • You're The Nearest Thing To Heaven • So Doggone Lonesome • Train of Love • Country Boy • Rock Island Line • The Wreck Of The Old 97 • The Ways Of A Woman In Love • Home Of The Blues

"Twenty Golden Hits"
Charlie Rich
Sun 1003
Another Place I Can't Go • Break Up • C. C. Rider • Caught In The Middle • Gentle As A Lamb • You're Gonna Be Waitin' • Jeannie With The Light Brown Hair • Lonely Weekends • My Baby Done Left Me • My Heart Cries For You • Philadelphia Baby • School Days • Sittin' and Thinkin' • Stay • That's How Much I Love You • There Won't Be Anymore • Unchained Melody • The Weddings Over • Whirlwind • Who Will The Next Fool Be

"The Original Jerry Lee Lewis"—
Jerry Lee Lewis
SUN 1005
Crazy Arms • End Of The Road • It'll Be Me • Whole Lotta Shakin' Going On • You Win Again • Great Balls Of Fire • Down The Line • Breathless • High School Con-

CURRENT SUN ALBUMS — 173

fidential • Fools Like Me • Break Up • I'll Make It All Up To You • Lovin' Up A Storm • Big Blon Baby • Livin' Lovin' Wreck • What'd I Say

"The Original Johnny Cash"—
Johnny Cash
SUN 1006

Don't Make Me Go • Next in Line • Home Of The Blues • Give My Love To Rose • Guess Things Happen That Way • Come In Stranger • The Ways Of A Woman In Love • You're The Nearest Thing To Heaven • I Just Thought You'd Like To Know • It's Just About Time • You Tell Me • Goodbye Little Darling • The Story Of A Broken Heart • Down The Street To 301 • Blue Train • Born To Lose

"The Original Charlie Rich"—
Charlie Rich
SUN 1007

Whirlwind • Philadelphia Baby • Rebound • Big Man • Lonely Weekends • Everything I Do Is Wrong • Sad News • Red Man • Who Will The Next Fool Be • Caught In The Middle • Easy Money • Midnite Blues • Sittin' And Thinkin' • I Finally Found Out • There's Another Place I Can't Go • I Need Your Love

"Sun Rockabillys" Vol. One—
Various Artists
SUN 1010

How Come You Do Me - Junior Thompson • Jukebox, Help Me Find My Baby-Rhythm Rockers • Truckin' Down The Avenue-Sonny Burgess • Daddy Blues-Sonny Burgess • Listen To Me Baby-Smokey Joe Baugh • Your Lovin' Man-Vernon Taylor • Blues Blues Blues-Hayden Thompson • Fairlane Rock-Hayden Thompson • Willing And Ready-Ray Smith • Shake Around-Ray Smith • Baby That's Good-Edwin Bruce • Miss Pearl-Jimmy Wages • Fine Little Baby-Dick Penner • I'll Change My Ways-Danny Stewart • Never Did I-Don Hosea • John Henry-Don Hosea

"Duets"—
Jerry Lee Lewis and Friends
SUN 10011

Save The Last Dance For Me • Sweet Little Sixteen • I Love You Because • C. C. Rider • Am I To Be The One • Sail Away • Cold Cold Heart • Hello Josephine • It Won't Happen With Me • What'd I Say • Good Golly Miss Molly

Appendix Three: Factual Follow Up

This section lists all the non-Sun Records mentioned in the text together with the original issue numbers and an album on which they are currently available. LP issues are always in brackets.

Elvis Presley
Arthur Crudup, *That's All Right*, Victor 20-2205 (RCA LPV 573)
Bill Monroe, *Blue Moon of Kentucky*, Columbia 20370 (Columbia—Harmony HS 11335)
Roy Brown, *Good Rockin' Tonight*, Deluxe 1093 (Route 66 KIX 6)**
Wynonie Harris, *Good Rockin' Tonight*, King 4210 (King KS 1086)
Kokomo Arnold, *Milkcow Blues Boogie*, Decca 7029 (Blues Classics)
Marty Robbins, *That's All Right*, Columbia 21351 (CBS 82993)*
Arthur Gunter, *Baby Let's Play House*, Excello 2047 (Excello 8017)
Delmore Brothers, *Blues Stay Away From Me*, King (Starday SLP 962)
Ray Charles, *I Got a Woman*, Atlantic 1050, (Atlantic 2/504)
Jimmy Wakeley, *I'll Never Let You Go*, Decca 5973
The Eagles, *Trying to Get to You*, Mercury 70391
Leon Payne, *I Love You Because*, Capitol 40238 (Capitol SM 884)
Shelton Brothers, *Just Because*, Decca 5872
Elvis Presley, *Heartbreak Hotel*, RCA 6420 (RCA LSP1707 & others)
Elvis Presley, *Hound Dog*, RCA 6604 (RCA LSP 1707 & others)

(*) English issue. (**) Swedish issue.

Memphis Recording Service
Jackie Brenston and His Delta Cats, *Rocket 88*, Chess 1458 (Chess 6641.125)*
Howling Wolf, *How Many More Years*, Chess 1479 (Chess 2ACMB 201)
Rosco Gordon, *Rosco's Boogie*, RPM 322
Rosco Gordon, *Booted*, Chess 1487 & RPM 344
Bobby Bland, *Letter from a Trench in Korea*, Chess 1489
Walter Horton, *Now Tell Me Baby*, Modern 809, (Polydor 2383.200)*
Earl Hooker, *Earls Boogie Woogie* and *Guitar Rag* (Arhoolie F 1066)
Joe Hill Louis, *I Feel Like a Million*, Modern 795
Joe Hill Louis, *When I Am Gone*, Checker 763, (Chess 6641.125)*

(*) English issue.

Sunrise
Willie Nix, *Trucking Little Woman*, Checker 756, (Chess 6641.125)*
Willie Nix, *Lonesome Bedroom Blues*, RPM 327 (Kent KST 9002)

Rufus Thomas, *I'll Be a Good Boy*, Talent 807, (Redita LP 111)**
Rufus Thomas, *No More Doggin' Around*, Chess 1492 (Checker 6445.150)*
Big Mama Thornton, *Hound Dog*, Peacock 1612, (Duke DLP 73)
Dusty Brooks, *That Jive's Got to Go*, Supreme 1525
Dr. Ross, *Dr. Ross Boogie*, Chess 1504 (Chess 6641.125)*
Bobby Bland, *Driftin' from Town to Town*, (Kent KST 9002)
Billy the Kid Emerson, *The Whip*, M-Pac 70207 (President PTL 1002)
Johnny Bragg, *Beyond the Clouds*, Excello 2091

(*) English issue (**) Dutch issue

Country Roots to Carl Perkins
Hank Williams, *Your Cheatin' Heart*, MGM 11416 (MGM SE 4755-2)
Hank Williams, *Honky Tonkin'* MGM 10171 (MGM SE 4755-2)
Hank Williams, *Jambalaya* MGM 11283 (MGM SE 4755-2)

Sun Country
Harmonica Frank, *Swamp Root*, Chess 1475, (Chess 6641.125)*
Buddy Jones, *Huntin' Blues*, Decca 5372
Chris Bouchillon, *The Medicine Show*, Columbia 15151-D
Bob Price, *Sticks and Stones/How Can It Be*, Chess 1495
Earl Peterson, *The Boogie Blues*, Columbia 21364
Hardrock Gunter, *Birmingham Bounce*, Bama 104
Bud Deckelman, *Daydreamin'*, Meteor 5014 (Redita LP 110)**
Jimmy Newman, *Daydreamin'*, Dot 1237
Carl McVoy, *Daydreamin'*, Hi 2002
The Hayriders, *Daydreams Come True*, Meteor 5027

(*) English issue. (**) Dutch issue

The Rockin' Guitar Man
Arthur Smith, *Guitar Boogie*, Super Disc 1004, (Starday SLP 173)
Carl Perkins, *Big Bad Blues*, Brunswick 05909*, (Bopcat LP 207)**
Carl Perkins, *Country Boy's Dream*, Dollie 505, (Dollie DLP 4001)
Carl Perkins, *Pointed Toe Shoes*, Columbia 41379 (Harmony HS 11385)
Carl Perkins, *Sister Twister*, Columbia 42514
Carl Perkins, *Restless*, Columbia 44723, (Columbia CS 9833)
Carl Perkins/Johnny Cash, [*Little Fauss and Big Halsy* Columbia S-30385N
Carl Perkins, [*Old Blue Suedes Is Back*, Jet KZ 35604]
Carl Perkins, *Where the Rio de Rosa Flows* and *That's All Right* (CBS 31454*)

Carl Perkins, *The Monkeyshine,* Decca 31709 (MCA COPS 6219)***

(*) English issue (**) Dutch issue. (***) German issue

We Called It Rockabilly
Bill Parsons, *The All American Boy,* Fraternity 853
Stan Freberg, *The Payola Roll Blues,* Capitol 4329 (UA. UAD 60093/94)*
Carl Perkins, *Hambone,* Columbia 42514 (Harmony HS 11385)
Delmore Brothers, *Hillbilly Boogie,* King 527 (Starday SLP 962)
Arthur Smith, *Guitar Boogie,* Super Disc 1004 (Starday SLP 173)
Merle Travis, [Best Of Capitol SM 2662]
Jack Guthrie, *Oakie Boogie,* Capitol 341
Tennessee Ernie Ford, *Smokey Mountain Boogie,* Capitol 40212
Bill Haley, *Rocket 88,* Holiday 105
Bill Haley, *Sundown Boogie,* Holiday 108
Bill Haley, *Icy Heart,* Essex 303
Bill Haley, *Rock the Joint,* Essex 303
Joe Almond, *Gonna Rock and Roll,* Trumpet 221
Johnny Carroll, *Wild, Wild Women,* Decca 29941 (MCA MCFM 2697)*
Bill Flagg, *Go Cat Go,* Tetra 4445
Billy Haley, *Rock Around the Clock,* Decca 29124 (MCA 161)
Elvis Presley, *All Shook Up,* RCA 6870 (RCA LSP 1707 and others)
Charlie Feathers, *Get With It,* Meteor 5032 (Redita LP 107)**
G.L. Crockett, *Look Out Mabel,* Chief 7010 (Chess 9124.213)*
Tarheel Slim, *Number 9 Train,* Fury 1016 (Island IWP 5)*

(*) English (**) Dutch issue

The Sun Sound
Eddy Arnold, *Cattle Call,* RCA 21-0133

The Sun Artists
Mac, Jake and the Esquire Trio, *A Gal Named Joe,* Meteor 5022
Jack Earls, [Olympic Rock Dial LP 004]
Hardrock Gunter/The Rhythm Rockers, *Jukebox Help Me Find My Baby/Fiddle Bop,* Cross Country 524
Roy Orbison, *Ooby Dooby/Tryin' to Get to You,* Je-Wel 101
Roy Orbison, *Tryin' to Get to You/Weldon Rogers, So Long Good Luck And Goodbye* Imperial 5457
Sid King and the Five Strings, *Ooby Dooby,* Columbia 21351
Johnny Carroll, *Hot Rock,* Decca 30013 (MCA, MCFM 2697)*
Gene Simmons, *Haunted House,* Hi 2076

(*) English issue

The Memphis Scene
Harold Dorman, *Mountain of Love,* Rita 1003 (MCA 2-8008)
Hoyt Johnson, *Enie Meanie, Minie Mo,* Erwin 555 (Redita 102)**
Don Willis, *Boppin' High School Baby,* Satellite 101 (Collector CL1020)*
Thomas Wayne, *Tragedy,* Fernwood 109 Reissued as Eric 45-160
Elmore James, *I Believe,* Meteor 5001
Mason Dixon, *Don't Worry 'bout Nuthin',* Meteor 5028
Junior Thompson, *Raw Deal,* Meteor 5029
Bill Bowen, *Have Myself a Ball,* Meteor 5033
Jimmy Lamberth, *I'll Pretend,* Meteor 5044
Charlie Feathers, *Tongue Tied Jill,* Meteor 5032 (Redita LP 107)**
Brad Suggs, *Bop Baby Bop,* Meteor 5034
Charlie Feathers, *Stutterin' Cindy,* Philwood 223 (Star 312)**
Tommy Tucker, *Lovin' Lil,* Hi 2014
Eddie Bond, *Rockin' Daddy,* Mercury 70826 (Redita LP 112)**

Eddie Bond, *Boppin' Bonnie,* Mercury 70941 (Philips 6336.257)*
Eddie Bond, *Monkey and the Baboon,* Diplomat 8856 (Redita LP 112)**
The Cochran Brothers, *Guilty Conscience,* Ekko 1005 (Rockstar JGR 001)*

(*) English issue. (**) Dutch issue.

Roots and Branches
Al Ferrier, *No No Baby,* Goldband 1031 (Goldband GR 7769)**
Buck Owens, *Hot Dog,* Pep 107, (Redita LP 109)**
Buck Owens, *Rhythm & Booze,* Pep 107 (Redita LP 109)**
Ronnie Hawkins, *Mary Lou,* Roulette 4177 (MCA 2-8008)
Sonny Fisher, *Rockin' Daddy,* Starday 179, (Chiswick 10CH14)*
George 'Thumper' Jones, *Rock It,* Starday 240, (Chiswick 10CH13)*
Rudy Grayzell, *Ducktail,* Starday 241
Jimmy Edwards, *Love Bug Crawl,* Mercury 71209, (Redita LP 112)**
Roy Hall, *All by Myself,* Decca 29697, (MCA MCFM 2789)*
Roy Hall, *Blue Suede Shoes,* Decca 29880
Hank Williams, *Roly Poly,* MGM 12727 (MGM E-3803)
Onie Wheeler, *Onie's Bop,* Columbia 21523
Johnny Horton, *Battle of New Orleans,* Columbia 41339, (Columbia CS 8269)
Johnny Horton, *Honky Tonk Hardwood Floor,* Columbia 41110, (Col. CS 8779)
Marty Robbins, *White Sport Coat,* Columbia 40864, (Columbia CS 8629)
Marty Robbins, *Mean Mama Blues,* Columbia 21477, (CCL 1129)***
Marty Robbins, *I Can't Quit,* Columbia 21545
Marty Robbins, *That's All Right,* Columbia 21351, (CBS 82993)*
Rusty & Doug Kershaw, *Louisiana Man,* Hickory 1137 (MGM-Hickory HR 4506)
Cleveland Crochet, *Sugar Bee,* Goldband 1106
Al Ferrier, *Hey Baby,* Excello 2105, (Flyright 525)*
Bobby Cisco, *Go Go Go,* Chess 1650, (Chess 9124.213)*
Billy Barrix, *Cool Off Baby,* Chess 1662, (Chess 9124.213)*
John Hampton, *Shadow Blues,* United 210
Bob Luman, *Red Hot,* Imperial 8313, (U.A. UAS 30101)*
Bob Luman, *Red Cadillac and a Black Mustache,* Imperial 8311 (CCL 1119)*
Weldon Rogers, *So Long Good Luck and Goodbye,* Imperial 5457 (U.A. UAS 30101)
Ricky Nelson, *Waitin' in School,* Imperial 5483, (U.A. UAS 9960)
Sanford Clark, *The Fool,* MCI 1003/Dot 15481.
Buddy Knox, *Party Doll,* Roulette 4002, (MCA 2-8001)
Buddy Holly, *Midnight Shift,* (Vocalion VL 73811)
Buddy Holly, *Rock Around with Ollie Vee,* Decca 30434, (Vocalion VL73811)
Johnny Burnette, *Tear It Up,* Coral 61651, (Solid Smoke 8001)

(*) English issue (**) Dutch issue (***) German issue

Cashing In
Onie Wheeler, *Run 'em Off,* Columbia 21193
David Houston, *Almost Persuaded,* Epic 10025 (Epic BN 26342)

Jerry Lee Lewis
Jerry Lee Lewis, *Pen & Paper/Hit the Road Jack,* Smash 1857
Jerry Lee Lewis, *She Was My Baby,* Smash 1906
Jerry Lee Lewis, [Return Of Rock Smash SRS 67073]
Jerry Lee Lewis, *I'm on Fire,* Smash 1886
Jerry Lee Lewis, *Another Place, Another Time,* Smash 2146, (Smash SRS 67131 & others)
Jerry Lee Lewis, [The Session, Mercury SRM-2-803]
Jerry Lee Lewis [Southern Roots, Mercury SRM-1-690]
Jerry Lee Lewis, [Jerry Lee Lewis, Elektra 6E-184]

End of an Era
Ed Bruce, [Shades of Ed Bruce, Monument 18118]
T.V. Slim, *Flat Foot Sam,* Checker 870
Rudy Grayzell, *Looking at the Moon and Wishing on a Star,* Abbott 145
Olympics, *Western Movies,* Demon 1508 (MCA 2-8008)
Ray Smith, *Rockin' Little Angel,* Judd 1016 (Reissued as Era 45-058)

Chapter 8 Sun in the Evening
Charlie Rich, *Mohair Sam,* Smash 1993, (Mercury SRM-2-7505)
Charlie Rich, *The Most Beautiful Girl in the World,* Epic 15-2343
Carl Mann, *Gonna Rock and Roll All Night,* Jaxon 502 (Collector CL 1023)*
Danny & The Juniors, *At the Hop,* ABC 9871

Roy Orbison, *Only the Lonely,* Monument 421 (Monument MP 8600)
Millie, *My Boy Lollipop,* Smash 1883

(**) Dutch issue

Chapter 9 The Memphis Sound
Paul and Paula, *Hey Paula,* Philips 40084, (MCA 3046)
The Markeys, *Last Nite,* Satellite 107, (Reissued as Atlantic 45/13091)
The Markeys, *Diana,* Satellite 112
Bill Black Combo, *White Silver Sands,* Hi 2021
Gene Simmons, *Haunted House,* Hi 2076
Billy Lee Riley, *Good Old Rock & Roll,* Southern Rooster 706-639
Sam The Sham, *Wooly Bully,* MGM 13322 (Original Sound 8860)

Appendix Four: Following the Sun

There follows a list of Memphis-based record labels which have operated between the fifties and the present. Where known, the label owners are indicated in brackets. It may clearly be seen that the emergence of Sun had a tremendous catalytic effect upon recording activity in Memphis.

The Early Fifties

Astral; Back Alley; B.B. and Blues Boy Kingdom (B.B. King); Buster (Buster Williams); Duke (Mattis/Fitzgerald); Fletcher; Meteor (Lester Bihari); Starmaker (J. Mattis); Steamboat; Sun (Sam Phillips); The Phillips (Dewey Phillips/Sam Phillips); Wasco.

Labels Whose Owners Were Associated With Sun

Honesty (Ernie Barton)
Louis (Bill Black)
Advance, Tab, Frontier, Millionaire, Western Lounge (Eddie Bond)
Arbur (Sonny Burgess)
Hi, Mach, M.O.C., (Bill Cantrell/Hi Records Corporation); Hi Country (Cantrell/Lewis Willis)
Goldwax, Beale Street, Bingo, Bandstand USA (Quinton Claunch/Rudolph Russell)
Summer, Echo (Jack Clement)
B.B., Cover, Light, Sound Of Memphis (Buddy Cunningham)
F&L (Frank Floyd/Larry Kennon)
Rolando, Hot, Ara, Bluffer, Renay (Roland Janes); Mountain (Janes/Bill Justis)
Play Me (Bill Justis)
Crystal, Dingo, Hut, Tune, Pen, Pepper, X-L (Stan Kesler)
Fonofox, Divine, Tempo, VU (Clyde Leoppard)
Stars Inc. (Bob Neal/Sam Phillips)
Rita, Nita, Good, Mojo (Billy Riley/Ira Vaughn)
Rhodes, Silver Star (Slim Rhodes)
Permanent (Shirley Sisk)
Racer, Chalet (Thomas Wayne)
1st (Bill Yates)
Ivy (James Van Eaton)

Labels Associated With The Phillips Family

Sun, Flip, Phillips International, Stars Inc., The Phillips, Holiday Inn; Judd, Black Gold, Knox, Philwood, SelectoHit, Solid Gold, Southern Rooster

Other Important Groups Of Labels

Erwin, E&M, Clearmont, Rivermont, Memphis, Wonder, Rebel Ace, Stompertime Zone (M. E. Ellis)
Fernwood, Boot Heel, Mid-South, Pure Gold, S&W, Whirlaway (Slim Wallace)
Home Of The Blues, Rufus, Zab (Reuben Cherry)
Stax, Enterprise, Hip, Satellite, Jaxon, Volt, Safice (Jim Stewart etc)
Glo-Lite, GMG, 625, Shelby, Tennessee Country Boy, UFO (Bill Glore)
Blake, Marble Hill (John Cook)

Labels From West Memphis

Alley; Astral; CMC (Sonny Blake); Razorback; Aaron, Maha, Cotton Town Jubilee (Gene Williams)

Other Memphis Labels
Ardent; AGP (Chips Moman); Aztec; Atlanta; Al-Be; Arbel; Allandale; Atomic; Bellemeade; Bubba; Castaway; Chimes; Co & Wi; Connie, Label (Jerry Jaye); Cathey; Chips (Chips Moman); Christy; C&F (Willie Cobbs); Chris; Cynthia, Delta Sounds, Dimac (Mack Allen Smith); D.W.A.; Dawson and Sandier (Mose Dawson); Eagle; Eastside; Eureka; Forrest; Flash; Eighth Street; E-Volve (C. King) Express (Robert Taylor); G-Zackie; Ford's (Scatman Ford); Gate; House Of Orange; House Of Sound (Johnnie James); Hurshey (Hurshel Wiginton); Kay; J.P.; J.W.; Moon; Marlin, Tap (Marlin Grissom); Memphis (Gene Miller); Mimosa (Steve LaVere); O.J. (Red Mathis/Bill Biggs); Peak (Lansky Brothers); Penthouse, Youngstown (Music Press/Chips Moman); Purl, Walmay; Plaza; P.A.C. (Tom Pleasants); Pine; Ru-Lu; Rainbow; Rebel; RCT; River (Jim Queen); Sandy; Santo, SanWayne (Bob McGinnis); Sharp; Shcok; Style; Safire; Shimmy; Showboat; Tri; Voll-Para; Von; Vendor; Wampus (Howard Chandler); Wescan (James Cannon); Wilrod; Westside; Walmay; Younger (Larry Rogers).

Appendix Five: Discographical Works and Recommended Reading

Record Research Pop/Rock 1955/1972, Joel Whitburn, Record Research, Wisconsin.
Top Country & Western Records 1949-1972, Joel Whitburn, Record Research, Wisconsin.
Rhythm & Blues 1949-1971, Joel Whitburn, Record Research, Wisconsin.
Blues Records: A Discography, Mike Leadbitter & Neil Slaven, Hanover, London, 1968.
The Sun Session Files, Escott/Hawkins and Twenty Years Of Elvis, Escott/Hawkins, Published privately, 1975. Available from the authors at 25 Lenham Rd., Platts Heath, Lenham, Kent, England.
The Encyclopaedia of Rock Vols. 1-3, ed. Hardy/Laing, Aquarius, London, 1977.
The Sound of the City, Charlie Gillett, Outerbridge, N.Y., 1970.
Country Music U.S.A., Bill C. Malone, University of Texas, Houston, 1967.
A History & Encyclopaedia of Country, Western & Gospel Music, Linnell Gentry, Clairmont, Nashville, 1961, rev. ed. 1969.
The Nashville Sound (Bright Lights and Country Music), Paul Hemphill, Simon & Shuster, N.Y.C., 1970.
Country Music: White Man's Blues, John Grissim, Paperback Library/Coronet, N.Y.C., 1970.
Mystery Train, Greil Marcus, E.P. Dutton, N.Y.C., 1976.
Urban Blues, Charles Keil, University of Chicago, 1966.
Nothing but the Blues, ed. Mike Leadbitter, Hanover, London, 1971.
Memphis Blues, Bengt Olsson, Studio Vista, London, 1970.
Elvis: A Biography, Jerry Hopkins, Simon & Schuster, N.Y.C., 1971.
Chicago Breakdown, Mike Rowe, Edison, London, 1973.
Feel Like Going Home, Peter Guralnick, Omnibus Press, N.Y.C., 1971.
Rock Folk, Michael Lydon, Dell, N.Y.C., 1971.
Sing a Sad Song, The Life of Hank Williams, Roger M. Williams, Ballantine, N.Y.C., 1973.
The Deejays, Arnold Passman, Macmillan, N.Y.C., 1971.
Some of the above may be obtained from Rock Culture Books, P.O. Box 96, Scarsdale, N.Y. 10583.

Periodicals
There has been a wealth of Sun info published in periodicals and fanzines over the years. It would be pointless to list these as most are long since unavailable. The following are still alive and flourishing at the time of going to press and cannot be too highly recommended. In all cases, send a stamped return envelope or international reply coupon for details of latest subscription rates.

New Kommotion: Quarterly, Superior fanzine for all oldies freaks with a decided slant toward rockabilly. Information from: Adam Komorowski, 3 Bowrons Avenue, Wembley, Middlesex, England.
Living Blues: Essential blues magazine emphasizing the current blues scene. Write to: Jim O'Neal, 2615 North Wilton Avenue, Chicago, IL 60614.
Blues Unlimited: Bi-monthly, dealing with all aspects of the blues. Write to: B.U. Publications, 36 Belmont Park, Lewisham, London SE13, England.
Time Barrier Express: Covering all aspects of rock & roll history. Professionally produced and well written. Essential reading. Details from: T.B.E., P.O. Box 206, Yonkers, NY 10710.

Index